MAP OF LOCATIONS

Bukhara• •Samarkand

Tehran• •Mashad

•Isfahan •Lahore

•Agra

:cca

J.G.D. I J.L.

TEMPLES,
CHURCHES AND
MOSQUES

To Mary who, as my constant travelling companion,
has added so much to the enjoyment of the buildings
described in this book

TEMPLES, CHURCHES AND MOSQUES

A Guide to the Appreciation of Religious Architecture

J. G. Davies

Basil Blackwell · Oxford

First published 1982
Basil Blackwell Publisher Limited
108 Cowley Road, Oxford OX4 1JF, England

British Library Cataloguing in Publication Data
Davies, J. G.
  Temples, churches and mosques.
  1. Church architecture   2. Architecture, Islamic
  3. Temples
  I. Title
  726   NA4600

ISBN 0-631-12887-5

Phototypesetting by Oxford Publishing Services
Printed in Great Britain by
The Pitman Press, Bath

CONTENTS

ACKNOWLEDGEMENTS

The author wishes to express his thanks to Basil Blackwell Publisher Limited not only for accepting this work so enthusiastically but also for the painstaking care and attention devoted to its production. He is grateful also to Anne Bowen and to Dorothy Stellinga, both of the Theology Department in the University of Birmingham, to the former for coping with the large volume of correspondence involved and to the latter for typing the manuscript; to R. C. Swift of the Geography Department for advice and assistance in connection with the photographs, and to Jean Dowling, of the same department, who drew more than half the diagrams and plans together with the two maps.

He is pleased to record his gratitude to the following who have provided the illustrations: Ashmolean Museum, Oxford: pp. 23, 26; James Austin: pp. 28, 32, 42, 54, 59, 146, 151, 158, 159, 170, 179, 181, 195, 196, 212, 225; Barber Institute, University of Birmingham: pp. 97, 105, 108, 112, 148, 161, 163, 165, 218; Courtauld Institute of Art: p. 174; F.H. Crossley: pp. 157, 172, 183, 192; J.G. Davies: pp. 2, 5, 49, 83, 86, 93, 162, 214; Egypt Exploration Society: p. 7; Embassy of Pakistan: p. 141; French School of Athens: p. 70; Hirmer Fotoarchiv: p. 232; A.F. Kersting: pp. 4, 9, 12, 13, 15, 17, 63, 82, 89, 92, 114, 115, 125, 127, 131, 140, 188, 205, 207, 209, 229, 236; Mansell/Alinari: pp. 94, 194, 198, 211, 221, 224, 227; Foto Marburg: pp. 122, 190; National Tourist Association of Greece: pp. 33, 38, 40, 46, 50, 68, 73; Dr Johannes Steiner: pp. 235, 237; Wim Swann (Granada Publishing): p. 119; Professor R.A. Tomlinson: pp. 44, 47; Roger Wood: pp. 123, 138; Dean and Chapter of Worcester Cathedral: p. 176.

PREFACE

Every year millions of travellers visit countless temples, churches and mosques throughout the world. They are frequently escorted around the sites by guides who provide a host of facts about the buildings: the dates of their construction, the names of the architects if known, the subjects of the mosaics or ceramics. In this way much information is purveyed but little understanding is communicated. These guides, and guide books too, are the source of much knowledge about these works of art but they are of little help towards appreciating them in themselves.

With notable exceptions the same observation could be made about the writings of many art historians. Their entirely legitimate interests concentrate upon dates, upon questions of origins and influences, of development and possible decay. But the enjoyment of architecture is not directly related either to facts about its history or to the recognition of those features that are derivative and those that are new: enjoyment rests upon immediate impact, upon what you see and feel as you look and move around. Granted that for a total view all possible factors are relevant, nevertheless appreciation of a Gothic cathedral, for example, is not greatly affected by determining whether or not the pointed arch was a western creation or an importation from Islam. This study is not concerned with these issues but faces instead such questions as: how are buildings to be enjoyed? What factors are to be looked for? Aesthetics rather than historical analysis are the prime concern.

It can be said then that this book is about delight, a term used by Sir Henry Wotton and one occurring frequently in the following chapters. Writing in the early seventeenth century and basing himself upon the Roman author Vitruvius, he perceived in fine architecture three factors: commodity, firmness and delight. The first of these refers to the accommodating of a building's design to its use, the second to materials and structural techniques, and the third to its aesthetic and symbolic aspects. While it is this last element that will receive most attention throughout this book, neither the first nor the second can be entirely neglected. Since the majority of buildings enclose a space that has been provided for a particular use, some knowledge of that function is indispensable to appreciation, and since this study is devoted to religious buildings, function means mainly worship.

This restriction is in part due to the author's own specialist interests. It also rests upon the recognition that throughout human history it is upon temples, churches and mosques that the greatest attention has been lavished; moreover, thanks to their strong construction, these have been the most durable of buildings. Consequently this book is not directly relevant to any and every place that may be visited, nor will it add much to the enjoyment of sites where everything is in ruins and there is virtually no architecture. In this last instance archaeology is primary and guide books indispensable. This study, then, will come into its own when you are contemplating the well-preserved temples at Paestum or Agrigento but not so much when you are confronted with the remains at Pella or Sparta. But even when sufficient of a building is still standing to enable it to be enjoyed, that enjoyment may be impaired because such components as reliefs and paintings that were essential to the original may have been removed, as were the Elgin marbles from the Parthenon to the British Museum and the carved panels from Selinunte to the museum at Palermo.

There is one other limitation. No buildings will be mentioned or described that have not been visited by the author. Since enjoyment involves both visual and physical experiences, to speak of what has been neither seen nor felt is to reduce the subject matter to nothing. A visual experience is involved because appreciation is in part a matter of seeing what is there, although often the eye has to be taught what to look for and how – this is a major theme throughout the book. Yet there is more than just the activity of the eye. For example, to move through the entrance door of a Palladian church into the nave is to have more than an optical experience. For full appreciation you must be aware of that something more, of the feelings of rhythm, liberation, and so on that arise as you advance through architectural space. It should be noted further that since architecture is made from material substances that are frequently

moulded or carved like sculpture, it may also be related to the
sense of touch.

Since the aim of this book is to provide an introduction to the
most rewarding way of looking at architectural masterpieces,
there is the problem of turning an experience that is visual,
physical and tactile into words. This has however never prevented artists from writing about their paintings or architects about
their buildings, and there is no reason to doubt that words,
hinting at how to approach architecture, may increase awareness and so contribute to understanding and further enjoyment.
But the difficulties do not end here. How is it possible to convey
the real quality of buildings by means of plans and photographs
which are two-dimensional and so only partially convey a sense
of three-dimensional space? A book is not an adequate substitute for a visit, but it is hoped that the combination of photographs, drawings and text – written in direct relation to the
illustrations – will convey something of the reality of the subject
matter.

As to the scope of this study, the ten chapters examine the
historical styles in chronological order, beginning with the
architecture of Egypt and concluding with Baroque and
Rococo. They thus cover the period from the earliest buildings
along the Nile to the eve of the stylistic revivals in the late
eighteenth century. No attempt has been made to adopt a
uniform plan for each chapter as this would suggest a greater
similarity between the styles than actually exists. Each one is
therefore treated in a way that seems most appropriate to it.
Moreover little explanation of changes from one to the other
has been attempted; in particular evolutionary categories have
not been used. Indeed the concept of evolution as applied to the
history of architecture has had ill effects in that it has suggested
that what is earlier is more primitive and less perfect than that
which follows. From this perspective Romanesque, for example,
was long considered to be mediocre in comparison with Gothic
and to be no more than a stage on the way to its realization and
as such incomplete. That Romanesque buildings had a beauty of
their own which is neither in competition with nor inferior to
the architecture of a later period was in this way overlooked.
Equally ideas of growth, maturity and decay are not discussed
here, for they, in their turn, have similarly impeded appreciation.
Thus Baroque was considered to belong to the era of the
decadence of Renaissance architecture – a view which success-
fully inhibited enjoyment of Baroque buildings in and for
themselves. Not that any style can be surveyed in total isolation;

it is easier to describe items in comparison and by contrast with others. Such an association draws attention to those aspects where they are alike and those where they differ, so shaping the perception of the particular qualities being examined.

In the body of the text technical terms are explained when each is first used, but there is an appendix for those who may lack an initial familiarity with the subject. This provides definitions of the different types of buildings, their ingredients, qualities and principles of composition and the categories to which they may belong. Finally there are some suggestions for further reading, indicating one or two books for each style that may be considered to make a major contribution to appreciation.

University of Birmingham   *J. G. Davies*

1

THE TEMPLES
OF THE NILE

There is one serious disadvantage in beginning this analysis of the various architectural styles with the Egypt of the pharaohs: the artistic vision embodied in the temples of the Nile is so entirely different from that which is familiar to people today that we have to learn a new way of seeing before we can appreciate Egyptian architecture. This vision was remarkably consistent; persisting virtually unchanged for nearly 3,000 years and expressing itself as much in painting and sculpture as it did in architecture. Indeed the best introduction to it is by way of examining a typical painting, since this is easier to understand by means of a reproduction on a flat page than is a building that occupies space.

THE EGYPTIAN ARTISTIC VISION IN PAINTINGS

A husband and his wife are depicted in the accompanying reproduction of a painting from the wall of a noble's tomb of the eighteenth dynasty (1545–1350 BC) at Thebes. Upon examination various odd features become apparent. First, the man's right foot shows his instep, which should be invisible from this viewpoint. Second, while the legs are represented from the side, his chest and shoulders and those of his wife are frontal. Third, although their heads are in profile, their eyes are as if seen full-face. What the artist has done is draw the figures not as they appear to be but as he knew them to be, and knew them in their most characteristic form. The instep is there because it is known to be part of the foot. Legs and heads in profile give a more complete picture than they do from the front, whereas shoulders and eyes from the side do not reveal their full reality and have therefore been drawn frontally. In effect this means that the artist was interested in the mental and not the visual image. Egyptian art has therefore an ideographic character.

Egyptian art is also ideographical in a second sense. Not only is the memory image primary but the paintings themselves express ideas: this one conveys a sense of permanence. Husband and wife are bathed in a uniform light: there are no shadows

Thebes, wall painting from noble's tomb

(although Egypt is a land of sunshine) because shadows change all the time. The transient is rejected in what is a sepulchral art depicting those unaffected by the altering conditions of life in this world. Durability, calm, aloofness, immutability but not lifelessness – the couple have passed beyond a fleeting existence through the door of death.

The dominance of the mental image may explain a further characteristic – the lack of perspective. A Renaissance painter drawing a road that meanders towards the horizon will make it narrower the further away it is – that is how it looks. An Egyptian, on the other hand, knows that a road stays the same width and so for him the correct diagram of it consists of two parallel lines. Egyptian art is consequently entirely lacking in depth; as we can see the husband's stool has only two legs. There is a pronounced ground line, everything being placed on it, so that nothing appears to recede. Overlapping seldom takes place as it might conceal important features; space is ignored, people and objects are not depicted in the round, instead there is emphasis upon line, i.e. linearity is a further general characteristic.

This graphic quality is also to be noted in connection with overall compositions, for many paintings are arranged in long, narrow, horizontal bands which give a sense of linear movement (lateral of course and not in depth). Placing one band above another is known as superimposition and a picture is then created by adding one item to another; indeed even the body in Egyptian design is really the sum of its most salient features. When the principle of addition is adhered to in this way symmetry is frequent and Egyptian art in general conforms to a 'law of frontality' which requires that an imaginary line drawn vertically through the centre of a figure divides it into two equal halves. The picture reproduced in this section is nevertheless unified by means of a focal dominant, namely the locked gaze of the couple.

Scale and proportion are further unifying devices. Egyptian artists used a square grid as the foundation for their designs. Parts of the body were then made to correspond with fixed locations. Equally important in achieving a harmonious effect were the colours, all carefully graded. Indeed the Egyptians delighted in colour – witness the brilliant jewellery belonging to Tutankamoun. The tomb paintings preserve much of this brilliance, being still as fresh as the day when the pigments were first applied to the walls.

By means of this brief analysis it has been possible to identify nine characteristics of the Egyptian artistic vision. It is ideographic, uninterested in perspective and so two-dimensional, linear, additive, symmetrical and conforming to a law of frontality, accentuated by means of a focal dominant, which, together with a uniform scale and a system of related proportions, serves to unify the design, and finally it favours bright colours. That these may also be characteristics of Egyptian architecture is not immediately evident since, to take but one example, how can

Karnak, hypostyle hall

two-dimensionality be applied to what is necessarily three-dimensional? However, rather than attempt to apply these characteristics to architecture straight away, it will make for an easier transition to buildings if these same characteristics are next illustrated from works of sculpture, looking first at reliefs and then at sculpture in the round.

RELIEFS

High up on the columns of the hypostyle or pillared hall at Karnak there is a series of reliefs that record the possessions, attainments and divine relations of Amenophis III and others. Those at the top, 79 feet above ground, are scarcely visible and were even less so originally when a roof kept out the sunlight. These reliefs are not so much visual images as a permanent statement in stone of essential ideas – they are ideographic and so exemplify the first characteristic of the Egyptian artistic vision. Moreover the technique expresses the durability of the image by providing it with highly distinct outlines. Indeed the carvings can be described as surface engravings, as if the face of the stone had been stamped with a seal. They are then two-dimensional; there is no perspective. Because the surface is primary, the designs have been created by a sequence of receding planes, i.e. they are sunk into the masonry and it is possible to speak of a 'plane-parallel' approach that produces a kind of stratification. Indeed because the figures are so surface-dependent

Edfu, rear wall of temple of Horus

they appear flattened and spread out in such a way that we cannot imagine their existence as solid bodies independent of the surface. In the light of this we can expect the designs to be strongly linear and this is indeed the case. Even from a considerable distance the figures on the rear wall at Edfu, for example, are prominent against their ground because of their outlines. In this way the form-obliterating effect of bright sunlight has been countered as the clear and assured shallow cutting produces a strong shadow or light line to define the contours. The design is linear too in the second sense of being arranged in a band and is disposed according to the principle of addition – one figure is juxtaposed against another on the same ground line. Balance, symmetry, frontality, occasional accentuation and uniform scale are as evident in these reliefs as in Egyptian paintings, while remains of pigment hint at how colourful they must once have been.

SCULPTURE IN THE ROUND

The façade of the temple of Ramses II at Abu Simbel consists of two pairs of colossal statues of the pharaoh on either side of the entrance. These huge figures, over 60 feet high, convey a sense of aloofness and majestic calm with no hint of human frailty. Ramses does not react to the earthly situation – he is emotionally impassive. But this does not mean that he is lifeless; rather he manifests a tranquillity deeper than repose. As ideograms of eternity these pieces of sculpture cannot be bettered.

At first glance these statues seem to negate the surface quality that has been noted as a characteristic of the Egyptian artistic

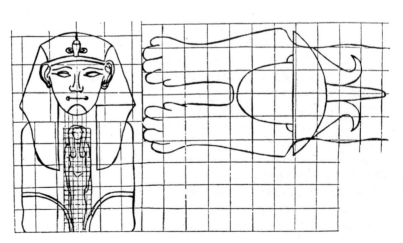

Fig. 1 Working drawing for a sphinx

vision. In fact this is misleading for each piece of sculpture in the
round is really an organization of four planes. Justification of
this terse statement is to be sought in a knowledge of Egyptian
sculptural technique. The sculptor, like the painter, used a grid
system, which appears quite clearly in the accompanying reproduction of a papyrus of the Graeco–Roman period (figure 1).
This is a working drawing for a sphinx, showing views from the
front and looking down on the top of the head. So outlines of
front, top, back and sides were sketched and then transferred on
to a squared block of stone. Next the artist began to cut inwards
from each face towards the centre and finally rounded off the
corners. The result was multifacial, the piece consisting of four
planes meeting one another at right angles and offering four
distinct views to the beholder. It was therefore planar, its depth
being derived from plane recession or stratification exactly as in
reliefs. The effect of following the method just described is that
each piece seems to be enclosed in an invisible rectangular box.
Naturally symmetry and the law of frontality are very evident.
This means that to enjoy the sculpture it should be contemplated
from a central position at front, back and each side. Oblique
views contradict the strong directionality of the Egyptian vision.

*Abu Simbel, temple of
Ramses II*

THE IDEOGRAPHIC CHARACTER OF EGYPTIAN ARCHITECTURE

By now the peculiarities of the Egyptian artistic vision should be familiar and we can consider its embodiment in the magnificent buildings that survive along the banks of the Nile.

If the statues of Ramses II at Abu Simbel express the idea of non-transience, the façade as a whole conveys an identical message. Awe-inspiring in its size, it represents sureness, conviction and firmness. It is a declaration of order, negating confusion and denying haphazardness. Since the afterlife is believed to be a prolongation into eternity of present existence, durability is essential. Impressive in its immensity, the temple is witness to continuity and changelessness.

These related themes do not however exhaust the ideographic content. Each entire temple complex, consisting of pylons, courts, halls and chambers, is an enclosed 'oasis', symbolizing the Egyptian cosmos. In a sense the entire land of Egypt is one large oasis with the Nile providing a central axis and the fields on either side forming a narrow band parallel with the waterway. The temple is a symbol of this world and relates it to eternity, in particular by means of the pylon, the hypostyle hall and the inner sanctuary. The pylon was formed of two quadrangular towers with an entrance gate between them – that of Philae is typical. Its outline corresponded to that of the hieroglyph for 'horizon' and so it denoted the limits of north and south between which the sun god was believed to rise and set. The hypostyle or pillared hall was like a vast papyrus thicket, with the floor often painted to represent water and the ceiling dotted with the stars of heaven. The columns were seen as fertility symbols, with their capitals reproducing the sacred plants that brought well-being and protection. Here the mental image clearly dominates. Finally the sanctuary was an inner chamber where the image(s) of the god(s) or goddess(es) indicated that this was their home.

TWO-DIMENSIONALITY

The pylon at Philae well illustrates the second characteristic that Egyptian architecture shares with its painting and its sculpture: the broad expanse of wall on either side of the entrance indicates that the building is surface-positive. There is an evident concern for the plane; primacy is given to area, which refers to a surface with length and breadth, and not to space, which involves three dimensions. Indeed the Egyptians have been described as space-shy. Certainly they were not interested in interior space at all – the voids within their buildings give the impression of being excavated, hacked out of the encompassing mass. The intervals between the walls and columns are neither planned nor modelled; they are simply voids. Consequently there is no architectural space, which exists when the relationship between voids and solids governs the design. Rather there is simply physical space with the surfaces as the controlling elements to which the voids are subordinate.

This disregard for space becomes very noticeable in the hypostyle hall at Karnak if the visitor stands in the centre of a square defined by any four adjacent columns. To right and left, before and behind, there are corridors formed by long rows of columns stretching into the distance until they are halted by an outside wall. There is precision and a rhythmic vista along each axis, but nothing is visible except these passageways. The visitor is aware that he is in a monumentalized papyrus grove but all he can see are the paths between the stems.

Philae, temple pylon

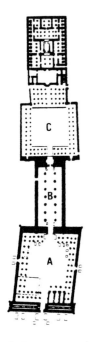

Fig. 2 Luxor, temple of Amoun

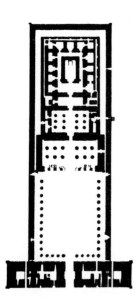

Fig. 3 Edfu, temple of Horus

LINEARITY AND THE PRINCIPLE OF ADDITION

To look to right or left along these corridors at Karnak is further to become aware of the extent to which Egyptian architecture is linear and orthogonal (right-angled). In exact accord with this are the avenues of sphinxes in regular parallel lines that lead to the entrances of many temples. The outlines of the buildings too are crisp, definite and precise so that there is absolute formal clarity, of which the pyramids probably provide the outstanding example. The temples are also planned in linear terms: they are long, narrow, horizontal and directional through pylon, court and hall to sanctuary. Indeed this unvarying sequence reveals the principle of composition to be that of addition achieved through juxtaposition. This building by accretion is most noticeable when temple plans are examined to discover how an original nucleus has been expanded. So the temple at Luxor (figure 2) first comprised a high colonnade (B), a colonnaded court (C) and a sanctuary, all the work of Amenophis III. Later Ramses II placed another court (A) and an entrance pylon in front of the existing three units.

SYMMETRY AND FRONTALITY

Being linear and additive, Egyptian temples are highly symmetrical about a longitudinal axis. Elements on either side are identical. Where balance, rather than bilateral symmetry, is used, it is normally in areas of secondary importance. In general, mirror imagery prevails, corresponding to the law of frontality, as previously illustrated by the pylon at Philae and the façade of Abu Simbel. In the former case the two quadrangular towers are identical, flanking the entrance gate; in the latter case two colossi sit in imperturbable majesty on each side of the door. Because the design is so symmetrical and, at the same time, orthogonal and planar, it should be contemplated from a central position in the same way as a portrait head. Of course this is not the case with a building that has been conceived in the round – then incompleteness is a characteristic of any particular aspect, since each view points beyond itself to those that adjoin. Egyptian temples, on the other hand, composed like Egyptian sculpture of four complete sides, present four independent views, each entire in itself. Hence the rear wall at Edfu is as self-contained as any part of a whole that has been planned according to the principle of addition. The plan of the Edfu temple (figure 3) also demonstrates the extent to which symmetry can dominate. The enclosing walls have been so drawn around and balanced that attention is focused inwards: containment is stressed, marking the outline of a special holy shrine in sharp contrast to the endless space around it.

ACCENTUATION AND PROPORTION

This bilateral symmetry, exemplified by Edfu, was one of the major ways by which the Egyptians unified their designs. They also employed focal dominants and observed a uniform scale throughout each building. Accentuation is very bold and consequently easy to detect; for example, there are the pyramids with their converging lines at the apex and there are the pylons which, because they are made up of such powerful flanking towers, draw attention to the prominence of the doorway. Even when unit was added to unit, at very irregular and often widely distanced intervals of time, harmony was preserved by ensuring that everything grew in size according to rules of proportion common to all parts of a complex. As with painting and sculpture, a grid was used, with preference given to rectangles built up from squares in the ratio 2:1 and to isosceles triangles whose height to base ratio was 8:5 – this last producing a close approximation to the Golden Section. Columns, capitals and obelisks too were cut with due regard to proportionality, and colour was normally applied to bring out salient features as well as enriching the reliefs on the walls.

STRUCTURAL ELEMENTS

While sharing with painting and sculpture all the characteristics of the Egyptian artistic vision, architecture has aspects peculiar to itself. It consists of structures that are to be used and so some knowledge of building components and more especially their forms is needed.

Egyptian architecture is essentially post-and-beam (trabeated) and its origins lie in simple reed or wooden structures, with an upright providing a support for a horizontal member carrying the roof. Walls too could play an important role as supports but the roofs were just flat lids with no effect on design. Wood was in greater supply in ancient Egypt than it is today and bundles of reeds were often used as props. Indeed many of the decorative features of the later stone bases, shafts and capitals derive from this primitive technique. So bundles of reeds were often erected in sockets of earth and hollowed stones; these continued to appear as a raised part of the pavement on which the later stone columns stood, although from a structural point of view they were not needed. The use of mud originally may also explain the batter or inward sloping of the pylons, the inclination being designed to avoid collapse.

In the light of this we can immediately understand why the capitals that formed the 'heads' of each column assumed plant forms: the papyrus, the lotus and the palm. The papyrus, common in the delta, was the sign used by the ruler of Lower Egypt, while the lotus was typical of Upper Egypt. When the two kingdoms were combined, the two plants were often linked as symbols of that union. This was not simply political symbolism: it also had a religious connotation. The plants were representative of the life-giving vegetation arising out of the waters of the Nile, while the ruler was the one who assured this life-sustaining growth and who accordingly hung his house with plants. They were tied to supporting posts which then became, as it were, the stems of the flowers. Thus the papyrus and lotus capitals express the idea of fertility.

Of the two flowers it was the papyrus that was the most

Karnak, Great Court of temple of Amoun

popular as a capital; few examples of the lotus survive and it was not used in temples. The flower could of course be either in bud or open and there were two capitals that corresponded with these two forms. The papyrus with open head appeared at the beginning of the third dynasty and consisted of a single plant, as in the Great Court at Karnak. The papyrus with unopened head or bud capital was in use from the fifth dynasty onwards and was employed to good effect in the court of Amenophis III at Luxor. Eight triangular stems were packed together with their flat bases against the central mass and the ridges outwards, the buds being grouped at the top. What is sometimes called a degradation of this last form was achieved by smoothing the shaft of all irregularities and rounding the capital into a blunt cone — examples are plentiful in the temple of Amoun at Karnak.

Luxor, temple of Amoun

Fig. 4 Palm capital

In addition to the different forms of papyrus and lotus, there were three other capitals. First was the palm, which was out of favour in the Middle and New Kingdoms but was renewed in the Graeco–Roman period and is well represented at Edfu. Second, there was the tentpole capital whose origin is indicated by its name. It is not a very attractive shape but may be studied in the Great Festal Temple of Thutmosis III at Karnak. Finally there is the Hathor capital, four-sided with four heads of the cow-eared goddess Hathor.

Once these unfamiliar forms have been assimilated and note has been taken of the graceful way they swell to meet the cross-beam, further appreciation depends upon grasping the architectural dynamics involved in this structure. A post is essentially a linear object with lines of force or dynamic vectors running along the vertical in both directions, upwards and downwards. The nature of this interplay depends upon the shape and proportions of the column and on the architectural elements with which it is connected. Short squat columns seem crushed by the weight above them; tall slender ones give the impression of thrusting upwards. The terminal elements of base and capital prevent the movement from continuing visually beyond the point of contact with either ground or ceiling, but they do not serve as barriers to interaction nor isolate the shaft. The clue to the major vector in Egyptian columns is provided by the base (figure 5). A base can express the fact that through it the column is fixed to the floor; it stands upon the pavement. But a base can also be a part of the floor, appearing to emerge from it. The Egyptian base, deriving as has been seen from containers for bundles of reeds, belongs to this second category, thus corresponding with the fertility symbolism of upward growth – the column then embodies movement towards the heavens. Moreover, most Egyptian columns have a swelling just below the centre (probably the relic of the sag of the pliable reeds) and this too emphasizes upward movement.

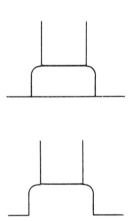

Fig. 5 The relationship of floor, base and column

In addition to post-and-beam, walls were important members of Egyptian buildings. They were in part structural – pylons, screens, and so on – and in part they satisfied the interest in surface. They were used as areas for display or ornament, the decoration spreading out in the plane and unfolding itself with little concern for depth effect. The result was twofold: on the one hand the possible heaviness of the walls was offset and on the other the surface was given greater significance because the reliefs constantly respected it, its structure being unimpaired because of their deliberate flatness. A play of light and shade was nevertheless created and contrasts were introduced into what could otherwise be a monotonous expanse. Further contrasts, in which light played a part, were produced within the building complexes by an alternating sequence of courts in bright sunshine and halls in virtual darkness. A different type of contrast, that resulting from texture, is to be noted between the polished sheen of the original facing of the pyramids and the soft warmth of the smooth temple columns.

PATHS

Every building tends to belong to the category of either a path or a place. Egyptian temples are of the first type: each one is a monumental processional sequence. The ancient Egyptians were very conscious that life is a journey. The sun god himself undertakes a daily voyage from the moment he arises in brightness to the hour when he descends into darkness. An essential part of the worship of Amoun-Ra was the bearing of his image in a sacred boat, symbolizing the diurnal progress of the sun. On high festivals this barque was transported from one temple to another, from Karnak to Luxor for example. The impressive ramps of the mortuary temple of Hatshepsut at Deir el Bahari

Deir el Bahari, temple of Hatshepsut

were there to receive Amoun when his barge was borne between the sphinxes of the queen to the sanctuary dedicated to him on the uppermost terrace. We can therefore expect that the conditions that are needed for the structuring and following of a well-designed path are likely to be fulfilled in the various temples.

A path requires strong edges so that there can be no uncertainty about its definition. Hence Egyptian temples have sharp contours, with each unit added in their creation possessing formal clarity. Further a path has to have continuity and this is emphasized by the linearity of Egyptian architecture, its longitudinality, axiality and symmetry, all of which stand out on the plan of any temple. That of Edfu (see figure 3) is an excellent example of this longitudinal disposition with bilateral symmetry, emphatic axis and a steady advance drawing the visitor from pylon to shrine. The complex is accordingly very directional and it is also horizontal in thrust; indeed just as sculpture in the round appears to exist in an invisible cube, so each temple could fit within a rectangular box that emphasizes the movement towards the cult image and uses horizontality as a witness to eternity.

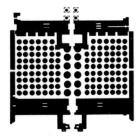

Fig. 6 Karnak, hypostyle hall

There is a certain staccato aspect to this relentless drive because, observing the principle of addition, the units are relatively independent; further, the hypostyle halls may seem to constitute interruptions. However they are not so much places as stages on a journey. Indeed a brief analysis of the Karnak hall (figure 6) reveals that it is a part of the processional path and is a passage rather than an internal volume. While it is true that it is much wider than it is long, the movement in length has been preserved by the creation of a central corridor out of two flanking rows of columns, 35 feet higher than the aisles. Moreover this taller 'nave' is wider than the corridors on either side. In addition some of the rows of columns at right angles to the nave are not in line with the nave colonnades: the effect is both a fragmentation of space to right and left, broken by the staggered columns, and also an accentuation of the east–west axis. What is more this central passageway was lit through high stone grilles, with narrow slits. Being not as dim as the areas to either side therefore, it was distinguishable from them. One may wander in the thickets of these halls and enjoy them, but they are not permanent resting places, and one returns to the main path to seek recognizable landmarks, in the way of statues, such as the pair that funnel the visitor from the court of Ramses II at Luxor into the colonnade of Amenophis III. Other prominent points were denoted by obelisks, themselves solidified rays of the sun. In all temples there is a sharp terminal (the holy of holies) and end-from-end differentiation – no one can mistake the god's bedroom for the entrance pylon.

THE PYRAMIDS

Within this same category of a path there fall what are probably the most familiar of Egyptian buildings – the pyramids. That they do belong to this type is not immediately obvious because they appear to be more or less solid structures of the crystal type. Nevertheless an examination can demonstrate the correctness of this classification and the extent to which the pyramids display all the main features of Egyptian architecture.

Pyramids of Giza

Whereas, as previously mentioned, reed and wood were the materials used for the earliest buildings, the move to stone was taken by one of the greatest architects of the world, Imhotep, the servant of Zoser (*c.*2750 BC). He it was who piled rectangular tomb upon tomb to create a royal resting place. One slightly smaller *mastaba* (Arabic for 'bench') was superimposed upon a larger one and so on to produce at Sakkara a pyramid in step form (figure 7). However the Egyptian preferences for precise outlines and for planes were not satisfied by this design and these aesthetic concerns led naturally to the true pyramid, so well exemplified at Giza with those of Kheops (*c.*2690), Khephren (2640) and Menkeros or Mykerinos (2600), where

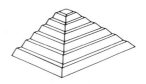

Fig. 7 Sakkara, step pyramid

huge blocks of stone are added together by juxtaposition and superimposition.

As an ideogram a pyramid unhesitatingly speaks through its material and its massiveness, demonstrating the timelessness of stone and denying the ravages of time by its size and permanence. Its broad horizontal base evinces immobility and stability, but a pyramid is also an up-soaring triangle and so connects with the heavens. It spreads and weighs downwards for the security of the dead pharaoh and at the same time constitutes a kind of path leading up to eternity. Its architectural dynamics, when it is viewed as an object in itself, correspond with this duality of ideas. A pyramid is a compact mass resting on the ground, but it is also a wedge-shape embodying an upward force (figure 8a). Both dynamic themes are present everywhere within it. Since these dynamics operate in two directions, there is a rising towards the apex and a simultaneous descent towards the base. This two-way dynamism is very evident in the horizontal layers, formed by the rows of blocks of stone, as they become narrower upwards and wider downwards. So the internal dynamism of a pyramid arises from the complementary relations of ascending and descending, or of contraction and expansion. This dynamism is the perfect vehicle for the twin ideas embodied in the shape. Like the top of an obelisk – which is a pyramid in miniature – a pyramid is a bundle of solar rays, emanating from the central point of the sun and denoting the care of Ra for the deceased, and it is also the Egyptian equivalent of Jacob's ladder, a way up to the divine presence. However it is the latter vector that is primary, but the justification for this statement rests upon the planar nature of a pyramid and must therefore wait until that has been investigated.

An Egyptian pyramid is more a picture than a structure. What is presented to the observer is the uniform plane of a triangle, whose sharply cut-off sides in no way suggest their junction with a three-dimensional body behind. Indeed the pyramid demonstrates more clearly than any other building the extent to which Egyptian architecture used the plane as its constitutent element, precisely because a pyramid is made up of four equal isosceles triangles converging on a single point. It has therefore four independent and complete faces and it was intended to be viewed squarely on from the centre of any one of these four sides so that there was no perspective but simply a single triangular surface visible at any one time. All that has been said previously about the two-dimensionality of the Egyptian artistic vision applies to the pyramid: it is surface-positive; it is planar. This means that to view it obliquely so that two sides are seen together is contrary to the original vision. This has a direct bearing upon the primacy of the upward or downward movement. When a triangle is looked at from a position opposite the midpoint of a base edge the principal impression is one of aggressive rising movement (figure 8b), whereas if two sides are visible, and therefore a double baseline comes into view, attachment to the ground is accentuated and the downward vector is predominant (figure 8c). To correspond most nearly to the intention of the design, the visitor should occupy a central position, thereby acknowledging the surface quality of the monument, its frontality and the bilateral symmetry of the shape. That this is the way to obtain the most rewarding view is endorsed by the focal dominant, which is the apex. A pyramid is so compact that the apex attracts the eye readily and serves as an accent although it has no separate existence.

There is yet another aspect of architectural dynamics that is relevant at this juncture. A pyramid is not only an object in itself, it is also an object in space. It displaces air as it pushes into the sky – again attention is being drawn to its summit (figure 8d). The surrounding space also presses in on it and seems to compress it to a mere point – the apex is further accentuated (figure 8e). Not only is there in this way an interplay between a pyramid and its surrounding space, the structure was also related to other features in a total complex of funerary design.

The body of the pharaoh was transported down the Nile and a halt was made on the bank where it was landed. Next a cortège conducted the corpse up a great processional road to the foot of the tomb that had been prepared for it. There it was made ready – by embalming, and so on – before it was enclosed in the heart of the pyramid. Corresponding to these several activities and movements, the entire funeral complex of Khephren consisted of a valley temple (originally on the bank of the Nile which has since receded), then a special causeway to the mortuary temple and finally the pyramid itself. Hence the pyramid, which was both a place where the body was entombed and a path leading upwards to heaven and downwards for the descent of the sun god, also functioned as a node or goal giving direction to the entire funeral way, with its clear directionality, landmarks, and so on. It was not an independent entity but the focus of the last rites.

The architectural complex just described prefigured the layout of the temples of the New Kingdom, such as those at Karnak and Luxor. The valley temple at Giza was the equivalent of a vestibule; the causeway led to the mortuary temple containing hall, courtyard and sanctuary and was at the foot of the shrine.

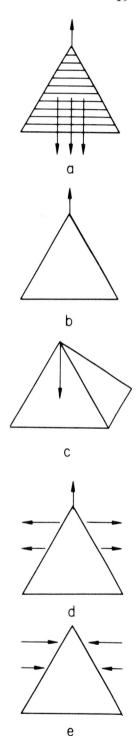

Fig. 8 The dynamics of a pyramid

There are evident parallels here with pylon, courtyard, hypo-style halls and the room for the cult image. The pyramid is itself replaced by the mountain in the temple of Hatshepsut, while the terraces represent the other units. The upward movement of the ramps, in this remarkable design by another outstanding archi-tect named Senmut, reproduces the vertical thrust of the pyramid and in this way vertical axiality has been united with a longitudinal path.

This last example is one of the few that reveals a deliberate attempt to relate architecture to landscape, whereas many Egyptian temples, such as the one at Kom Ombo, are indepen-dent actors in space. At Deir el Bahari however the colonnades echo the drop of the cliff behind, beyond which lies the Valley of the Kings. The whole is freely integrated with its setting: the beauty of the severe lines accords well with the horizontality of the cliff top and the vertical sheerness of its face. Again at Abu Simbel the façades of the two temples do not break the line of the hill in which they have been excavated. The smaller temple of Hathor and Nofrotere has its pilasters between the statues sloped parallel to the incline of the hill – temple and mountain are united as the mountain becomes part of the temple and the temple part of the mountain. Other temples may be related to the Nile, the highway for the transportation of the god's ceremonial barge – but often they stand up stark, like oases in a vast amorphous desert, eternally waiting.

2

AEGEAN ARCHITECTURE

To speak of Aegean architecture is to leave the pharaohs and conjure with such romantic names as Agamemnon ruler of Mycenae, the hero Hercules, born according to some at Tiryns, and Minos the priest-king of Knossos. Indeed in this chapter are to be considered both the palaces of Crete and, on the other side of the Aegean, the citadels of Argos. The distance between the two regions is great, but there were relations between them, as indicated by the fragments of paintings recovered at Mycenae which are in exactly the same style as those unearthed at Knossos and also, roughly midway between the two centres, on the island of Santorini or Thera. The precise nature of the relations between Crete and Argos is still a matter of dispute and turns largely upon the interpretation of an ancient form of writing known as Linear B. Nevertheless, whatever the ultimate outcome of this debate, it need not be pursued further here because it does not directly affect our delight in the remains; whatever their date (and the possibilities range from 1400 to 1200 BC) it is their present condition that is the basis for architectural enjoyment.

Apart from foundations, the Tholos Tomb and the Lion Gate at Mycenae, together with the walls and galleries at Tiryns, neither of these two mainland sites, nor Pylos, has much to offer in the way of architecture. At Knossos, on the other hand, thanks to the efforts of Sir Arthur Evans, much of the palace has been subjected to restoration or, as he preferred to call it, 'reconstitution'. He was sensitive to criticism from purists and defended his action with several arguments. He pointed out that, in the very process of digging, the archaeologist cannot avoid a choice: either he removes and so destroys the upper layers in order to reach those beneath or he must resupport them; by obviating the danger of collapse in this way he also preserves them. He chose the latter course because in his view an adequate record comprises not only reports, photographs, drawings and objects removed to a museum, but the site and building conserved as far as possible.

Not only did Evans reconstitute pillars, stairs, walls and so on, he also put up replicas of frescoes – the originals having been lodged in Herakleion museum – and this further helps to preserve the archaeological record by indicating in corridors and rooms where they were found. This certainly adds interest to a visit, while his reconstitution programme prevents the non-expert from being misled, renders the plan comprehensible and gives clues for the enjoyment of other sites that have not been so conserved. It justifies too the inclusion of these places within a study of architecture – but were these palaces in any sense religious buildings?

The palaces were not temples. Indeed the Minoan civilization appears not to have had specialized sanctuaries. They were however essentially sacred edifices, being, according to Evans, 'interpenetrated with religious elements'. In the West Court at Knossos, for example, there are the bases of two altars, while another is to be seen in the middle of the Central Court at Mallia. Within the palaces there are numerous shrines – like chapels in bishops' palaces – together with pillar crypts, i.e. dark cellars enclosing a cluster of piers and probably associated with chthonic or earth rites. There are also lustral basins or baths for purification. Everywhere are examples of the sacred symbol known as the Horns of Consecration – along the eaves and in other prominent places. Many double-axes, which were probably used for the sacrifices, were placed about in pyramidal bases. Their outlines were incised upon pillars and walls and were represented in paintings. Indeed the double-axe as a sign of Minoan religion was as omnipresent as the cross in Christianity. Nor was it confined to Crete; examples are forthcoming from the mainland as well. Then the so-called magazines, with double-axes engraved on the upright slabs (orthostats) that line them, were less rooms to store provisions as treasuries for religious offerings – see figure 14 (I–XVIII). Processions bearing these gifts were depicted on frescoes along the corridor walls.

Granted that all the palaces, whether on the mainland or in Crete, had a sacred character and granted that there were other similarities between them, such as a common fresco style and the use of identical symbols, yet they are sufficiently distinct for the two areas to be considered separately, beginning with the Minoan palaces.

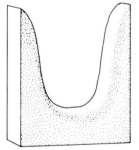

Fig. 9 Horns of Consecration

Fig. 10 Double-axe

MINOAN PALACES

PALACE AND LANDSCAPE

It was Evans himself who remarked that the Central Court at Knossos is dominated by Mount Juktas, but he did not pursue what this might mean in terms of the relationship between the palace and its landscape setting. This investigation was delayed until the 1960s and the publication of a remarkable study by Vincent Scully who was able to demonstrate the existence of a clearly defined pattern at Knossos that was reproduced at the other main palace sites. Three elements are involved in this pattern: an enclosed valley within which the palace is located; a rounded hill on the north–south axis of the palace and, in line with this, a double-peaked mountain. The profile of the last is that of a pair of horns, suggesting upraised arms and the female cleft. As such it serves as a symbol of the active power of the Earth Mother, while the rounded hill, with the breast-like outline, has the same association.

Knossos, Central Court and Mount Juktas

The harbour of Knossos was to the north of the palace which was approached through a valley. Passing into the north entrance – figure 14(8) – one eventually reached the Central Court which was on the north–south axis aligned with both a moulded hill and beyond it with the notched peak of Juktas. Similarly at Phaistos, the entrance is in the north-west corner and the visitor eventually descends to the Central Court which is on the north–south axis with the horns of Mount Ida, while at Mallia Mount Dikte presents the same split summit. This is the climactic shape that draws the gaze and causes it to rest within its cup. The eye is directed thither by the elongated court and the result is an emphasis upon the natural order that derives from the goddess. The recognition of this reciprocity of palace and landscape is an essential part of appreciating the architectural achievement of the Minoans.

The palaces do not confront the landscape; they are essentially hollows that receive and are controlled by it. Their inhabitants were in this way safe within the embrace of the Earth Goddess, and so the architecture, adapted to the shapes of the sites, expresses harmony with the forces of nature. It is in a sense 'natural' architecture in that it almost takes its colour from the countryside, grouping itself along its contours and spreading outwards from a central court which is to be found in all Minoan palaces and is the focus of the whole plan.

THE CENTRAL COURT AND THE BULL GAME

All Minoan palaces, including that at Zakkro, where excavations began only in 1962, have centre courts. These are usually twice as long or more from north to south as they are wide from east to west, all measuring about 170 by 80 feet. This standardization suggests that they were built to definite specifications and they are certainly key features, the palaces growing from the inside out, sprawling or spilling over from this primordial unit. It was therefore the organizing nucleus of the plan, at once dividing and uniting the parts of the complex. It was both a traffic hub and a centre for daily activities. At all four sites can be seen the column bases of the porticoes that diversified the façades, which probably had upper galleries on the long sides and were given some monumental treatment.

According to many commentators the Central Court was also the place where the Minoans held their bull games. As depicted on frescoes from both Knossos and Tiryns, this was a kind of dance in which young men and young women engaged. As the bull charged, the acrobat sprang upwards, seized the horns for greater leverage and, when the animal tossed its head, performed a somersault along its back and landed beyond the tail. This passage through the bull's horns was a form of religious ceremonial, possibly initiatory in character. Now the full import of the Horns of Consecration becomes evident. They are the horns of the sacred bull and at the same time they correspond to the mountain cleft and so constitute a fertility symbol.

The bull game requires vigorous rushing to and fro and for this a terrain free from obstacles is needed. But in the middle of the court at Mallia there is the base of an altar, while at Zakkro there is also a base, slightly off-centre. It is difficult to reconcile the presence of such large fixed objects with the bull game. Moreover all these courts were paved and this does not provide a firm surface for either charging bulls or somersaulting acrobats. Consequently it has been argued that the courts were not used for this game, but this does not deny their sacred character, confirmed as this is by the presence of altars.

OTHER COMPONENTS OF THE PALACE PLAN

Outdoors

At Knossos, Mallia and Phaistos, in addition to the Central Court, there is a second one to the west. There is also at Knossos, at the end of the Royal Road, an open-air section known as the Theatral Area – see figure 14(9). This consists of a paved courtyard in front of shallow steps or terraces, and is obviously a place of public concourse. Similar terraces border the West Court at Phaistos. Various ideas, all plausible, have been advanced about what activities drew spectators thither. A fresco from Santorini and a miniature from Tylissos show that boxing was a favourite sport and bouts could have been staged here. Again, the Theatral Area was well suited for the ceremonial reception of important guests, for the hearing of lawsuits or to serve as a station for a religious procession on its way to the Central Court. It could also have been the scene of dancing which was certainly a feature of Minoan life.

Transitional

Some of the main entrances of the palaces were marked by porches of a monumental character. The South Propylaeum at Knossos provides a notable example – see figure 14(3). It is an H-shaped room with two columns at each end and constitutes a formal entrance hall of some grandeur.

Equally transitional between interior and exterior are the colonnades which, as already mentioned, were stationed along the sides of the Central Court. They were also adjuncts of the residential quarters, allowing pleasant views of the surrounding gardens and the access of light, its brilliance tempered by the shade thus provided.

*Knossos, South
Propylaeum*

Indoors

Within the palaces accommodation was differentiated according to the function of its parts. At Knossos, for example, the northern section was where the principal workshops were located. Among the religious features we have already noted the pillar crypts and lustral basins. An example of the latter is connected with the Room of the Throne at Knossos – figure 14(6) – which itself may have been the place where a priestess presided over the cult of the Earth Goddess. Other rooms of public venue were often, though not exclusively, on the first floor, being halls with their ceilings supported on columns and piers.

The domestic quarters (figure 11) all have similar nuclei made up of a corridor, two rooms and a light well, plus the occasional bathroom. The rectangular rooms were formed of both simple walls and screens of piers with sets of double doors between them. When the doors are opened, they fold back and fit into a panel in the face of each pier; when closed, they constitute a temporary partition. Of the two rooms in each nucleus, the sides of one can be either one wall and three pier screens (1) or two walls opposite each other and two screens. The second room (2) has one side of piers, which it shares with the first room, and then one side opening through columns on to a light well (3) with walls on the other two sides. They have been planned on the 'but-and-ben' or 'in-and-out' system which requires traversing one room to enter the second beyond or parallel with it. The effect of this and of the use of partitions is that the rooms are not self-contained boxes; there is an interpenetration of space that produces a kind of lightness and fosters movement, which is the fundamental characteristic of this architecture, and requires some attention being paid to the means of circulation.

All parts of the palace are joined by a vast number of sinuous corridors on each level, with staircases providing a vertical link and light wells the illumination. These last produce a suffused, gentle light so helping to create a cool interior in sharp contrast to the intensity of the heat and sun outside. The stairways too are light and graceful and this effect derives both from the openness of the rhythmical balustrades and from the constancy of the distance between them and the flight above with which they descend or mount in parallel. The stairs have normally a

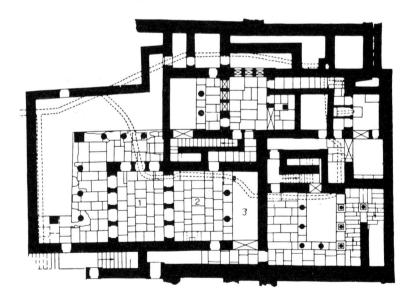

Fig. 11 Knossos,
domestic quarters

minimum of two flights, arranged either in an L, with one at right angles to the other, or in a U, with the two parallel and connected by a landing.

STRUCTURE AND COMPOSITION

Without question Minoan palaces are mass-positive, built from huge blocks of stone, although the mass also serves to define space for movement. Columns were used for porticoes and verandas but they were not really essential to the basic structure. The system is post-and-beam, which is revealed in doorways, yet the supporting and protecting functions have not been fully differentiated, so that it is the walls that constitute the distinctive feature. The pillars that create internal divisions are themselves really part of a wall, being what remains when holes have been pierced through it.

Minoan columns on circular stone bases were mainly of *Knossos, North Entrance* wood; at their summit is a rounded capital supporting a block, *Passage* on which rests the beam (architrave). Above this there is usually

a frieze of circles, which probably represent the ends of another wooden component, namely, logs. In considering these elements, it is natural to begin at the bottom and work up.

The Minoan base, like the Egyptian, is part of the floor pushing up to engage the shaft. This vertical movement is continued by the column which tapers towards the bottom. In other words, while most columns are wider at the bottom than at the top, the Minoan is narrower at ground level and broadens out as it mounts to meet the beam. The effect is not one of compression but of exuberance, of upsurging energy. Although it has vectors in both directions, up and down, it is the burgeoning thrust that predominates – movement is its characteristic. The shaft, with its skywards dynamic, thus corresponds with the Horns of Consecration.

The third part of the columnar structure is the capital which is rather like a base reversed; it avoids the appearance of the post burrowing up into the beam and it facilitates the movement from the vertical back to the horizontal. In this way it overcomes the twofold problem presented by the trabeated system: first, how to prevent the vertical movement from seeming to continue visually beyond the interface (figure 12a), and, second, how to prevent the abruptness that occurs when a circular support is placed under a rectangular lintel (figure 12b). The Minoan solution, which is continued in the period of classical Greek architecture, is to gather the shaft together by a necking or narrow moulding that begins the transition from shaft to capital. Then there swells out a rounded form to meet a square block (abacus) that itself corresponds with and joins the beam (figure 12c). So the upward flow of forces splays outwards to engage the architrave and the descending flow runs through the capital, like a funnel, into the pipe-like shaft. There is no isolation of column from superstructure nor any barrier to interaction between them. There is a two-way continuity that conveys delight as the dynamic stream is grasped and appreciated.

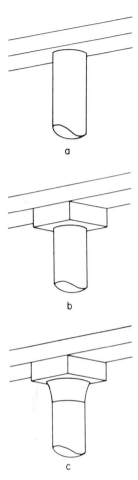

Fig. 12 *Relating shafts to beams*

While some columns have vertical grooves or flutes, thus emphasizing the thrust upwards, most are plain. Colour was however applied to reveal the distinctness of the parts. On the evidence of frescoes, black capitals crowned red shafts and red capitals topped black shafts, with mouldings that were sometimes white, sometimes yellow. This provides a clue to the Minoan principle of composition. The parts are differentiated by the pigment and are in this way to be seen as so many sub-wholes. This is demonstrated beyond question by pictures of buildings on seals; invariably they show the necking as separate from the shaft and capital, as well as the capital from the

Fig. 13 Architectural details on a seal

necking and the beam: each is a semi-independent entity, the whole being created by the assembling of distinct units (figure 13). This means that the principle of composition is undeniably addition. The same conclusion is supported by the palace plans where unit after unit is juxtaposed. Superimposition, which is another pointer towards addition, can be seen in the wall frescoes with their two-band designs, one above the other.

CHARACTERISTICS OF MINOAN PALACES

When a plan is drawn up on the principle of addition, unit is stuck on to unit in what has been called an agglutinative manner. But in the case of the palaces, despite the accentuation provided by the dominant Central Court, it is impossible to detect any concern for the coherence of the parts. No attempt has been made to arrange them symmetrically for example; on the contrary, any one of the sites reveals a certain disorderliness which must be regarded as one of the leading characteristics of Minoan architecture. Its second main characteristic has already been encountered when analysing the column: this embodies the concepts of force and energy and so emphasizes the importance of movement. Delight in these buildings then arises in large measure from recognizing how this irregularity and this endless motion have been given form.

Irregularity immediately confronts the modern visitor to Knossos. Opposite the present-day entrance, across the West Court is a long façade; built of well-cut limestone masonry, it is anything but straight. The wall is interrupted by shallow breaks and recesses and it advances and retreats in a series of projections and bays. Functional explanations are not convincing, for example the suggestion that the bays may have corresponded with windows in the floor above, while the projections were produced by the pushing outwards of interior units of different sizes. The fact remains that the Minoans were not concerned to enclose buildings in neat rectangles, preferring broken outlines. They used flat roofs so that the palaces straggle vertically as well as horizontally; the levels are not uniform, the number of storeys varying from one to three. The profiles are consequently as uneven as the ground lines. The defining shape is not provided by the structure but by the natural setting: the building is indeed a partner subordinate to the landscape.

Irregularity is further apparent when you attempt to go inside the palaces: you then discover that the entrance points are all off-centre and that there is a multiplicity of choice. Even when a choice is made, access meanders. To take Knossos as an illustration (figure 14): the entrance is not in the middle of the western façade but in the south-east corner of the West Court (1). This opens into the Corridor of the Procession Frescoes (2), which wanders round to the South Propylaeum (3). There you can either pass through the porch and up the stairs (5) to the main rooms on the first floor or continue into the Corridor of the Priest-King (4) and so on to the Central Court. There is thus no obviously direct way to follow.

Minoan irregularity is also embodied in the endless corridors that are such a feature of the palace plans. Scarcely a single passageway is straight; instead they are bent and each one is either dog-legged or L-shaped. They change direction abruptly and the line of communication is unpredictable. Examples, typical of all, are the North Entrance Passage, figure 14(7), and the Corridor of the Procession Frescoes, both at Knossos. It is the existence of this circulation system that underscores the ceaseless movement which, after irregularity, constitutes a main characteristic of these buildings.

Fig. 14 Knossos

This movement is by no means always smooth; rather it is restless, and inconsequential. This is exemplified by the but-and-ben arrangement which requires one room to be traversed before the second one can be entered. It is further evident in the disposition of entrances which, as previously noted, are either off-centre or located in corners. What is more, any clear passage through them is inhibited by the positioning of the supports. Instead of space corresponding with space, the entrance columns obscure the openings between the piers. Such deflection of movement can be experienced at the top of the Grand Staircase at Phaistos where pillars and piers do not match and neither do the intercolumnar spaces. Indeed at Phaistos while the sweep up the steps is unimpeded, it has to split when it reaches the shaft that stands in the very centre of the entrance to the first antechamber.

The bifurcation of the motion is continued in some rooms by a central row of columns, with further conflicting lines of movement being introduced by means of counter-axes. The Room of the Throne at Knossos, figure 14(6), illustrates this duality: one axis starts from the entrance and crosses the chamber along the short row of columns on the left to the exit on the far side; the other axis, at 90 degrees to the first, is created by the throne

Phaistos, Grand Staircase

which projects from the right-hand wall. Similarly the Theatral Area has two tiers of seats or steps set at right angles – there are therefore counter-axes. All this means that the Minoans delighted in contrasts: not only those inherent in divided movement and counter-axes but also in differences of structure, of colour and texture and even between light and shade. To follow the winding corridors is to plunge into darkness and then re-emerge into bright sunlight; to experience closure and openness.

Knossos, Room of the Throne

ORNAMENT

The impression of movement was everywhere intensified by the decorations, and sufficient traces remain for their contribution to be appreciated. The subjects of the frescoes that ran along the corridors included gambolling dolphins, charging bulls and graceful dancers. Vivacious and active, they correspond with the movement of the architecture and complement it. Even when the designs are abstract, the same impulse to rhythmical advance is present. There is an inescapable zest for life, a love of nature and an exuberance that echoes the burgeoning of the Minoan column. There is however no attempt to impose a rigid order (this was to become a characteristic of classical architecture). Here there is no analytical clarity but fluidity and freedom of mobility.

There is a concern for line as well, emphasized by the many

dadoes and superimposed bands, and this is yet another con-
comitant of the passion for movement. Indeed the time has
come to recognize that these buildings are anything but static
and so do not belong to the category of places – they are rather
paths.

THE PALACES AS PATHS

Clearly defined paths have six principal characteristics: our
immediate task is to see how far these can be identified and so
appreciated in the palace architecture. A path requires strong
edges and this is certainly a feature of the endless corridors
which are defined by walls with decorated surfaces. Continuity
is ensured by the patterning of the floors; for example, the
corridor of the Priest-King at Knossos had uninterrupted border
strips of blue-green slate faced with red stucco, and there was a
central seam of gypsum slabbing. The figure processions also
contribute to continuity and at the same time mark directions.
These frescoes act as companions along the way, and even when
a corner is reached, the middle blue bands that separate one
register from another undulate onwards and turn without halt-
ing, so sustaining the forward movement.

The slightly elevated paved ways, too, which are found in all
the palaces, especially in the West Courts, indicate directions.
Gradients also stress this directional element, as when the North
Staircase at Phaistos descends to the Theatral Area, while from
the North Entrance at Knossos – see figure 14(8) – the passage
mounts to the Central Court. Finally there is to be noted the use
of linear configuration for this purpose – spaces are long and
narrow so that movement, both real and optical, is canalized in
one direction, leading to and from the Central Court.

Nevertheless it has to be acknowledged that the primary
direction is not always as clear as just represented. Many of the
units that make up the network of passages can be read as
two-way: stairs lead up but also down; to enter a dog-legged
corridor is not to see its opposite end. The Grand Staircase at
Phaistos is anything but directional. You arrive at a blank wall
and even if you do find the two small exits and choose one rather
than the other, which direction to take beyond them is not at all
apparent. Does this mean that the paths in Cretan palaces are
ill-designed? Not necessarily so: it could be that they are paths
but that they also belong to a very special kind of path that
would justify this ambiguity. However before exploring this
possibility, there remain three other path characteristics to be

noted. Recognizable landmarks, that give character to a path and assure the traveller that he is indeed on the way, are by no means lacking; altars, Horns of Consecration, double-axes, fresco scenes such as the charging bull in the North Entrance Passage at Knossos, stretches of colonnade – all these help orientation. But there are no sharp terminals to show where a path finishes, nor end-from-end distinctions to prevent confusion about where one is.

It might be supposed that the Central Court constitutes at least one sharp terminal, but this can be questioned. It is not to be identified as a place, because while it was a focus and is indeed limited in size and has pronounced borders – all place characteristics – it is neither an inside in contrast with a surrounding outside nor is it truly closed in upon itself because of its essential relationship and openness to the landscape. Rather it is a junction of paths, a node or central point, which is both centripetal, drawing people towards it, as well as centrifugal, urging them out into the circulation system that surrounds it. Because all corridors start from and eventually lead back to the Central Court, there can be no clear end-from-end distinction, even while it remains the principal goal of every movement. It is not surprising therefore to find that its paving, unlike that of other courts, is not patterned and has no direction indicators.

The whole palace system is in fact a kind of web built up from meandering alleys and thin, elongated rooms. No one path stands out as more important than another; all are interconnected to create a remarkable network. But – the question must be faced – what kind of paths are these that have strong edges and continuity with recognizable landmarks but are directionally ambiguous and possess neither sharp terminals nor end-from-end distinctions? The inescapable answer is that a network made up of such paths must be said to constitute a maze. This conclusion means that the enjoyment of a tour of the palaces must in part be of the same kind as that which accompanies the penetration of a labyrinth.

THE LABYRINTH

The delight to be derived from visiting a maze is related to the human interest in pathfinding: we are all would-be pioneers and explorers. The converse of this, of course, is the fear of being lost. Consequently a maze is pleasurable to the extent that there is no danger of ultimately not coming out and as long as it is not entirely chaotic but has a shape that can eventually be apprehended. Both of these conditions are fulfilled in the Minoan palaces. Visual clues are provided to help you find your way around; each clue, such as a double-axe in a pyramidal base or an altar, has a character of its own that enables it to be identified and reassures you that you are on the right track. Confidence is preserved by the knowledge that there is an exit, and as you become familiar with the route there is enjoyment in recognizing the landmarks. There is also the pleasure of encountering the unexpected – secret nooks, turnings that had not been anticipated, passages that double back and that rise and fall, rooms that open into one another.

There is further delight in being temporarily lost. This is quite appropriate to the maze situation where movement can be interpreted as involving a sequence of unexpected vistas, stimulating in their variety and not predetermined by a very simple map indicating an overall order. An environment such as a maze is more a texture than a design. It is held together by its homogeneity which refuses to assign to any one element a particular place fixed by the structure of the whole: it is, as already suggested, a network.

Yet another aspect of appreciation concerns the possibility of relating a maze to a larger area so that it is not just an incoherent fragment. The Minoan palaces, with their strong north–south axes and their reciprocity with the landscape, achieve precisely this. At the same time they present a challenge. There are baffling choices of direction. There is a need to remember the way back or at least, if you have a plan in a guide book, to discover where you are and decide where to go next. As this is accomplished there is a feeling that a problem is being solved, akin to finding the answer to a riddle, except that in this case it is not so much a matter of the intellect nor just of visual perception but of bodily motion. Indeed the essence of a labyrinth is movement; such a structure only takes on meaning as you walk through it. You follow the path and since this special kind of path is a maze, it is not to be looked upon as a way to a goal – the delight is in the journey rather than in any arrival – path and place tend to coalesce. Yet whoever penetrates a maze finds himself time and again at its centre, like the *Three Men in a Boat* at Hampton Court, and as do visitors to Crete who emerge repeatedly into the central courts. It is here that architectural character and legend come together, for at the very heart of the maze, according to Greek mythology, there dwelt the Minotaur.

The Minotaur was the man-bodied and bull-headed offspring of Pasiphaë, wife of Minos, priest-king of Knossos. The monster was confined within a maze and was there eventually killed by

Theseus with the aid of Ariadne, Minos's daughter. The designer of the maze, which wound round and about like the River Maeander, was said to be Daedalus who also constructed at Knossos a 'dancing ground' for Ariadne. Accompanied by a troupe of young men and women rescued from the Minotaur, Theseus left Crete and called at the sacred island of Delos; there, according to Plutarch, he led them in a Crane dance that 'imitated the inward and outward windings of the labyrinth'. It is not difficult to appreciate how Knossos, with its Theatral Area, Central Court and sinuous corridors, could have given rise to such traditions – it was indeed the House of the Double-axes. The Greek word for this ritual object was *labrys*, which in time was applied to the twisting and intricate character of the palaces and so 'labyrinthine' gained a meaning that has endured to this day.

PALACES AND CITADELS OF THE PELOPONNESE

The most striking contrast between the palaces we have just been considering and those at Tiryns and Mycenae derives from the fact that the former were not built to withstand hostile attacks whereas the latter were great strongholds with huge, defensive walls. Both citadels rear up and are silhouetted against the sky. At Mycenae the walls are from 10 to 23 feet thick and in some places as much as 33 to 46 feet. At Tiryns many of the massive stones weigh up to 14 tons, and it was very fitting that Pindar should apply to them the adjective Cyclopean (i.e. erected by the Cyclopes or giants), and that Homer should sing of 'wall-girt' Tiryns, while Pausanias compared it with the pyramids. Sufficient of these fortifications remain to impress by their rugged strength and by their domination of the countryside. Here too, as in Crete, there was reciprocity between the buildings and the landscape.

Tiryns was set in a plain with a conscious relationship to the natural features that symbolize the goddess. Like the Minoan palaces there is a strong north–south axis; to the north is the Heraion of Argos and to the south the horns of the ridge of Palamedes. At Pylos the main axis is similarly in line with a conical hill and the cleft peak of Mount Mathia – the sexual symbolism is undeniable. At Mycenae, while the entire citadel is erect and arrogant in its posture, in its disposition it is subservient to the goddess. You enter past a round tomb, itself a symbol of the womb of nature, through the Lion Gate whose central pillar is yet another symbol of fertility, and so mounting past the grave circles, where the heroic dead still watch over the stronghold, you ascend to the hall or megaron where the king sat in majesty and power.

Tiryns, Gallery

Fig. 15 Pylos, palace of Nestor

The megaron in the palaces of Argos has a forecourt, but this is not to be compared with the great central courts of Crete. It is always subservient to the royal hall – an annex, as it were, simply freeing the approach, so although easily identifiable on a plan, it is in no sense a general focus. It is the megaron itself rather that exercises the principal centralizing role, retaining its identity as a separate shape to which other units have been added although it is surrounded by a conglomeration of other structures. As exemplified at Pylos (figure 15) it usually comprises a main room (6), preceded by an antechamber (5), a portico (4), a small court (3) and an H-shaped porch (2,1). Within the Presence Chamber there is a throne to one side and a round hearth in the centre. This latter is another feature distinguishing these buildings from the Minoan ones, because on Crete the mild climate meant that only portable heating appliances, such as braziers, were required; on the mainland the greater winter cold had to be countered by fixed hearths well protected against the draught. Fluidity and dispersion have given way to concentration. The palaces of the Peloponnese are not pathways but places, even though they have a circulation system within them. So they have pronounced borders, are limited in size and constitute foci for gatherings; they are enclosed and condensed in form.

A further contrast with the Cretan buildings is to be noted in the way the units forming the central nucleus, i.e. the megaron, were axially planned with symmetry to the fore. So at Tiryns (figure 16), penetrating through the porch (1,2) and across the court (3), you find that the two columns of the portico (4) are aligned across the antechamber (5) with the two pairs of columns around the hearth (6). The casualness of Minoan architecture has been rejected, although there remain a confusion of small rooms and a number of irregular passages with some abrupt turns that preserve hints of a maze. Add the traces of frescoes in the same technique; add further columns tapering downwards and supporting friezes with circular log ends; add also the occasional pillar in an entrance dividing movement – then there is some similarity in terms of vigour and dynamism.

Also common to Crete and the mainland, although the majority of examples are in the Peloponnese, is the round tomb (tholos) which is a circular, underground stone chamber. Each course is built out beyond the one below (corbelling) to create a dome and to produce a beehive shape. An approach was laid out to the doorway in the form of a passage (dromos) which has been likened to a railway cutting ending at the mouth of a tunnel. Essentially symmetrical and well proportioned, a very

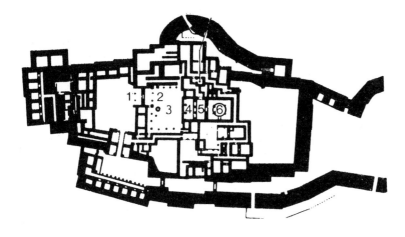

Fig. 16 Tiryns

Mycenae, Treasury of Atreus

fine example may be seen at Mycenae: the so-called Treasury of Atreus (1330–300 BC). You are drawn inwards, partly by the traces of a monumental doorway and partly by the sides of the dromos that open out like a pair of inviting arms. The rounded security of the enclosure gives a sense of peace: it is unquestionably a 'place' embracing and enfolding in Mother Earth. In this way you can share the experience of the funeral cortège as, bearing the body, it made its way into the tomb. The infilling of the dromos that took place immediately after the burial has been removed so that what was skilfully planned originally for the welcome and repose of the dead is today exposed for the delight of the sightseer. Indeed the joy of these places lies very much in historical recollection and the recalling of heroic legends: Mycenae was the home of Agamemnon, captain of the Greek hosts, whose death at the hands of his wife Clytemnestra was to be avenged by his son Orestes; it was to Pylos that Nestor, the former Argonaut, returned after gaining renown for his wise counsel at the siege of Troy. Yet there is also architectural delight not to be missed in such structures as the powerful galleries at Tiryns, the Lion Gate at Mycenae and the Tholos Tombs.

3

THE SANCTUARIES
OF CLASSICAL GREECE

Perched on the low knoll of Kolonos Agoraios overlooking the main square of ancient Athens, the temple of Hephaistos, founded in 449 BC, is one of the most complete examples of a Greek sanctuary to have survived from the classical period. A description of its principal parts will provide an introduction to every Greek temple because the ancient Greeks, having devised what they regarded as a perfect plan, varied it very little: all temples are in fact members of a single family and share common features.

THE PARTS OF THE GREEK TEMPLE

The Hephaisteion stands on a large stone platform (crepidoma) and its top step (stylobate) bears along its four edges a continuous row of columns (peristyle). There are six along the front and so it is called hexastyle, as distinct, for example, from the Parthenon which, having eight columns, is octastyle. These columns support a superstructure, known as the entablature, which itself holds up the roof. They also enclose a walled unit (cella) where the statue of the god or goddess was preserved. This has an entrance porch (pronaos) formed by the prolongations of the side walls, each terminating in a solid masonry support (pilaster or anta), with two further columns between them – the technical term for this arrangement is 'distyle in antis'. The porch is balanced at the rear by another section (opisthodomos) that is identical except that it has no means of access into the cella. Because it is surrounded by a single row of columns the Hephaisteion is known as peripteral.

The core of this structure is readily identifiable as a megaron or hall with porch, of the kind we have already encountered at Tiryns and Pylos. It has simply been elongated and then sur-

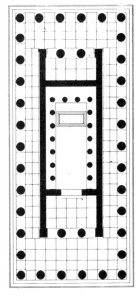

Fig. 17 Athens,
Hephaisteion

rounded by a colonnade. After all, the Olympian gods and goddesses were men and women writ large, and nothing was more natural than to provide their images with dignified houses. Despite this, however, it is not the inside of a Greek temple but the outside that is the principal source of delight.

Athens, Hephaisteion

THE EXTERNALITY OF GREEK ARCHITECTURE

The temple of Segesta (426–16 BC) in the mountainous region of north-west Sicily also stands on top of a hill but unlike the Hephaisteion it is by no means complete, not because it is in ruins but because the building programme was never finished. All that had been erected before the plan was abandoned was a stylobate with a peristyle bearing an entablature and, at each end, a triangular pediment. What is of interest to note is that there is no cella; the construction was proceeding from the outside inwards. Consequently it was the exterior that dictated the form and not the interior.

Externality is also evident from the fact that most temples had few openings for the access of light, apart from the main doors, and so this dim, more or less impenetrable abode of the deity was not enclosed space but a closed-off hole, falling within the category of excavated architecture on the inside and the crystal type on the outside. Clearly the internal volume did not interest the architects; instead they concentrated upon external form.

What may be called the 'all-roundedness' of the Greek temple is demonstrated by the existence of the false porch behind the cella: since this makes the rear façade exactly the same as the front one, there is no special emphasis to distinguish one from the other. So far from inviting movement inwards, for example through the pronaos, the two identical ends encourage movement *around* the building. It is virtually impossible to differentiate between the two façades of the Parthenon, for example.

The front is in fact at the end opposite to the monumental gateway (Propylaia) and it was there that the altar was situated directly before the pronaos. Around this stone of sacrifice worship took place, and so there was no need for space to be provided inside the building.

That the Greek temple is to be viewed in the round is further endorsed by the continuous four-sided platform upon which it stands, as well as by the way the steps discourage anyone mounting them, since only rarely are they low enough to be used as stairs. The temple is then not a container of space but an externalized sculptural object.

This view is supported further by the way in which the colonnade around the cella is arranged. The peripteral design is not functional; the gap between pillars and walls is frequently too shallow to afford protection from the elements or to accommodate processions. But then it was not intended to; rather the colonnade serves to articulate the surfaces of the temple, giving them some depth. It is a narrow element acting as an edge or border. The columns form lines parallel to the cella walls and direct the gaze away from them – the walls themselves being an impassable barrier. In fact the colonnade is not an inward-indicating but an outward-regarding system and so the principal ornamental areas, such as the frieze, are on the exterior.

In sum a temple like that of Aphaia on the island of Aegina can be described as a box with a fence around it and so it is essentially extrovert. It really has no inner life, but it has the perfect exterior. In this way what was an architectural package to envelop a statue has become a symbol of the splendour and greatness of the deity. Indeed it represents the presence of the god or goddess and is itself the monument and sculptural embodiment of that presence. It is therefore no surprise to learn that many of those who designed temples were sculptors. Skopas, for example, was responsible for Athena Alea at Tegea and the great Phidias was closely associated with the Parthenon.

THE MASS-POSITIVE AND SCULPTURAL CHARACTER
OF THE TEMPLE

The Greeks of this period had a passion for the perfect shape and each separate building, standing free on all sides, had to correspond to an ideal form with every detail crisp and clear. The carving is sharp and precise; the figures in solid geometry are simple and unambiguous – rectangles, cylinders, triangles. The entire construction is remarkable for its lucidity. Each

Aegina, temple of Aphaia   temple is not simply a mass, although each can be properly classified as mass-positive; each is an articulated plastic volume with emphasis upon the solids and not upon the voids; that is, it is not the hollows and spaces that have been given form but that which is substantial, firmly contoured, and, in short, sculptural. Without some understanding of the character of Greek sculpture in the classical era, however, this last word will not mean very much.

In the immediately preceding archaic period (*c.* 700–480 BC) the artistic vision of the Greeks had been similar to that of the Egyptians in that pieces of sculpture were regarded as combinations of four cardinal faces. The squarely cut *kouroi* or young men to be found in museums all over Greece are ample evidence of this. In the fifth century BC however the Greeks began to model in three dimensions, but even so the resulting figures were not free in space and there persisted a tendency to restrict movement to one direction and to preserve the old frontality. Correspondingly their sculpturesque temples are constituted by the juxtaposition of four rectangular sides and can be viewed squarely on from the centre of any one of them, in the same way as the pyramids. Yet it has to be noted that the Greeks, unlike the Egyptians, were interested in perspective and this allowed the possibility of oblique views so that more than one side can be contemplated together. It allowed this because Greek perspective was partial in contrast with that of the Renaissance theorists. The latter held that whatever is represented in a picture should be regarded from a fixed position and that all receding lines should converge to a vanishing point. The Greeks did not have this outlook, and so when their attitude was expressed in buildings they demanded no fixed locations from which they were to be viewed – you can move round them. In the process oblique views present themselves, so that while the temples are a fitting together of four surfaces, they are also entities in the round.

Further insight into the sculptural character of this architecture is possible if we compare it with classical Greek reliefs. In these figures do not project beyond the front face of the slab of stone from which they have been carved; subjects occupy a volume between two parallel planes – between the background and the front surface. The latter creates an invisible barrier, confining the action to the space between the planes from which the spectator is excluded; there is no relationship between the subjects within the block and the space outside. When embodied in an entire building, this artistic vision denies any relationship with the space in which it is set. Therefore, while being mass-positive, these sanctuaries are also space-negative in that no attempt was made to relate adjacent structures – the volumes between them are empty voids. Each one is isolated and none is treated as a constituent part of a complex. This explains the apparent chaos at such a centre as Olympia, because the numerous shrines are so many independent sculptural entities without any contact between them. The Greeks were however concerned to establish a relationship with the landscape. While clearly separate from the natural environment, their temples are in balance with it and so the previous insistence that they are objects in and for themselves must be qualified by the recognition that they are also objects within a setting. This reveals an interest not in space but in location. The sites contribute to the architecture just as the buildings embellish the landscape.

TEMPLE AND LANDSCAPE

The Greeks, regarding different natural features as expressive of holiness, sought to make their sacred buildings complementary to the landscape as the Minoans had done with their palaces before them. Appreciation is then bound up with discerning how the two fit together.

*Sounion, temple of
Poseidon*

On the edge of the cliff at Cape Sounion there stands a
hexastyle temple that was probably designed by the architect of
the Hephaisteion in Athens *c*.444 BC. Reared upon a high crepidoma, it presents a dazzling white appearance although its
columns are actually of a grey-veined marble from a nearby
quarry. It is the dedication of the temple to Poseidon, god of the
sea, that provides the clue to its position and to its interaction
with the natural environment. Seen from a ship heading for the
safety of the Piraeus, it dominates the coastline, while standing
in front of it, looking out to the horizon, the worshippers would
have been conscious of its sovereignty over the ocean. The
building both thrusts upwards in lofty majesty and, with the
rhythm of its columns and the horizontal lines of its entablature,
is like the shaft of a trident pointing across the deep. As lord of
the sea, Poseidon could smooth its waves when he rode over
them in his chariot and he could equally whip up the calmness
into a terrifying storm. Thus he controlled the fate of all who
voyaged in ships. This temple, hard and crystalline against the
liquidity of the water below, is a perfect embodiment of the
god's potency and an assurance of his protection both on land
and sea, for Poseidon was described by Homer as 'the earth-
shaker', the one who can 'break through the crust of the ground',
the one therefore whose favour you do well to seek wherever
you are.

Below the southern slopes of Mount Parnassos is the temple
of the Pythian Apollo, containing within itself the holy place of
the Delphic oracle. This temple attracted around it a multitude

of statues, altars, tripods and treasuries, all strung out along the Sacred Way from the south-east corner of the site up to the god's abode. From the entrance the temple can be seen high on the mountainside but is lost to view as the ascent begins between the ranks of monuments. Each of these is a separate unit, the spaces between them being simply unfilled voids. Each treasury, which is an offering in itself, takes the form of a small, non-peripteral temple although none housed a cult statue. They are all independent entities, sculptural and clear-cut, but they set off the slope with their platforms and by the way they face on to the path or, disposed at an angle, mark a bend. The first section of the way is straight, but then there is a sharp turn right by the Treasury of the Athenians where the west end of the temple becomes visible, only to disappear as the climb continues. One hundred feet above the entrance, the shrine again comes into view and, mounting to the left, more and more of the façade is disclosed until the great altar is finally reached. The arrangement of the entire site splendidly matches the contours, with the

Delphi, Treasury of the Athenians

V of the towering cliffs dominating above and picking out the terrace upon which the temple was erected and so unequivocally asserting that here is the centre of the world. Buildings and nature combine to make this the most impressive sanctuary in the whole of Greece.

THE ORDERS

Having established that a classical temple is to be experienced as a sculptural object within a natural setting, it is important not to forget that it is also a structure. The Greeks however were not pioneers in construction methods. Having adopted the post-and-beam system, they found in it adequate means to realize their ideal of perfection. The only change in column and lintel could be by modification and so efforts were devoted to their refinement in order to achieve the greatest aesthetic effect in terms of beauty of line and of form. The Greeks were motivated in this quest by a desire to discover an order that could explain existence and allay anxiety at the apparent irrationality of life. Rejecting the indeterminate, they favoured ideal types and hence there emerged what are known as 'orders'.

An order is a column-and-superstructure unit and the term itself indicates that the position and shape of each part varies little. The three classical orders then are so many combinations of special pillars with particular types of entablature. The two principal ones, the Doric and the Ionic, derived their names from the forms of spoken Greek – Dorian on the mainland and Ionian in eastern Greece or Asia Minor – although their geographical distribution did not exactly correspond with that of the dialects. The third or Corinthian order was not widely popular with the Greeks and only came into its own in the Roman period. However to describe all three in turn by noting the differences between their several components is a necessary preliminary to identifying the principle of composition that underlies and unifies them and indispensable to the appreciation of the architectural dynamics of each whole.

Doric

As exemplified by such buildings as the Hephaisteion at Athens and the Athenaion at Paestum *c.* 500, the Doric order can be subdivided into load (A), supporting member (B) and stepped base (C). Moreover within each of these three there are a further three subdivisions. Reading downwards, the lintel element (A) has a border (cornice) at the top (a); then there is a frieze (b)

which rests upon a beam, known as an architrave or epistyle (c). The post element (B) consists of a capital (d), formed of an abacus (e) on a rounded moulding or echinus (f) with which the shaft (g) is then engaged. The entire structure stands upon a crepidoma (C) made of three steps of which the uppermost is the stylobate (h).

Paestum, Athenaion

In the interest of clarity some of the subordinate features of these several components have been passed over and it is now necessary to draw attention to them. So, this time reading upwards, we note first that the Doric column stands directly on the stylobate (h) and that its shaft (g) is much wider at the bottom than at its summit. It is decorated by shallow, concave grooves or flutes rising vertically. As it approaches its termination, the shaft swells out into a kind of cushion and since this resembles the shell of a sea urchin it is called an echinus (f). Above this, the rectangular abacus (e) corresponds with the shape of the beam (c) which is the first member of the entablature (A). Next there is the frieze (b), which is divided into panels, each alternate one having two vertical channels in the centre and half channels at the edges so that the whole is termed a triglyph (i). Between these are the metopes (j) which can be unadorned but frequently bear reliefs. Above and below each triglyph and

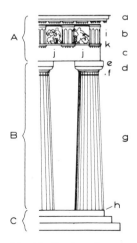

Fig. 18 Doric order

at the top of each metope there are rows of small drop-like projections or guttae (k). These look like the tips of wooden pegs, just as the triglyphs recall beam ends and the circles on Minoan friezes log ends. It is in fact generally supposed that these are reminders of wooden prototypes drawn upon by the architects as a repertory of forms and adapted as decorative features; indeed the postholes, 6 feet in from the walls of the tenth-century BC building recently excavated at Lefkandi on Euboea, strongly suggest that the entire peristyle had a wooden precursor.

Crowning all is the cornice (a) in the shape of a moulded, horizontal projection.

Ionic

The Ionic order, exemplified by the Erechtheion at Athens, which was completed by 405 BC, seems to have crystallized into a conventional system some 50 to 80 years after the formation of Doric. The cornice (a) was given a row of small square blocks (dentils) that may originally have been joists carrying a flat roof.

Athens, Erechtheion

The frieze (b) has lost metopes and triglyphs and can be either plain or bear a continuous relief, like the one around Athena Nike (see page 54). The architrave (c) has been divided into three sections, each superior one projecting slightly. The abacus (e) is still there, but with its lower edge decorated. The capital (d) presents two spirals or volutes at the front and a similar pair at the back. The shaft (f), which is taller and narrower than the Doric, has a base (g) which fixes it to the stylobate (h).

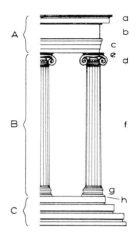

Fig. 19 Ionic order

Corinthian

The third and final order, the Corinthian, was probably invented in Athens in the fifth century BC. In the classical period it differs little from the Ionic except for its capital. This is made up of acanthus leaves, arranged alternately high and low into two rows that are surmounted by volutes – these are however less prominent than on Ionic columns. Bases, shafts and entablatures follow the established patterns.

Different characters were attributed to these three orders by the Roman architect Vitruvius, writing probably at the end of the first century BC under the Emperor Augustus. He declared that Doric is masculine and so appropriate to such deities as Hercules or Mars, while Corinthian is elegant and suitable for a shrine to Venus. Between the two he placed Ionic as tempering the severity of Doric but less delicate than Corinthian: in his view it was best adapted to such goddesses as Juno and Diana. That there are indeed differences between the characters of the orders will become evident if the elements from which they are composed are examined in greater detail. Leaving aside the stepped base that was in any case uniform, the elements fall into two groups, one consisting of the supporting members (post) and the other of the supported (beam).

Fig. 20 Corinthian capital

SUPPORTING ELEMENTS

Bases

It seems natural to begin with the base, although Doric does not have one: indeed it does not need one. The explanation for this is to be sought in an aesthetic interpretation of this architectural element. A base may be viewed in any one of three ways: as part of a floor, as the terminal element of a column or as a link between that which it supports and that on which it stands. The Greek base is of the second type and so it indicates, in contrast to both Egyptian and Minoan examples, that the column is not

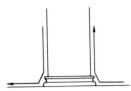

Fig. 21 The function of the base

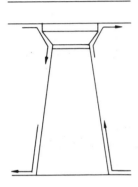

Fig. 22 Two-way movement

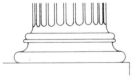

Fig. 23 Attic base

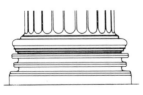

Fig. 24 Asiatic base

part of the floor, growing out of it as it were, nor does it bore down into it – instead it rests firmly upon it. At the same time the classical base does function as a link in that it assists movement from the horizontal to the vertical and vice versa (see figure 21).

It will now be apparent why a base is unnecessary in the Doric order. The column is very large indeed at its bottom end so that there is never any suggestion that it is continuing downwards. Its very girth, where it stands on the stylobate, is the means of passing from the horizontal to the vertical (see figure 22). Such monumental solidity does not require the interposition of any other member.

The much more slender Ionic and Corinthian columns do need bases to fulfil these aesthetic functions, and in fact two principal forms were created: the Attic and the Asiatic or Ephesian. The Attic base (figure 23) has three parts, separated by narrow flat bands (fillets). First, at the bottom, there is a rounded convex moulding (torus), surmounted by a concave one which, because it creates a shadow, is called a scotia (Greek for 'darkness'). The third section is another torus. The profile contracts upwards so that its broadest part lies on the horizontal floor and its narrowest fits close to the shaft. The mouldings create bars of shadow and their parallelism with the stylobate reinforces the impression that the whole structure is stable by expressing the levelness of the foundations. The Asiatic base (figure 24) conveys a greater feeling of verticality because it stands on a cylinder or drum (spira) articulated by fillets and scotias on top of which there is a torus.

Shafts

In essence a Greek column is a simple support that is subject to compression since it carries a load. If short shafts had been used, they would have appeared to be squeezed between burden and thrust, whereas tall ones – and in general Greek examples are of considerable height – are primarily linear objects with dynamic vectors running along the vertical in both directions, skywards and earthwards. The thickness of Doric shafts could have militated against this, since the greater the circumference the more inertly columns seem to repose within themselves. However this was offset by two means: entasis and flutes.

Entasis denotes a swelling introduced into a shaft about one-third of the way up so that its profile is like that of a tense bow. It counteracts the appearance of midpoint thinness that often accompanies a straight-sided column. It is very evident, for example, in the colonnade of Hera II at Paestum where it gives life and resilience to the stone supports by making them seem to react to the load they bear. An entasis further decreases the tendency for the eye to be carried exclusively upwards and in this way safeguards the two-way character of the vectors. Indeed it creates a centre of energy from which forces issue up and down.

The potential heaviness of Doric is also counteracted by the flutes that emphasize the upward thrust. At the same time these channels operate to make a shaft seem slenderer than it actually is and also avert an appearance of flatness. Although there are exceptions, Doric shafts usually have 20 flutes which meet in sharp edges or arrises. Ionic columns, which in any case are more slender, normally have 24 which are separated by blunt fillets – the result is to give greater expression to the skyward movement.

The Greek column is not to be perceived as the remnant of a pierced wall, like the pillars in Minoan domestic quarters, as if a colonnade were nothing but a wall opened at intervals. On the contrary the classical column is always a semi-independent sculptural unit, although for its full effect its relation to its capital has to be taken into account.

Capitals

The classical capital, like its Minoan predecessor, is a device whereby a two-way transition is achieved between the energies that thrust skywards and those that bear downwards. While acting as a terminal element at the top of the column, and so corresponding to the base at its other end, it is not needed for structural purposes but helps to lock support and superstructure together in a way that is aesthetically pleasing.

If you follow the upthrust of a Doric column (see figure 22), you eventually reach the capital, which effects a smooth junction between the shaft and the beam. It is a terminal element that is both linear and geometrical and also, with its squared-off abacus presenting corners to the viewer, partly planar. Narrow where it grows out of the shaft and widening to meet the epistyle, there is structural continuity which provides the experience of delight as the dynamic flow is perceived and appreciated.

The Ionic order, with its greater upsurge has a capital whose volutes rise and roll outwards to rear the entablature into the air. The capital thus provides a visual climax to the momentum of the several forces, allowing them to gush up the shaft and spring outwards. It attracts the eye by its clear profile and also appeals to the sense of touch because it is fundamentally a relief capital and as such is planar in character. This creates a difficulty at each corner of a building however where a capital really faces two ways and so should present two pairs of volutes at right angles. The solution, which was not entirely successful visually, is to be seen at the corners of the temple of Athena Nike. Instead of four volutes, there are three, the centre one, at the corner, being placed diagonally so that it forms one pair with the spiral to its right and a second pair with the spiral to its left.

The Corinthian capital (see figure 20), which had to await the Roman period for widespread use, invests the somewhat static relationship between its core or bell and the abacus with a semblance of organic growth. The bell shape is hidden by acanthus leaves, from behind which the volutes spring up as if directed by an inner life force. The abacus, seeming to respond to this movement, rests lightly on these resilient supports. The vertical dynamic in this way disperses into a branching pattern of considerable beauty. The graceful harmony of the foliage helps to animate the otherwise possibly severe lines of a building. More fully than the other two capitals, the Corinthian is a 'mid-space' object, i.e. it is something that quite evidently occupies space; the eye moves round it. As such it was very suitable to the later Hellenistic and Roman styles in which space was to assume a primary importance.

Athens, temple of Athena Nike

SUPPORTED ELEMENTS

Beams, friezes, cornices

The entablatures of the three orders are alike in that each is made up of the same three members: beam, frieze and cornice, but the treatment of them in the Doric differs from the Ionic and Corinthian.

The Doric architrave is broad with a plain surface, apart from the series of six guttae beneath each triglyph. The next band, the frieze, is divided into sections by metopes and triglyphs. The size and positioning of these have to conform to certain rules that regulate the relationship between them and between the entablature and the columns beneath. First, every triglyph must be oblong and every metope square, but all are to be of the same height so that they fit side by side into the frieze. Second, one triglyph is to stand exactly above the centre of each column and one over the middle of each intercolumniation. The Hephaisteion exemplifies this very clearly (see page 42). These requirements are not difficult to meet along the sides; it is less easy to succeed with the treatment of the corner of the buildings where the frieze along one side meets the frieze along another. The rule covering this is that triglyphs alone, and neither metope nor half-metope, are to be placed in contact at the angles. This immediately presents a problem when the attempt is made to reconcile it with the other conventions. If the triglyphs are to touch and yet at the same time each is to be centred over the supporting column, then these corner ones have to be much wider than the rest and this conflicts with the Greek concern for overall proportions. Since such an increase in size was unacceptable, this rule had to be broken, and it could be that this was one reason for the eventual supercession of Doric.

The Doric frieze is not structurally necessary; it simply serves to increase the height of the entablature which is then in balance with all that is below it. Equally the cornice above – formed of a narrow band (fascia) with a second projecting one superimposed – is primarily aesthetic. It is a terminal element bringing the upright face of the building to its climax. What is more, the cornice gives harmony to oblique views because it continues around the corners of a temple and crosses the gable ends. On the two façades it is supplemented by a raking cornice that marks the edge of the roof and both completes and frames the triangular shape of the pediment; the latter therefore stands out very clearly, as, for example, on the front of the temple of Concord at Agrigento (450–40 BC) in Sicily.

The Doric entablature is to be read as a counterweight to the upthrust of the columns, but the Ionic opposes the ascending movement more as a boundary. As we have seen, it replaces the solid one-part beam with triple, projecting bands. If the gaze is reversed, there is a diminishing downwards that creates a lighter impression than its massive Doric counterparts. In time these fascias were capped with mouldings that could be either small and circular in section (astragal) with a bead and reel enrichment or have a wider quarter-round profile (ovolo) decorated with egg and dart.

Consideration of the Corinthian order may be postponed until the next chapter, beyond noting that it was all but identical with the Ionic, apart from the capital and a preference for curved friezes with the cornices supported on ornamental brackets (consoles).

After this further analysis, it should now be evident that Vitruvius's characterization of the orders was not without substance, especially as related to Doric and Ionic. The former embodies austere restraint, rejects the unessential and expresses great strength. It manifests a grand and simple monumentality, with all its elements united in a single cuboid body. Ionic is less rigidly uniform; it is charmingly elegant and, with its slender columns and light entablature, expresses gracefulness. Its greater use of carved decoration enables a fleeting vital force to play over its surface, and every part seems to burgeon with life and growth. Yet despite differences, the orders each exemplify the same principle of composition, and share similar ingredients such as proportion, rhythm, symmetry, and so on.

THE PRINCIPLE OF COMPOSITION: ADDITION

The Greek quest for meaning amid apparent chaos, which impelled them towards the creation of the orders, also induced them to analyse forms into their component parts. They examined constituent elements so that they could reshape them in accordance with their conception of how things should be: thus they advanced from multiplicity to unity. This multiplicity also stems from the sculptural vision that is embodied in both figures and temples. Sculptors of the classical period were intensely interested in anatomy, in the various parts of the body. Architects, in similar fashion, became interested in the anatomy of their buildings, in the different parts of the structure. This is why some knowledge of these many elements – tedious though it may be to acquire – is necessary. However sculptors and architects were not only concerned with the articulation of the several members but also with their relationships and integration. Like the figure of a god, a Greek temple is an organic whole. It is a single body made up of many parts with its own balance and clear contours.

To say 'made up of many parts' is to identify the principle of composition as that of addition. The units are added together, either by superimposition (capital on shaft, and so on) or by juxtaposition (metope between triglyphs, and so on). This arrangement emphasizes the components and brings out their individual characters. But despite their semi-independence, interest is distributed over the whole building, since they are subordinate to the temple in its entirety. Indeed they are so linked that the spectator's eye is constantly on the move; every line points to another. Not even a capital is intended to distract attention from the whole – but then, as we have seen from the previous analysis, each one is a means of uniting shaft and beam so that there is an evenness of dynamic flow and no hiatus of movement. In a sense this can be said to be the result of inflection. After all, a base is the inflected bottom end of a column as the capital is its inflected summit – these inflections enable them to relate to other elements. Shaft, base and capital are then distinct entities, but in Greek architecture they are so unified that they become a single member and a true harmony is achieved.

REFINEMENTS, PROPORTION AND SYMMETRY

Harmony is attained not only by modifying parts to relate to one another but also by paying attention to refinements and to proportion. While the Egyptians represented things as they knew them to be – their concern being with the mental image – the Greeks represented things as they wanted them to be – their concern was with beauty of form and appearance. Consequently a Greek architect, wanting his temple to look as if it was standing upon a flat platform but aware that if he constructed it entirely level it would seem to sag in the centre, countered this effect by a curve upwards from each end towards the centre of the stylobate. So, for example, the east and west façades of the Parthenon are 3 inches and its two sides 4½ inches higher at their midpoints than at their extremities. The same treatment was accorded the architrave to avoid a similar effect. A further refinement was the entasis or slight bulge that serves to offset the possible concavity that may occur in a column with perfectly straight sides. Angle columns too were specially designed: on the one hand, their diameter was slightly increased to avoid any semblance of weakness when seen in silhouette against the sky and, on the other hand, they were made to incline inwards in order to counter any suggestion of their falling outwards, which could have been made if they stood absolutely upright. These Doric refinements were not completely accepted by the designers of Ionic, but they do contribute to the harmony of the whole and reveal considerable visual sophistication.

Nevertheless it was to proportion that Vitruvius attributed the major role in unifying the subwholes. In his *De architectura* he declared 'Proportion is a due adjustment of the size of the different parts to each other and to the whole. . . . The parts of a temple should correspond with each other and with the whole.' These are quite intelligible statements but they give rise to the question: what is the basis of the correspondence or adjustment in size? By the time that this Roman architect was writing a widely accepted formula had been devised, but this belongs to the Hellenistic and Roman periods. From the era that is our immediate concern – *c.* 480–323 BC – no contemporary account has survived. That there was a system of proportion is a reasonable assumption, but there does not seem to have been an immutable canon and the basic module is uncertain. Evidence suggests that the overall dimensions of each element were derived from something that already existed when the building was under construction. This may have been the interaxal, i.e. the distance from the centre of one peripteral column to the centre of the next, or it may have been the diameter of a column's base. Whatever it was, it determined the height of a shaft, the measurements of a capital, and so on. To increase or decrease one affected every part. Variations were created in this way between buildings and between the orders. Doric columns, for example, were usually 5½ to 6 diameters tall, while Ionic were 8 to 10. This produced a difference in the ratio of entablature to column height which initially was 1:2 but by the early fourth century had become 1:3. The intention underlying all this, whatever the exact basis for calculation, is readily grasped, namely to achieve a consonance of the parts with one another and with the whole.

Unity in design can be intensified by the use of axiality and symmetry, both of which are found in the standard temple plan. As can be seen from figure 17 there is a horizontal axis running straight down the centre of the floor from one end of the Hephaisteion to the other; on either side of this line there are mirror images creating a perfect bilateral symmetry and demonstrating the cohesion of all the parts. Even the pronaos and the opisthodomos are symmetrical. In elevation too symmetry is

observed: the two long sides are identical; the two façades
likewise and if a façade is divided down the centre each part
reflects the other.

Athens, Parthenon

RHYTHM AND DYNAMICS

This symmetry does not mean that the buildings are static.
Greek temples have rhythm and movement and their dynamics
counter any suggestion of inertia. The rhythm is beaten out by
the procession of columns along the four sides and, in Doric, by
the regular sequence of triglyphs and metopes along the architrave. All this constitutes an invitation to the visitor to move
around the building. This movement involves the body as a
whole, until a corner is reached and a façade presents itself –
this is formed of two simple geometrical shapes: a triangle upon
a rectangle. Now the emphasis shifts to visual motion.

Contemplation of a façade begins with the low horizontal of
the steps, to perceive how they rise from the earth and how this
vertical movement is extended by the upward thrust of the
columns. But the colonnade itself, constituting a broad and
horizontal rectangle, patterned by the dark of the intercolumnar
spaces and the light of the shafts, makes the movement broaden

out. Then the fluting on the columns accentuates verticality and leads up to the horizontal line of the entablature, being carried smoothly around the swelling capital without any sense of shock as the circular meets the rectangular and the perpendicular encounters and is transformed into the horizontal. This horizontality is however broken by the short verticals of the triglyphs which echo the fluting and prolong the movement of the columns, tying entablature and support together and alternating with the dotlike guttae. Ultimately this visual journey reaches the horizontal cornice and may either continue to right or left and mount the raking cornice to the summit or halt where there are statues within the tympanum so that they may be enjoyed. In this latter case, attention focuses eventually on the dominant central figure and the ascent to the apex is completed. Then the movement may be reversed and the descent begins.

This visual adventure corresponds with the architectural dynamics which in turn counter even more convincingly any idea that Greek architecture is inert. It is of course stable but that does not mean the absence of tension. If, for example, two men of equal strength pull on a rope against one another, the rope will remain stationary although it is loaded with energy. A Greek temple is similarly imbued with energy and this arises from the adoption of the trabeated system and its refinement. In accordance with this construction method, each temple is made up of verticals and horizontals and a harmonious balance has to be established between them if the resulting building is to give delight. There has to be a rhythmic equilibrium that symbolizes the laws governing support and rest. This has in fact been achieved by the Greeks in a standard design whereby the forces remain alive but are mutually absorbed. The energies are pervasive, free and continually active but kept within broad, simple channels. The temple becomes alive: vectors mount and descend, branch out sideways, curve back, push skywards and root themselves in the earth. Soaring and downward-pressing forces counterbalance to create a steady state of rest in movement and movement in rest.

ORNAMENT – SCULPTURE

Not only is the Greek temple a sculptural object in itself, it is also a vehicle for sculpture. However the individual pieces of carving are always subordinate to the building; they are there to heighten its effect and not to stand out as objects in themselves. Indeed it can be said that the architecture has determined the sculpture, as may be readily illustrated from the treatment of the pediments. Although gable figures were infrequent in western Greek temples, elsewhere they were in use, their size and shape invariably made to correspond with the triangular frame within which they were included. The tallest one was placed in the centre, and there was then a gradation downwards from the apex to the reclining figures in the two lower angles.

While contributing to the enlivening of the surface, sculpture also served both to articulate the parts and to unify them, thus underscoring the additive character of the architecture. The mouldings were not intended to prettify the surface, like the attachment of a coloured ribbon to a wrapped parcel. They function as so many elements in an additive composition to allow the clear differentiation of its parts to be grasped. In Ionic, for example, the mouldings are not arbitrarily stuck on to empty surfaces, rather they blossom forth to clarify the structure of the temple. The joints between the architrave and the projecting blocks of the dentil course are marked by ovolo mouldings with an egg and dart pattern. The treatment of the entablature defines the lintel as a lying object, while the flutes on the columns indicate that they are upstanding entities. It is not surprising too, in view of the supporting function of columns, that this should be expressed either in the form of human beings bearing the weight of the entablature, like the graceful Caryatids in the southern portico of the Erechtheion (see page 50), or of giants sustaining the load on their forearms and heads, like the colossal male figures (telamones) from the temple of Olympian Zeus at Agrigento. In these ways sculpture emphasizes the essential nature of that to which it belongs. At the same time it contributes to the harmony of the whole.

This unifying function of sculpture is to be detected in the way the guttae of the Doric order bind together decoratively the epistyle and the frieze, and the triglyphs and metopes repeat at a higher level the sequence of column and interval below. The Ionic decorated frieze actually seems to embrace a building, acting as a girdle and underscoring its all-round nature.

COLOUR, LIGHT AND LINE

Although few traces remain, pigment was applied by the Greeks to pick out architectural details. Paint in this way serves articulation because it distinguishes the limits of what is coloured. If, for example, one object is made blue and another red, their differentiation is emphasized. By this means the semi-independence of the parts of the structure could be preserved and the outlines of the mouldings thrown into high relief. Hence details of friezes and of cornices were accentuated in strong blues and terra-cotta reds, while sculptural groups were gilded and coloured with reds, blacks, browns, yellows, blues and greens. Little of this has survived, but this does not seriously impair appreciation because the use of colour was always strictly subordinate to form.

Yet another ingredient that the Greeks favoured was light. Light can bring out selected coloured elements, but it can do more. There are in fact two kinds of architecture that use light and shade differently. The one draws forms with darkness upon light; the other draws forms with light on darkness. Gothic, as we shall see later, belongs to the first category; Greek to the second. The Greeks cared for shadow only as a dark field from which the light figures may be intelligibly divided. In this way readableness and clarity of accentuation were attained. The play of light and shade is also another aspect of delight in a Greek temple. The shadows themselves are kept constantly in motion by the changing light, while they also create duplicate lines within the building. They are essentially modelling shadows which define three-dimensional form. Precise edges and contours are produced in this way and the linear character of the architecture is brought to the fore. Both exterior and interior lines carry the eye to and fro, up and down: edges of steps, shadows in bases, flutes on columns, the profile of mouldings – all these contribute to our delight in the building.

PATH OR PLACE?

It remains to consider to which category of buildings the classical temple belongs: is it a path or a place? It is evidently not a ladder to heaven, like the pyramids, nor a processional way, like the temples of Karnak or Luxor, nor a maze, like the palace of Knossos. Equally it does not fit into the alternative category of a place, since a place is a gathering point to be experienced as an inside, whereas the Greek temple, as has been repeatedly emphasized, is essentially an external, sculptural object. We have then to seek some other classification and it could be that the concept of a 'domain' may prove appropriate.

A domain is an area defined by a particular human activity. Hence it is possible to speak of an agricultural domain or a sports' domain (a whole complement of recreational facilities). The Greek temple is unquestionably intended to provide for religious observances and it is placed within an area set apart for such activities. So the Athenian Acropolis is a domain, with an entrance gate and several temples within its precincts. Indeed a temple is to be understood as a particular feature within a religious domain, housing the statue of the deity and having an altar for sacrifice in front of the backdrop of its façade – in this way it contributes to the identity of the area. Moreover because it is in a reciprocal relationship with the surrounding landscape, it helps to define the character of the whole and, while not itself a place, creates a sense of locality.

THEATRES

The initial difficulty we have just encountered in trying to categorize the classical temple has to be faced again when we turn to another feature that was not infrequently included in the religious domain, namely the theatre, examples of which are plentiful, as at Athens, Delos, Delphi or Sparta. They were all accounted sacred since the performances for which they provided were originally rituals in honour of Dionysus, with the spectators as so many members of a religious congregation.

Epidauros, theatre

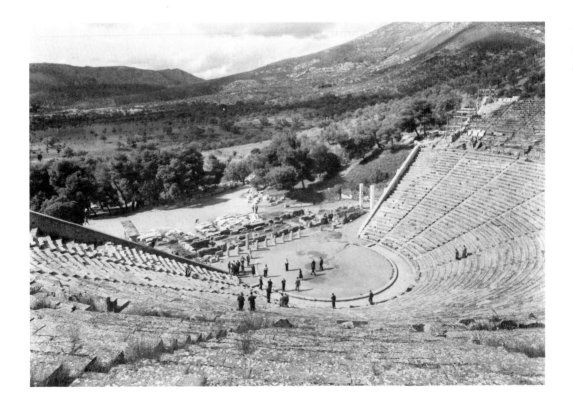

Obviously not paths, are they not equally obviously places?
Certain considerations would suggest that this conclusion is too
simplistic, but before criticizing it we need to know more about
their actual design.

Initially the theatre was just a flat area, sometimes paved but
more often of beaten earth, for the chorus and dancers associated with the cult. The congregation sat on a slope or on
wooden benches. In the late fifth century BC a few rows of stone
seats were introduced and this initiated a development that
continued into the Roman period. The structure became monumentalized and achieved its standard classical form in the fourth
century with the theatre of Epidauros. The plan has two main
constituent elements linked by a third. First there is the auditorium (cavea) and then the stage: these are related by means of
a circular orchestra or dancing floor. The stage building (skene)
is set at a tangent to the orchestra and constitutes a backdrop.
The seating wraps around the orchestra to a point just beyond
the half-circle where it meets two retaining walls and where
there are two open entrance passages.

*Fig. 25 Epidauros,
theatre*

Although this plan, which is typical of all, suggests that this is
a carefully designed place and that consequently there is no
problem about categorization, in fact the three elements of
which it is composed are not really integrated to produce a
single, unified building like the later Roman examples. Indeed
the Greek theatre, while it is a focus for gathering, is not an
inside in sharp contrast to a surrounding exterior. On the contrary, like the temple, it is intimately related to the landscape
within which it has been set. It is an architectural shape that
embodies and expresses the earth's hollows and from which the
rolling countryside beyond can be contemplated. The arc of its
seating nestles into the hillside so that the man-made and the
natural become one. Interior and exterior fuse. Unroofed, the
theatre is an open form that fits the landscape exactly. In effect
nature has been transmuted into geometry: the orchestra is a
perfect circle, the hillside the interior of a truncated cone and the
backdrop a simple cubic form. Whether you occupy a seat at
Delphi and look out over the shrine guarding the oracle to the
far horizon or mount the cavea at Segesta and see range after
range of hills extending into the distance or take your place on a
bench at Syracuse and behold the sparkling waters of the bay
beyond, the sites and their applied geometry are breathtaking.
Delight in this further element within a religious domain is
inescapable.

THE END OF THE CLASSICAL AGE

The death of Alexander the Great in 323 BC is usually taken to mark the end of the age of classical architecture and the beginning of the Hellenistic period. Not that there was any immediate and obvious break; indeed there had already been some anticipation of what was to come in the form of an unclassical interest in space. This interest is noticeable in the Propylaia at Athens (437–32) which is an interior space leading from one kind of exterior to another. The inside of the temple of Apollo at Bassae (430–400) is another example looking to the future, like certain temples in Magna Graecia, such as Temple C at Selinunte (*c.* 550), which with its deep pronaos and no opisthodomos at the other end denies the all-round character typical of most classical sanctuaries.

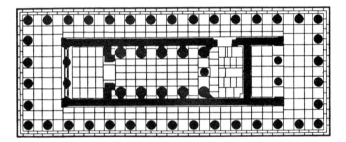

Fig. 26 Bassae, temple of Apollo

4

THE HELLENISTIC
AND ROMAN PERIODS

The Hellenistic period, which began with the death of Alexander in 323 BC, is usually considered to have come to an end with the victory of Augustus at Actium in 31 BC, when he became the undisputed master of the Roman world. From then until the fourth century AD, when the first Christian churches were designed, imperial architecture extended all around the Mediterranean basin.

THE HELLENISTIC PERIOD

INTEREST IN SPACE

The interest in space that began to emerge towards the close of the classical era, e.g. as at Miletus in Asiatic Turkey, is most obvious in Hellenistic town planning which became widespread in the third and second centuries with the founding of new cities after the conquests of Alexander. Buildings were no longer treated as isolated entities, but as units within an overall design relating houses, temples and places of public concourse.

A key element in these plans was the two-storeyed stoa. A stoa is a covered gallery with one of its long sides designed as an open colonnade. Stoas constitute frames within which clear spaces can be fashioned. They were used for perspective effect and introduced order and regularity even where there had been none before. Their function in this last respect is nowhere better displayed than in the agora at Athens (see figure 27). In the second century BC at least five stoas were erected to give greater definition and coherence to the entire area. The east side was closed by the stoa of Attalos and the East Stoa. To the south the Middle Stoa was built and parallel with it the Second South

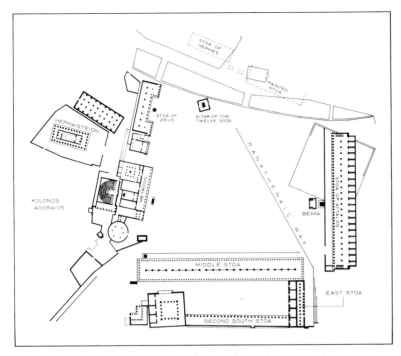

Fig. 27 Athens, agora

Stoa, while on the west a colonnade in front of the Metroön continued the line of the Stoa of Zeus. In this way two essential aims of the Hellenistic period were fulfilled, namely the creation of a regularized design and of protected volumes of space.

Part of the enjoyment of this architecture derives from appreciating the contribution made by the stoas to the harmony of the whole. They are space-definers, marking out a volume within which more focal monuments may stand, and they can serve as viewing platforms from which to enjoy them. In themselves they are space-frames, combining the qualities of cave and grove that are characteristic of most roofed structures. They are shells for human activity, in particularly for converse and commerce.

TEMPLES

Since Hellenistic buildings were treated as elements in a harmonious composition, temples have to be considered in their setting. Components of a specially designed architectural landscape, they often constitute the climax of a carefully arranged vista with horseshoe or L-shaped stoas acting as backgrounds. The precise form of any layout is influenced by the terrain available. The Acropolis at Pergamum, for example, has its various temples in a closely knit pattern that follows the contours of the hill. To visit these sites is to have the opportunity to

Lindos, Sanctuary   admire the skill with which the several parts have been brought
together. One outstanding example will serve as an introduction
to all: the sanctuary of Athena at Lindos.

Perched on the top of the Acropolis above the village of
Lindos on the island of Rhodes, this imposing, though now
much ruined, sanctuary consisted of two flights of stairs, two
terraces (each with its own colonnade) and the shrine itself.
Access was obtained up steep steps to the first level which was
occupied by a stoa with wings; its colonnade was unbroken
throughout its length but lack of space meant that the stairway
to the next terrace had to begin within its interior. This led up to
a Propylaea with a ten-column façade and a bastion on either
side. Passing through one of the five door openings, you
emerged into the court which had porticoes on all four sides, but
the eastern section was a false one, only 3 feet wide so as not to
mask the temple itself. This is an outstanding example of the use
of colonnades and ascending levels to create a monumental
composition. There is a rhythmic progression upwards to the
climax at the summit. The altar is placed on the axis of the
monumental staircase and only the temple, which retains its
original sixth-century place close to the cliff edge, breaks the
symmetry. The repetition of the four-columned façade of the
stoa wings in the bastions of the Propylaea and in the façade of
the naos creates a sense of harmony. Yet the temple itself is the
smallest architectural feature on the Acropolis and is reduced to
the role of a space-definer.

To fulfil this last role satisfactorily, special attention has been

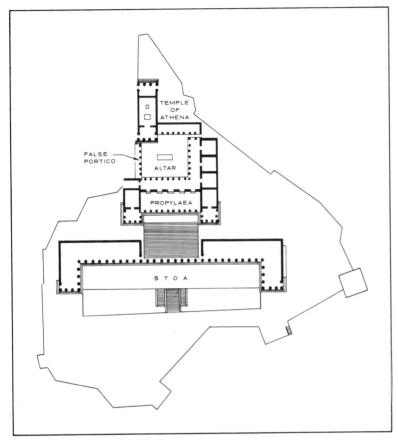

Fig. 28 Lindos, Acropolis

paid to the façade of the Lindos temple as it declares the culmination of the approach to it. Emphasis has been provided by
placing a row of four columns across its entrance so producing a
new type of temple known as the prostyle. In contrast to the
classical plan, with two or more columns between pilasters,
there was now virtually a detached porch. Examples of this
design were frequent in the Hellenistic period – no less than five
may be seen at Pergamum alone. The temple of Isis on Delos is
another striking illustration, standing with its brilliant white
columns on the slope of Mount Kyrkos. Further stress on the
entrance is evident in this instance in the greater width of the
central intercolumnar distance compared with the two flanking
ones – a device promoted by the great Hermogenes (*c.* 150 BC).
Flights of steps constitute an additional accent, used with striking effect on the theatre terrace at Pergamum with its 25 treads
mounting to the Temple of Dionysus (second century BC). One
effect of all this was for the pronaos to become deeper while the
rear of the temple was demoted in importance and either wasted
away, as at Pergamum, or was reduced in size, as in the temple of
Artemis at Magnesia on the Maeander (figure 29).

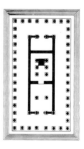

Fig. 29 Magnesia, temple of Artemis

Delos, temple of Isis

This Artemesion, according to Vitruvius, was the work of Hermogenes, who is also credited with inventing the pseudo-dipteral temple. Such a shrine, although designed as a cella surrounded by two rows of columns, has the inner colonnade suppressed. This innovation was not to create an area for concourse; the intention was aesthetic, to bring empty space into play as an element in the design. Hermogenes maximized the openness of the colonnaded corridor; he dissociated the rows of columns from the cella walls to produce an independent space into the depth of which the core of the structure withdraws almost entirely. In this way the bodily connection of cella and peristyle, like that between trunk and limb, was relinquished in exchange for an effect of bounded spaciousness.

Not only the pseudo-dipteral but also the dipteral temple of this period was intended to be an inner landscape rather than a sculptural presence. The later Artemesion at Ephesus must have suggested a forest of columns. In the façade the central pair were wider spaced than the others and directed attention inwards, but with nearly 100 columns, there must have been a tendency to wander about. The lower parts of the shafts had reliefs depicting figures in procession and so they defined a curving march. Since there was now an interest in interior space, visitors were encouraged to enter by the architecture. The temple of Asklepios on Kos was thronged by those wanting to enjoy the paintings on display. Moreover the spread of oracular cults necessitated entrance to obtain the divine messages; hence the practice arose of excavating crypts beneath the area where the statue was located as at Didyma. At the same time devotees ceased to be content with the mystic hidden presence of the image; the inner room was then abolished and the statue set up visibly at the back of the shrine – this is quite evident in the Pergamum examples (figure 30).

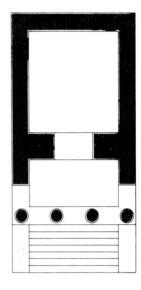

Fig. 30 *Pergamum, temple in middle gymnasium*

THE CLASSICAL ORDERS MODIFIED

In the construction of their temples, the men of the Hellenistic age employed the classical orders, but a certain exuberance and a pleasure in scenic display brought austere Doric into disfavour and led to the increased ornamentation of Ionic and Corinthian.

Although few temples were designed in Doric, it continued in use for stoas, being modified in certain respects. To lighten the effect columns were made slimmer with little in the way of entasis. Flutes were outlined but were frequently not executed; often the lower section of the shaft is smooth and only the upper part channelled. Capitals were decreased in size, the profile becoming almost rectilinear with few curving lines – examples abound on Delos which is preeminently the home of Hellenistic Doric. The strict canon of classical perfection was also broken by architrave, frieze and cornice being merged into a single beam and by a multiplication of triglyphs and metopes between columns made necessary by their greater spacing.

Ionic was already less heavy than Doric but now its capitals become smaller and overall height is increased. Pediments are made to appear to have less weight by piercing them with openings. Decoration is also a device to reduce an impression of bulk and so floral motifs were added to Ionic capitals with palmettes and leaves spreading outwards from and between the volutes. Historiated capitals came into vogue, i.e. those ornamented with human or animal heads, such as the bull capitals at Ephesus. All these features were now designed to be seen from a distance as befits a monumental complex in which the former detailed calligraphic design is out of place. This concern for visibility led to a preference for the Attic base, which is simpler and more compact than the Asiatic (see figures 23 and 24), although it too was soon enriched. The torus was covered with overlapping leaves and was supported on an eight-sided figure with its panels bearing palmettes or sea creatures, as on the two from Miletus preserved in an inner courtyard of the Louvre or the one still to be seen in place at Didyma. An additional square plinth was eventually introduced below the moulded base thus stressing the verticality of the whole and differentiating between a flat rectangular element, appropriate to the paved floor, and the more cylindrical shape suitable to the circular shaft. In this way, the function of the base is well realized, and it sits admirably on the floors now patterned with mosaics. Made of pebbles or stone cubes, they take the form of either geometrical figures, as frequently on Delos, or of actual scenes, such as those at Pella.

Above the supporting members, friezes in the Asiatic region were few before the year 300 BC, despite the love of decoration, and the dentils of the cornice rested directly on the architrave. In mainland Greece, on the other hand, the frieze was the norm but it had no dentils, although in time there was a combination of the two.

Hellenistic taste was undoubtedly more eclectic than that of the classical period and this made it possible for Doric and Ionic to be regarded as interchangeable. Hence by the second century many buildings had above the columns, whether Doric or Ionic, entablatures composed of Doric architraves and friezes and Ionic cornices often with dentils. Others had Doric capitals, architraves and triglyphs supported by Ionic columns and bases. Unacceptable to the classical purist, these combinations nevertheless manifest a liveliness and a willingness to experiment that is most appealing.

THE TWO-STOREYED STOA

In many ways then the architectural vocabulary of the classical era was pressed into the service of the Hellenistic vision and modified in the process, but what has been referred to as one of the greatest achievements of this age, namely the two-storeyed stoa, presented a considerable problem. Classical buildings were essentially single-storeyed and, in their vertical elevation, they culminated with the cornice. A cornice marks the uppermost termination of a wall; as such it has no logical place beneath a second storey because the entire design in which it has its place is intended to be a single continuous form. To put one floor above another and to fuse them into a whole, the Hellenistic architects adopted a principle of continuous tapering. They used Doric, with its greater girth, for the ground floor and gradually reduced the width from the lower column shaft through its capital and architrave up the Ionic shaft above. The diameter at the foot of the second-storey column was slightly less than that at the top of the lower column. An architrave and a thin band of masonry articulated but did not separate the two parts, which then reached their climax with the traditional cornice. In this way a unified interior volume was freely related to an exterior space, and this is created in two dimensions by the breadth of the stoa itself and in the third by the implication of movement towards and away from the façade and within and up and down the interior.

Athens, Stoa of Attalos

THEATRES

The interest in two-storeyed buildings had an effect not only on stoas but also upon theatre design. Few examples of the Hellenistic period remain intact, since most were refashioned in the imperial era, but the generally accepted layout can be recognized as constituting a half-way stage between the classical and the Roman. The Hellenistic plan represents a movement towards the unification of auditorium, orchestra and stage structure arising from a greater concern for space. The orchestra ceases to be a circle and becomes instead a horseshoe (in part enveloped by the cavea), while the stage is increased in size. Plays, previously confined to the orchestra, now had some of their scenes presented on the roof of the proskenion which was a raised platform in front of the stage building. This last, as at Priene, was a two-tiered structure forming a kind of ornamental façade and giving greater spatial definition to the area of the performance. Not yet a fully fashioned volume, the Hellenistic theatre certainly paved the way for its Roman successor, yet despite its more elaborate structure, it still existed in reciprocal relationship with nature and many a breathtaking vista awaits the visitor.

PROPORTION AND RHYTHM

Despite the new aspects in Hellenistic architecture that differentiated it from that of the classical period, there was a continuous respect for proportion. Indeed Vitruvius has preserved a detailed formula, devised by Hermogenes, that was now accepted and used as a basis for design. He gives a list of five ideal proportions calculated in terms of the diameter of the columns at their base in relation to their height. The view was taken that the sum of the interaxis, i.e. the distance from the centre of one column to the centre of the next, together with the height should always be 12½ diameters. The complete list is as follows:

pycnostyle (close-columned) = interaxis of 2½ diameters
                    + height of 10 diameters = 12½ diameters

systyle (narrow-columned) = interaxis of 3 diameters
                    + height of 9½ diameters = 12½ diameters

eustyle (well-columned) = interaxis of 3¼ diameters
                    + height of 9¼ diameters = 12½ diameters

diastyle (wide-columned) = interaxis of 4 diameters
                    + height of 8½ diameters = 12½ diameters

araeostyle (lightly-columned) = interaxis of 4½ diameters
+ height of 8 diameters = 12½ diameters

Sometimes the intercolumniation, i.e. the distance between two columns from edge to edge, is used and this can be confusing because it is not the same as the interaxis and indeed must always be 1 diameter less, just as the sum of the intercolumniation and the column height must be 1 diameter less, i.e. 11½ and not 12½.

By adhering to one or other of these, although with a preference for the eustyle, Hermogenes and his followers were able to relate the main elements of a building to one another, so that the dimensions are proportional. Part of the enjoyment of these buildings then lies in an appreciation of the harmony created by these and by the rhythm of the regularly spaced columns.

The Hellenistic architects also favoured a greater emphasis than previously upon the vertical dimension. This was achieved in part by making columns taller in proportion to their thickness and in part by reducing the entablature and so decreasing its force as a termination to the upward thrust. The proportions of the ground plan were also altered to stress verticality: classical temples have a length that is slightly more than twice their width, whereas the length of Hellenistic temples is slightly less than twice their width.

After the fifth century BC, with the decline of Athens, the creative development of temple architecture took place outside mainland Greece in Asia Minor where special attention was given to the Ionic order. Indeed Hellenistic temples having any structure left apart from their groundworks are rare in Greece and the Greek islands. This means that interest in Hellenistic architecture has to be mainly, though not exclusively, archaeological simply because of the dearth of surviving examples. Nevertheless its achievements are not to be belittled and some knowledge of them is essential if only as a preliminary to enjoying Roman architecture for which it undoubtedly prepared the way.

THE ROMAN PERIOD

The similarities between Hellenistic architecture and its successor will become apparent as this analysis proceeds. However it is important from the outset to be aware of the revolution in structural method carried through by the Romans: in brief, instead of the post-and-lintel system, they made use of the arch, i.e. the trabeated gave way to the arcuated.

THE ARCUATED SYSTEM

In place of the classical principle of using horizontal and vertical relationships between forces bearing downwards and others supporting them, the Romans chose a system in which the downwards pressures were absorbed and diverted diagonally. So while the classical structures give the impression of concentrated loads, in Roman ones the loads are distributed. This is achieved by employing the round-headed arch. The dynamics of the arch are relatively simple to appreciate: its rounded section is like a bent bow of which the two tips are always liable to spring outwards, which means it has sideways thrusts to left and right as well as an upward surge. Stability is achieved by the wall bearing down on the top and to the sides of the arch, thus counteracting the outwards spread.

The arch not only affects the upright parts of the structure, it can also influence its roofing. From it therefore derive the three main types of vault used by the Romans. There is, first, the barrel or tunnel vault which is really no more than an arch prolonged in depth. Next there is the transverse or groin vault which is produced by the intersection of two tunnel vaults. Thirdly there is the dome, which is simply an arch rotated on itself; indeed since 'vault' derives from *volvere*, 'to roll or turn about', the dome, perhaps more than the others, stresses the extent to which arcuated and vaulted architecture is one of turnings, replacing the straight lines of the trabeated by curves.

To produce this result the Romans laid courses of broken stone or brick and filled each one with liquid mortar to penetrate and solidify them. Their domes were consequently solid bells of concrete and were somewhat static. In general Roman vaults are like so many rigid lids embodying the principle of inert stability. But it was this use of concrete that freed the Romans from the tyranny of the rectangle. No longer had they to be subservient to the demands of a rectilinear system. They could enclose large volumes without a forest of columns to hold up the roof; they were able to express the continuity of part with part and to exploit the three-dimensional curve. Not only the major vaulted spaces, but their entrances, openings, niches and decor were evolved from a preoccupation with the embracing and focusing qualities of circular lines and surfaces. This deliberate use of curvilinear features is very evident, for example, in Hadrian's Teatro Marittimo at Tivoli, AD 118–25, where the enfolding and sheltering forms reinforce an impression of permanence.

However for the first main advance in vaulted architecture, it is necessary to go back some 50 or more years to the Golden

House of Nero in Rome, although not a great deal of it now remains to be enjoyed. Whereas previously domestic quarters consisted of rectangular boxlike rooms, bounded by flat planes and constituting so many unintegrated parts simply added together, now under Nero the rooms became carefully proportioned interiors with concave ceilings and often curved walls – further, they interpenetrated each other, so that there was a continuous flow of space. In this way the Romans created envelopes enclosing shapes and, like the Hellenists, produced space-positive buildings; walls and ceilings thus acquired a space-shaping, or space-bounding, function.

INTERIOR SPACE

Architectural interest now focused not upon masses but upon the spaces they could define. Light and space became more important than the actual masonry and so the pre-Hellenic concern for solids was replaced by a delight in the volumes between them. The result was to turn architecture outside-in. The externality of classical buildings gave way to the interiority of Roman ones. However large or elaborate traditional interiors had been, they were always conditioned by the proportions of a unified, coherent exterior. Under the empire, this was reversed and the exterior was conditioned by and conformed to the interior, becoming an expression of the inside form. The Pantheon was in fact composed entirely as an interior and an analysis of this remarkable building will illustrate further this key aspect of Roman design.

THE PANTHEON

As far as its structure is concerned, the Pantheon, dating in its present form from the reign of Hadrian, was created by adding two elements together: a temple front and a domed cylinder. The first of these was constructed of a row of eight columns bearing a pediment and leading into a vestibule of three aisles, of which the left and right culminate in semicircular niches and the central one in the bronze entrance doors. This is a transitional element that screens the main part of the building, giving no hint of the breathtaking volume beyond, and in this way and by its rectangular shape it heightens the contrast to come.

The second element is a dome upon a circular drum united by superimposition. The proportions of these certainly contribute

Fig. 31 Rome, Pantheon

to the overwhelming sense of harmony: the height of the drum is equal to its radius, which is identical with that of the dome, so that if the circumference of the dome were continued to form a complete sphere it would just touch the pavement. The dome, supported not by the walls but by invisible relieving arches within them, has at its apex a great round opening or oculus which is the sole source of light that floods downwards, over the curving wall. The space is all-encompassing and bounded. It impresses first by its sheer immensity; surprise is combined with a sense of liberation, followed by a feeling of relaxation and calm as the visitor realizes how he is being embraced within a vast unity. It is only then that details begin to be noticed, because in effect the interior is seamless with no primary focal point, while manifesting all the essential features of a place. Consequently the articulation of the surfaces by niches, apses, panelling, twinned columns, and so on, is entirely secondary because these exist only in virtue of the hollow they surround. This is why no photograph can convey an adequate impression of this building. To delight in the Pantheon is not to linger on the outside but to stand in the centre, beneath the oculus and to experience how the space spreads outwards on all sides, sometimes distended into apses and niches or indented by columns but never dissipated.

'EXTERNAL' SPACE

When the Romans came to plan their places of public concourse, they continued the Hellenistic programme by creating significant configurations out of undifferentiated space and in this way gave even external space an interior quality. Witnesses to this are the many fora in North Africa, such as that at Thuburbo Maius, which are enclosed by a capitol and three stoas. Space is now shaped around ritual and there is provision for formal patterns of action such as triumphal processions. So, making use of both axiality and biaxiality, together with a consistent symmetry, the Romans produced open-air structures that coerce the observer and compel him to follow a path that has been laid down by every detail of the design.

In this way self-contained environments were created to which even nature was subservient and from which it was sometimes excluded. No longer a partner, as with classical temples, the landscape was levelled or built up as required and all was organized according to the will of man. Order – imperial order – was all important and linear design was the most prevalent system of organization, but monotony was avoided by

sequential variety. These several qualities can be enjoyed nowhere better than at Tivoli in the villa of Hadrian and in Rome
in the imperial fora.

Axiality and symmetry are most evident in the latter, in
particular in those of Augustus and of Trajan (see figure 32).
Entering the first, you find colonnades to right and left, which
originally accommodated shops, these two aisles framing a kind
of central nave leading to the temple of Mars Ultor which is
reared up on a great podium at the far end against the Quirinal
Hill. On either side of the shrine are two hemicycles or semicircular recesses which shape and define the expanding space.

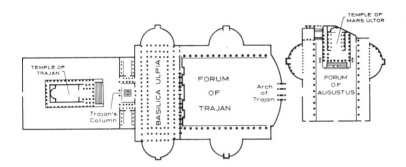

Fig. 32 Rome, imperial
fora

Between these hemicycles there is a lateral axis that crosses
the central one running up to and through the middle of the
temple. On either side of the longitudinal axis there are mirror
images, making this a fine example of bilateral symmetry: the
two halves match and mutually complete each other and add up
to a well-organized whole. The entire forum was surrounded
by a wall over 100 feet high, of which some parts remain.
This masked the slope of the hill behind and the adjacent
buildings, emphasizing that this open-air public place was also
an interior. Here the designer succeeded in enclosing space
without closing it.

Next to the forum of Augustus is that of Trajan which was
even more complex and subtle and covered an area equal to all
the others put together. One passed through a great archway in
the centre of a curved wall into an open court, flanked by
colonnades and two immense hemicycles. The space thus
created was biaxial, the one axis running between the semicircular recesses and the other crossing this and advancing from
the entrance to the Ulpian basilica on the opposite side. The
basilica itself fulfils something of the function of a Hellenistic
stoa in that it serves as a border element of the open court. It was
created by interiorizing colonnades which had previously been

external features and so it consists of a central nave and four aisles. It has a longitudinal axis between the apses at the narrow ends, crossed by a transverse one at right angles. This latter then passes through the column of Trajan beyond, joining the longitudinal axis of his temple which completes the series of spaces. Here the basic scheme of Roman spatial organization is very much in evidence: there is symmetry and biaxiality with the axes, as usual, concluded by a protecting and engulfing building-shell such as a hemicycle, or, as in the two temples in these fora, by an apse. Here too sequence, rhythm and movement are to be enjoyed by physical progression. There is spatial definition with additive volumes which are sinuously flowing and horizontally directional. Each form is a combination of paths and places: the temples belong to the latter category, the open spaces to the former while the basilica has features of both.

The colonnaded street was equally a path. This was very much a Roman development which took place (especially in the eastern part of the empire) where rows of columns were constructed to march along either side of the principal urban thoroughfares. The effect is to stress horizontality and to stimulate directional movement. These monumental avenues create an aesthetic of the street out of a combination of stoas, fountains, exedrae (semicircular marble seats) and triumphal arches. All the features of a well-defined path were then assembled – strong edges, continuity, recognizable landmarks, and so on.

Many of the columns and bases of these streets remain *in situ* and to proceed along Harbour Street (the Arkadiane) at Ephesus (a rebuilding by Arcadius *c.* AD 400 of a Hellenistic original) is to enjoy the leisurely movement and elegance of this kind of disposition, with its two pedestrian walks in colonnades 5 metres wide paved with mosaics. Similarly at Pergamum the Via Tecta provides a magnificent approach to the Asklepieion, itself possessing its own very fine colonnades, and at Perge two such streets divide the whole city into four quarters.

UNITING ORDERS AND ARCHES

A colonnade is of course a row of columns supporting an entablature and it is an example of post-and-beam construction using one or other of the classical orders. The buildings of the Roman era were however often arcuated and it is therefore necessary to consider how orders and arches were actually related.

Roman buildings are examples of wall architecture and this

means that the arches are simply holes – for light and access – through walls that bear the vaults. Walls and vaults are not distinct but complementary: the differentiation between load and support is hidden as everything is merged into an envelope to enclose a shape. In such a system the classical orders have no place as structural elements and they become instead decorative features. By this means the monotony of the blank wall can be relieved. An empty surface is without expression but apply to it, for example, a row of columns and its dynamic character is spelled out since it becomes visibly a pattern of vertically oriented forces. In this way a conventional element which previously carried a load was given a changed use and, no longer corresponding with the technical structure of the edifice, became an ornamental adjunct, although retaining some of its past meaning as a support.

The character of Roman architecture becomes more intelligible when it is realized that it is the outcome of the combination of a system of mass construction with a skeleton one to enclose and cover a particular volume. In other words, to a mass made of vaults and walls that enclose and cover space fictive members have been applied and these give the impression of being parts of a skeleton structure, although in fact they do not function as such at all. In this way the Roman architects realized their greatest achievement, namely the marriage of the classical orders – which belong essentially to trabeated buildings – to arched and vaulted multi-storeyed buildings. One can be integrated with the other in various ways. It is possible to have three-quarter or half-columns with the other quarter or half buried in the wall. Pilasters, i.e. flat representations of columns carved in relief on the wall, can be used and treated as vertical strips of ornament in conjunction with the well-established horizontal accent of entablature and cornice. The orders are applied as frames around the arches, but this is never a haphazard exercise. On the contrary, the orders usually dominate any building to which they are attached and act as controls of the overall design. This control operates because the arches have to harmonize with and be proportional to whatever order has been selected.

These various factors are all plain to see and to enjoy on the outside of the Colosseum. Elliptical in shape, this immense amphitheatre is really one continuous wall which is divided into superimposed sections. The first three storeys are pierced with arches so that each is a curving arcade; the uppermost one has simply rectangular windows at regular intervals. The classical orders have been attached to this structure so that each arch is framed by a pair of three-quarter columns bearing an entablature, Doric at ground level, Ionic next and Corinthian above, while the top band, which acts as a terminal element to bring the huge wall to a satisfying climax, is decorated with Corinthian pilasters on lofty pedestals. This imposing façade reveals the Roman taste for the spectacular and for the rhetorical: it proclaims imperial power and strength. Its size is not just the result of multiplying the dimensions of something essentially small; instead it has been conceived from the outset as large and so it impresses by its magnitude and grandeur. Delight is to be obtained from contemplating the relationship between the static and decorative functions of the architectural members, their proportions and unity. The whole is enlivened by the syncopated rhythm of the arcades and the successive bays which are themselves enhanced in daylight by the shifting shadows. Scenic architecture has here reached a zenith. Spatial effects too have been achieved, because the exterior is in effect a trabeated screen of superimposed orders that stand visually in front of the series of arches, which are in this way thrown back in space, providing both depth and a glimpse of interior volumes. The attached columns introduce recession into the design as the walls project and then withdraw.

Rome, Colosseum

*Ephesus, Library of
Celsus*

There was yet another way of decorating façades that was widely favoured in Asia Minor and also influenced the Roman theatre: this involved constructing a screened wall. Such façades were conceived as objects in themselves to provide the culmination of a vista, as, for example, the Library of Celsus at Ephesus which is the visual climax of Curetes Street looking down the hill. This is a load-bearing wall screened and ornamented by columns that are not engaged but stand in front of and are connected to the main wall by a zig-zag entablature. It can be said that the wall has been encrusted with plastic projections each of which consists of twin columns, with Corinthian capitals, linked by an architrave. The upper storey is displaced, as it were, so that it straddles the spaces in the ground floor and it has a central triangular pediment flanked by curved ones. The entire wall has become an interlocking decorative system with niches or aedicules as its most prominent features. The break with classical models could scarcely be more marked. While the columns have an entablature, they do not support a roof; the architrave is not straight but bends through a series of right angles, while the flanking pediments have borrowed a semicircular contour from the arch. The orders are being treated with a freedom that would have been inconceivable in the days of Pericles, although some move in that direction had been begun in the Hellenistic period.

THE ORDERS

Fig. 33 Tuscan capital

As already noted when discussing the Colosseum, the Romans continued to use the three classical orders – Doric, Ionic and Corinthian – but they added two others. From the Etruscans they took the Tuscan (figure 33), which has a capital very similar to the Doric with echinus and abacus. They themselves developed the Composite, which can be regarded as a combination of Ionic and Corinthian in that it has the volutes of the former and the acanthus leaves of the latter, the volutes being much more prominent than in the classical Corinthian.

Since these orders were employed as decorative elements, it is not surprising to find that the Romans preferred the Corinthian, precisely because it is more ornamental than the others. They systematized the double range of leaves and gave a greater sense of support to the abacus by accentuating the spiral tendrils at the four angles. Their delight in elaborate ornamentation also manifested itself when on occasion they replaced the volutes with other forms such as the rams' heads in the temple of Concord at Rome.

Neither Doric nor Ionic found much favour in the design of temples. When used, the Doric differs a little from its prototype in that the column is provided with a base; there is a plain moulding below the echinus; the necking at the top of the shaft is smooth while the guttae are not cylindrical but conical. With the Roman Ionic the projection of the volutes is less marked than previously and the diagonal capital is favoured. The Attic base is the norm; plinths are regularly employed, but fluting is infrequent.

To treat the orders as decorative elements inevitably further relaxed strict adherence to the classical relationships between the parts which, in any case, had already been modified in the Hellenistic age. Now the orders were disassembled into their constituents to be used entirely as ornamentation: columns were turned into free forms that could exist without any structural responsibility and became fields for additional carving in spirals or other patterns; capitals appeared without columns; pediments were broken or were placed above arches; lintels were arcuated, as in the centre of the façade of the temple of Hadrian at Ephesus so that the horizontal architrave suddenly rears up into a semicircle. Corbels or stone brackets (modillons) were introduced into cornices. Arches were placed on columns, for example in the peristyle court of Diocletian's palace at Split in Yugoslavia, where the columns neither embrace nor frame the arches but support them directly, thus anticipating many an arcade in the Christian basilicas. Despite all this, the overall effect of the remains is not as sumptuous as it must have been originally since many of the mosaics on the floors, the paintings on the walls, or the marble veneers, have long since been destroyed.

TEMPLES

The characteristics of Roman architecture are of course present in every building type, including the temples. The preoccupation with space is certainly very evident both in their interior design and in the way they are integrated within the urban setting. The cella is increased in size laterally, often taking up the entire width of the platform on which the temple stands. The curve is to be seen in the apses within which cult statues could be placed, as in the temples of Mars Ultor and Trajan in Rome. It determines the plan of the Pantheon and of other circular temples, such as that of Vesta in Rome.

However it is in understanding the way that the Roman temple, almost invariably Corinthian, forms a visual climax to exterior space, that appreciation mainly lies. Whereas the classical Greek shrine had been a prismatic solid isolated in free space, the Roman temple, in the line of the Hellenistic sanctuary, is an organic part of the space it generates. It is this fact above all else that explains the peculiarities that differentiate it from its predecessors. Since it is a focal point, it is raised upon a high platform and so, given a dominating position, embodies the power and strength that is habitual to Roman imperial art as a whole. Frontality is emphasized by a flight of steps usually at one end only, and this accentuates the façade as with the Capitol at Dougga. Widely spaced and relatively slender columns, with the central intercolumniation broadened to stress the longitudinal axis, draw further attention to what has become a frontally directed entity. This skeletal openness of form gathers space between the columns and beneath the jutting beams of the roof, while the porch, as in the Hellenistic era, becomes deeper. Indeed the columns along the façade of the developed temple are really those of an expanded prostyle porch rather than part of a continuous colonnade.

In the early days of the empire there were some peripteral temples. Such was the temple of Castor and Pollux in Rome (AD 6). This had a podium 22 feet high, with a flight of steps leading up to a porch three columns deep. There was no opisthodomos and columns embraced the whole. However the colonnades tended to shrink to a mere series of half-columns engaged in the walls of the cella and this resulted in what is known as the pseudo-peripteral plan. Peristyle and cella walls merge, as in the Maison Carrée at Nîmes of the reign of Augustus. While a consequence of this is a certain loss of identity of walls and colonnade, the continuation of the columns along the sides and back binds the composition together and unifies porch and cella. In this way there was produced a single-celled temple, extended by a deep

Dougga, Capitol

Nîmes, Maison Carrée

porch and having a simple plan, organized symmetrically along an unambiguous longitudinal axis.

It remains to be noted that the proportions of these temples reproduce those of the Hellenistic period set down by Vitruvius. Each set has its own rhythmical character. Whereas pycnostyle has its columns so close together that it is almost a palisade and, being tense and forbidding, suggests little movement, systyle can be described as a quick march, eustyle as a dignified walk, diastyle as a serene and stately progression, with araeostyle as a slow, leaping motion. Delight arises from the enjoyment of these different tempos through physical movement.

THEATRES AND AMPHITHEATRES

The Roman delight in space is probably best shared by visiting examples of two other quasi-religious building types, namely theatres and amphitheatres which have survived to the present day in large numbers. Auditorium or cavea coalesced with the stage to form a single structure, as exemplified by the theatre of Orange in the south of France or at Aspendos in Asiatic Turkey. The semicircular seating wraps around the semicircular orchestra. The side entrances are covered with barrel vaults and lined up parallel with the stage. The elaborately decorated back wall

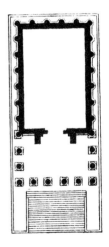

Fig. 34 Nîmes, Maison Carrée

Fig. 35 Orange, theatre

of the stage is heightened to the level of the top of the auditorium. In this way there was created an interior volume enclosed within one uninterrupted perimeter. The steeply sloping seats and the lofty *scenae frons* create a strong feeling of interior space, within which the performers were confined to a narrow stage and appeared like so many figures in a relief. In this way they became dependent elements of a dominant space which was axial in that over the main door of the rear wall was the statue of an emperor or other dignity.

In the theatre space is shaped to funnel the attention of the audience towards the dramatic spectacle; in the amphitheatre (the name of which suggests the combining of two theatres, although the form is invariably elliptical) an oval is used to create a multifocal bowl. This spatial concavity is reflected in the contours of the exterior which is perforated to channel the flow of large numbers of spectators in and out. Many amphitheatres are supported by a structural web of radial and concentric vaulted passageways, framing the area where the primary action is located. Each of them, like the Colosseum, presents tiers of open and enframed arches, so spaced and proportioned as to suggest from a distance stability and from close at hand attraction. Perhaps the amphitheatre is most remarkable as illustrative of the Roman passion for devising new spatial forms. There were no Greek precedents and it was never popular in the eastern Mediterranean, though in western Europe and in North Africa many splendid examples remain.

AQUEDUCTS AND TRIUMPHAL ARCHES

To contemplate the exterior of any amphitheatre, such as that at El Djem in Tunisia, *c.* AD 230, is to be acutely aware of the marching arches along the superimposed storeys. A similar effect is presented by the Roman aqueducts. There is, for example, sufficient remaining of the one built by Valens *c.* 375 at Istanbul for us to enjoy the way its massive legs stride across the valleys between the several hills. But despite the fact that an aqueduct has an inside channel for the water, it is not a building, although it is a formative element in external space. When a bridge crosses a river it changes the character of the banks; it makes them face one another, otherwise they would go on and on as indifferent border strips. So the Pont du Gard, near Uzès, animates and establishes relations within the river valley.

Like the aqueduct, the triumphal arch has no interior s it does dominate its surroundings and is therefore a

Rome, arch of Constantine

external space. Immensely popular – it is estimated that there were some 64 in Rome alone by the end of the empire – they were a kind of monumental billboard proclaiming, through the reliefs and inscriptions, the victories and achievements of one emperor or another. They were often designed as pedestals for a group in bronze or some other materials, which naturally affected the proportions. For example, the arch of Trajan at Ancona, AD 112, which has lost its surmounting figures, appears now too elongated simply as an arch. At first they had a single opening, but later, as with the arch of Constantine in Rome, they were provided with two smaller arches to flank the large central one. Variety, differing accents, linear rhythm, make of such a structure a fitting climax to a vista and offer an invitation to explore the space beyond.

The western empire came to an end with Romulus Augustulus whose ignominious reign lasted scarcely a year from 475 to 476. Nevertheless for nearly 200 years before that architecture had been given a fresh impetus by a rapidly expanding new religion, i.e. Christianity. Its early buildings owed much to imperial Rome but in its turn it devised its own forms to suit its own religious needs.

5

EARLY CHRISTIAN ARCHITECTURE AND THE BYZANTINE ACHIEVEMENT

One of the charges brought against Christianity by its pagan opponents was that it was a new religion. While defenders of the faith sought to counter this by stressing continuity from Judaism, nevertheless in one important respect at least Christianity was new – unlike all the other religions of the ancient world it had no place for bloody sacrifice. Indeed for its two main acts of devotion it required no more than some water and some food and a drink – the first, for baptism or initiation, could be supplied by a stream or even the sea, and the others, for the eucharist or Lord's Supper, could be consumed in a dining room. Such materials and functions do not of themselves engender special buildings and for 250 years there was really no Christian architecture properly so-called.

EARLY CHRISTIAN

In the early fourth century, after the conversion of Constantine, Christianity became a legalized religion. Accommodation for large numbers of adherents had to be provided; the house-church was then no longer adequate. The expedient adopted can be described as the turning of the classical temple outside-in. This literally happened in the case of the temple of Athena at Syracuse. A hexastyle building of the fifth century BC, this had pronaos and opisthodomos, two columns in antis and side colonnades of 14 Doric columns. In the seventh century AD it was transformed to become the cathedral of Syracuse which to this day visibly incorporates the classical building. The spaces between the peristyle columns were filled in to create an external wall; openings were cut through the walls of the cella to produce arcades. The result was to turn the cella into the nave, the former corridors between colonnades and cella walls into aisles, with the division between cella and opisthodomos destroyed for the latter to become the sanctuary.

THE BASILICA AND INTERIOR SPACE

So at Syracuse, out of an object-in-the-round, with little interest in the inside, an interior volume was produced that corresponds with the Christian understanding of worship as the meeting of a community with its God. The church is not a house for the deity; rather it is a house for the people of the deity. There was consequently little interest in its external aspect.

Basilicas do not impress from afar. They are plain, presenting broad surfaces, with windows and doors practically flush with the masonry and with few recesses or extrusions. They rely for effect on the simple juxtaposition of contrasting planes. The façades are awkward in shape and simply reflect that of the nave and aisles. The single triangular pediment of the classical temple has been divided into three portions, of which that in the middle has broken away and is raised above the wings, which, with their lean-to roofs, have each a triangular fragment. In contrast the inside is highly decorated – the glory, it may be said, is all within.

This does not mean that the basilica is to be understood as a receptacle, like the Hellenistic temple. Rather the interest lies in its content, i.e. in the nature of the space that enables the all-important eucharistic action to take place. This space is dynamic because it embodies a forward movement to the east where the altar is placed and where the climax of the Lord's Supper is reached in the act of communion. Every architectural feature is subordinate to this: indeed none can be properly appreciated without understanding how each contributes to the dominant and essential pathlike quality of the basilican design.

THE NAVE

A nave is virtually an oblong box with base and lid formed of pavement and ceiling. Its two long sides are walls in three bands:

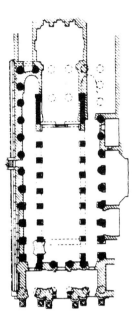

Fig. 36 Syracuse, temple (in black) transformed into cathedral (shaded)

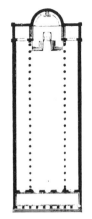

Fig. 37 Rome, S. Maria Maggiore

Rome, S. Maria Maggiore, nave

columns at ground level, an expanse of masonry above and a series of window-openings on top of that. As such a nave is characterized by horizontality, self-containment and inward-lookingness. Its very shape beckons forward because this is how rectangles affect human beings, i.e. if one enters through a short side one is immediately drawn to the side opposite, and in the case of the basilica this means towards the altar. Indeed floor, roof and walls all have a part to play and much of the delight lies in being able to recognize the subtle ways in which this is achieved.

Since seating was almost entirely absent from the Early Christian basilica, the floor was unencumbered and mosaic patterns, indicating forward movement, were readily visible. The marble inlay pavement (*c.* 1150) in S. Maria Maggiore in Rome (432–40), though much later than the original church, faithfully represents this way of marking a dominant direction. A clear pointer towards the further end was also provided by the central

ridge of the open timber roof which was initially common. It was however on the walls to right and left that the most care was lavished.

The treatment of these differs from anything that had gone before. Wall design in the Hellenistic period involved placing a colonnade to stand freely in front of a solid wall, thus producing the stoa. Under the empire the columns were attached with half or three-quarters protruding and the remainder imbedded. The Early Christian method was to draw back the columns entirely within the plane of the wall so that the lower zone in a basilica was in effect an open wall beneath a closed section. There is then the suggestion of a continuous surface, which is particularly noticeable as one looks down a nave and sees how the columns press together and appear to have no spaces between them, like an avenue of trees leading on into the distance.

At first an uninterrupted architrave carried the entablature and provided another directional indicator. This was soon replaced by a series of archivolts, which are really the architrave bent upwards to form semicircular mouldings around the tops of arches. This also stresses the surface quality because whereas a column may be regarded, in the light of classical prototypes and despite its inclusion within the wall boundaries, as a self-contained sculptural unit, an arch is quite obviously cut out of a

Ravenna, S. Apollinare in Classe, nave

wall and its supports are read as residues. In this way the arcades emphasize the two-dimensionality of the sides of the nave, but at the same time they stride along as in one of the zones of an aqueduct. With their curvilinear rhythm whereby one part runs on into the next they promote a flow of movement, accenting it by the 'spring' of the archivolts from column to column.

Above these, the second band, which is frequently an unpierced expanse of masonry, makes the nave sides even more like the faces of a canyon so that they act as space-definers of the volume between them. They are sheathed with polychrome and highly polished materials, that leave the envelope of space smooth and inviolate. The most supple and flexible of these textures to emerge was the mosaic.

Movement was introduced and a recessional perspective was accentuated by having either a row of figures processing toward the east end, as in S. Apollinare Nuovo in Ravenna, or a succession of panels, as in S. Maria Maggiore in Rome.

Ravenna, S. Apollinare Nuovo, nave arcade

The upper stage of the nave wall is known as the clearstory or

clerestory because, with its windows, it allows illumination in from outside. The windows are set at regular intervals creating rhythmic alternations of light and shade and so continuing the horizontal thrust towards the sanctuary. Since the light shines downwards, the possibility of losing oneself in the roof space is counteracted; after all it is only a wooden lid.

Within the boxlike nave there is a relatively undifferentiated continuum of controlled and channelled space and it forms essentially one single unarticulated unit. Delight in a basilica however involves more than concentration upon this volume alone. Most Early Christian churches had aisles, usually two but sometimes four, and these affect both the character of the nave and of the building as a whole.

AISLES

The word 'aisle' originally meant a wing and its derivation points to its dependent role: an aisle is not the main body of a building but an adjunct. While parallel to the nave, the aisles are strictly secondary and are shown to be such by either their lesser illumination or their size. When the width of a nave and of its aisles is set in the ratio of 2:1, the aisles are subordinate spaces, and if they are made even narrower they become mere passage-ways. They have less prominence too because they are lower than the nave, their lean-to roofs usually abutting just below the clerestory.

However the impression of a central promenade flanked by tunnels is seldom conveyed as views between the columns or through the arches provide interlocking vistas. There is then a flow of space from the nave into its wings, while the uninter-rupted expanse of the pavement suggests an open unity. The character of the nave itself can be more precisely defined by the aisles which are similar, though smaller, units of space. They visually reinforce its direction; they accompany the main high-way on its eastward progression; they serve as porticoes to the principal thoroughfare so that the nave can be enjoyed as a colonnaded street, a kind of processional way leading to a triumphal arch. Indeed contemporary writers referred to the basilica as a royal road and others stressed its on-flowing move-ment by comparing it to a river.

THE BASILICA AS A PATH

It is now important to explain what is meant by interpreting the basilica as a path. That a nave has firm edges has already been demonstrated when analysing its side walls. The three zones coalesce to form very clear boundary lines. However to be strong an edge does not have to be impenetrable, and so, while the arcades do divide the nave from the aisles, they also keep them in visual relation. Hence arcades not only divide the dominant space from the subsidiary ones, they also unite them, thus creating a dynamic tension. They may be considered not as barriers but seams along which the differing volumes are sewn or joined together.

The aisles themselves contribute to the framing of the nave, while at the same time they too are paths defined on either side by the arcades and outer walls. At first however they had no obvious goal, simply accompanying the nave part of the way to the sanctuary. In the eastern Mediterranean, however, apses were soon added to their terminations, probably to reinforce their pathlike quality.

Continuity and directionality are obviously necessary if a path is to be easily recognizable. Attention has been called to both of these above in terms of floor patterns, the ridge lines of roofs, the mosaics and the windows. Moreover when an element is cumulative in one direction, there is no hesitation about which way to go and this is achieved by the rows of columns. Converging lines perform the same function: the nave walls appear to draw together thus focusing the eye on the altar and emphasizing its importance as a goal with columns constituting a sequential series of landmarks. Identity is also given to paths when they have a sharp terminal and end-from-end distinction.

TRIUMPHAL ARCH AND APSE

Advancing both visually and physically along the nave in the direction so clearly indicated, the next architectural feature to confront the visitor is the triumphal arch. Originally an open-air Roman creation, the Christians employed it as an interior feature to mark the approaching climax of their own *via triumphalis*. Such an arch summons one to approach it and to pass through it: it is a kind of gateway to the altar. Architecturally the arch also functions like an aqueduct joining two sides of a river valley together. In the basilica the arcades could be indifferent boundaries going on and on with no reason ever to come to an end, but the triumphal arch bridges the space between the two sides so that they are brought into relation and face one another; at the same time it provides a frame for the apse and in this way helps to create a sharp terminal.

The Early Christian apse is half an upright cylinder sur-mounted by a quarter sphere; it is clearly distinct from the rest of the building which is rectangular. Its concave shape suggests the shelter of an embrace. Space flows into it and it holds its arms out in welcome. It is not then an abrupt terminal, like a flat east wall; instead it evokes an impression of expanding hollowness. With its unbroken concave surface, it both enlarges and shapes the primary space, unifying it and reinforcing its containing quality.

An apse has a semicircular vault that, like every vault, suggests an invisible centre line in a way that is not so in rectilinear space. In the latter every line drawn from floor to flat ceiling is the same length and no one is emphasized: in an apse however the much greater vertical distance at the centre is thrown into prominence. This middle line corresponds with the main axis of the entire basilica which is characterized by bilateral symmetry. Axiality is the dominant; the design develops around the centre line which unifies the whole and further stresses the eastward direction. In other words, path and main axis coincide and advance together until the central line of the force which they embody is caught and cupped in the curved shape of the apse. The axis culminates in this terminal hollow. An apse is a subordinate feature only in scale; in fact it is an essential element in the whole design, both fixing the axis and expanding the larger volume, following the method of organizing space already evident in the imperial fora.

THE ALTAR

Delight in this design is obtained by movement as much as by sight. Entering the nave, one feels compelled to walk forward, but this advance cannot go on indefinitely without losing significance; it has to be concluded in a way that gives satisfaction – the apse provides an admirable closure. It exists however for the altar (as does the entire building) and being a very clear and defined space it serves as a frame. It fulfils this function whether or not the altar is placed on its chord, which is the norm, or in front of it.

The importance of the altar is due to the fact that it is essential for the celebration of the eucharist. In addition, since Christ himself was believed to be the place of encounter between God and humankind, the altar, which serves a similar end, was regarded as an effective symbol of his presence. Indeed many early writers referred to Christ himself as the altar and so the basilican path leads to him and proclaims that the path of life too finds its end in Jesus Christ. Unlike, for example, the later religion of Islam which recognizes God primarily as pervasive throughout his creation, Christianity sees the divine influence focused in a particular manifestation and its basilica embodies the desire to centre and celebrate architecturally this specificity. Apse and altar together present a geometry of sovereignty. By locating the altar at this point, Christ's surveillance of the cosmos is suggested through the enfolding surface, free from angles and curving around the symbol of his presence.

The architectural dominance of the altar is thus achieved by making it the object to which the eye is first attracted. Of course every object in a visual field constitutes a small gravitational centre of its own; but give it the importance of the altar in the basilica and it is bound to draw special attention. Moreover while repetition can devalue elements, isolation throws them into prominence; in this way the altar, standing either on its own or beneath a baldachin or ciborium (a small dome carried on four columns), is given positional enhancement. The handling of space contributes to the same effect. Space declares the 'where' of things; it can also reveal the 'how' of things. The way space is moulded (the 'how') indicates 'where' the centre of interest lies. Thus the pattern of the arcades leads forward to the apse, but so does the shape of the space between them, i.e. the elongated form, narrowing in perspective, means that attention is directed to the far end. One cannot escape it; if one looks upwards, there is the roof and the downward-flowing light to bring one back to the horizontal; if one follows the line of the windows, one reaches the triumphal arch and is forced to descend into the frame of the apse and so be led again to the altar. The arcading is really a directing of attention by the use of planes, but the elongation of the rectangular boxlike nave and the decrease of space into the apse are also spatial means for guiding observation. This is 'how' space functions to affirm 'where' interest must eventually be concentrated.

Because entrance into the basilica is usually at the west end, there is a tendency to think of it entirely as a forward march to its climax in the apse, but in fact the building can be conceived as planned from its east end with the vault of the apse as the dominant factor from which the rest of the building flows. So the space sweeps outwards and upwards through the triumphal arch, broadening, lengthening and expanding right down to the exit doors. Then the nave is apprehended as a westward elongation of the sanctuary and as a path in the reverse direction. Altar and apse thus constitute both an introvert centre or node, drawing the visitor towards them, and also an extravert node in so far as they can equally be a point of departure towards the outside world once the act of communion has taken place.

TRANSEPTS

There is another spatial unit to be noted before leaving the east end of the basilica and that is the transept. This is the transverse part of a church at right angles to the nave. While not infrequent, it was by no means universal in the early period of Christian architecture. It can take one of two main forms. When the nave colonnades are brought to an end just before it, as in old St Peter's, Rome, there is a continuous transept in that the transverse space is undivided. The effect is to increase the volume in front of the apse. When the colonnades continue, turning at right angles into the wings and then envelop them on three sides, a cross transept is produced: this is really a swelling of the nave, for example as at St Menas, Abu Mina, Egypt.

However neither shape is to be regarded as constituting a cross-roads because when they are reached it is immediately apparent that there is no real choice of direction. Whether they have a flat end or are rounded to combine with the apse in a trefoil plan, they are obviously cul-de-sacs and their effect is to concentrate even more attention upon the sanctuary.

OTHER CHARACTERISTICS

That the principle of composition is addition needs little demonstration. Aisles are added to the central nave and a transept to its east end; its walls are superimposed, semi-independent layers; the focus is on a half-cylinder juxtaposed against the short side of an oblong box. The cohesion of the parts does not derive from structural integration, rather it is the result of a kind of sewing together of adjacent volumes and expanses. The composition is successive, as witness the linear rhythm of the colonnades. The elements face the viewer orthogonally and so frontality is noticeable in that the walls face the central axis, the arch confronts the nave and the apse itself turns round a midpoint.

Because the basilica is formed in this way out of clearly distinguishable parts and also comprises a union of paths and places, it is possible to draw a diagram of each building. Such a diagram is not concerned, as are plans, with the structure but with making visible the architectural functioning of the various features to reveal the underlying pattern made up of edges, seams, nodes, and so on. The Church of the Nativity at Bethlehem can be taken as a typical example. The present building is not exactly that constructed by Constantine; it has been reordered by Justinian, although its original nave and aisles remain intact. On either side of the nave are two aisles, while the nave itself terminates in a continuous transept with rounded ends, and the altar is set in a central apse. Entering at the west end, we become aware that the central axis runs straight down the middle of the nave. The direction of the building thus leads towards the sanctuary. Next it is to be noted that the plan is symmetrical, two identical aisles on each side, two arms to the space in front of the altar, rows of columns corresponding with rows of columns. Here is bilateral symmetry so that the aisles are not separate corridors but parts of a whole. The building can then be grasped as a unified space through which to move to the focus of attention at the far end. All this can be derived from a study of the plan. A diagram (figure 38) brings awareness of other features. From this it is evident that the centre of the building is a wide path, flanked on either side by two subsidiary paths which are also edges. The central highway is framed not only by these but also by other edges in the form of columns which are both landmarks and seams. This *via triumphalis* eventually conducts to a wide space with place characteristics; this is a node which has at its centre a prominent landmark (the altar). The entire building is contained within very clear borders.

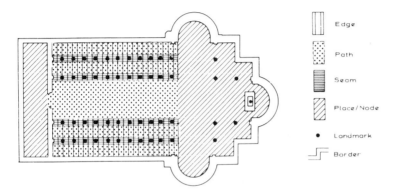

Edge

Path

Seam

Place/Node

Landmark

Border

Fig. 38 Bethlehem, diagram of Church of the Nativity

TOMBS, MARTYRIA AND BAPTISTERIES

Although undergoing some elaboration, the basilican plan persisted as the norm for western Europe for over 1,000 years. This means it can be illustrated not only from buildings of the fourth and fifth centuries but also by such eleventh-century examples as the cathedrals of Torcello or Pisa, the abbey of Pomposa or the church of S. Clemente in Rome. However from the beginning of Christian architecture there was another group of religious buildings that had a different character: they were designed as places and were used as tombs, saints' shrines and baptisteries.

Among the first to be erected *c.* 350, was the mausoleum of Constantine's daughter, Constantina, in Rome, now the church of S. Costanza. This is a round edifice with a domed centre room rising from an arcade carried by 12 pairs of composite columns. This in turn is encircled by a barrel-vaulted ambulatory and the whole was originally enveloped by a continuous colonnaded porch. S. Costanza is what is known as a centralized building, i.e. it has been planned around a vertical central axis and it is characterized by rotational symmetry. Movement inside is slow because it is not a path to be pursued but a centre, concentrated in form, limited in size, with a continuous bounding surface largely isolating it from the exterior. Being circular it has no directions and so rests in itself. While it does have an ambulatory, which is a kind of round path that eventually joins up with

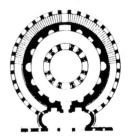

Fig. 39 Rome, S. Costanza

itself, to enter it is not to feel that one is being led anywhere; on the contrary this corridor enfolds the central volume in a kind of gentle but firm embrace. However not the least important factor giving character to the interior is the dome, not simply because it moulds the space but because of the meaning that the shape was believed to embody.

The dome was read as an image of heaven. It gave assurance of an eternal home for the departed. Hence domed structures were used for tombs, and also to shelter sites that witnessed to the Christian faith. These martyria either referred to events in the life of Christ or were shrines to those who had testified with their blood. Hence the Anastasis of Jerusalem, built by Constantine, was a circular building around the rock tomb of Jesus, while at Bethlehem the cave-stable was originally enclosed in an eight-sided figure which itself, to the early Christians, was the equivalent of a circle.

The octagon was also favoured, particularly in the west, for baptisteries where believers sacramentally died and rose with Christ, because the number eight was understood to refer to the first day of a new week and so to Sunday when the New Age dawned with the resurrection of Jesus. The fonts that provided the gravitational centre of these buildings were accorded the same ideological content. They also could be octagonal and hexagonal as well, the latter referring to the sixth day of the week or Friday when Jesus died on the cross – hence also cruciform fonts. Others were rectangular but even then it was the shape of a sarcophagus with its associations that the designer had in mind.

Mosaics further contributed to setting forth the meaning of the baptismal rite. The two octagonal baptisteries at Ravenna – that of the Orthodox (400–50) and that of the Arians (*c.* 500) – have in the centre of the dome a representation of the baptism of Jesus by John (the prototype of all Christian baptisms), surrounded by prophets and apostles whose ranks the neophytes join in order to bear similar witness.

ORNAMENT

Mosaic was indeed the outstanding decorative element in centralized buildings and basilicas, with painting used when the more costly technique was out of the question. Sculpture was less favoured because the prevalent interest was in the modelling of space rather than in the creation of objects in space. Relief (particularly on the sides of sarcophagi) and not figures in the round was therefore most frequently adopted. The effect of this was to subordinate the sculptural details to the architecture. Capitals were given a surface quality to preserve the two-dimensional nature of the nave walls as space-definers. On the Corinthian capital the acanthus leaves were reduced in number and simplified in outline, making them less plastic. The volutes were allowed to atrophy and the overall design became more like a block than a bell with an inner life. The actual decoration was achieved by deep undercutting and drilling, which produces a sharp contrast between the white outer face and the dark incisions.

In the late fourth century, as a consequence of the replacing of the architrave by archivolts, a new device – known as the impost block – was produced that was to help the transition from the top of the capital to the footing of the arch. It is an inverted and truncated pyramid whose sides splay outwards and upwards to meet the arch. At first it was quite plain, sometimes decorated with a single cross on the side facing the nave. While in the Byzantine era it was to be much developed, in the Early Christian period it serves mainly to illustrate the lack of concern for sculptural detail.

Mosaics are a different case. Although they too were to achieve their zenith in later centuries, there are sufficient examples – S. Costanza, S. Apollinare Nuovo, S. Pudenziana, the Ravenna baptisteries, and so on – to show how admirable a form of decoration for basilicas and baptisteries they can be. Mosaic is a method of placing small pieces of differently coloured materials closely together to form a patterned surface. Prior to its use by Christians, mosaic had been employed for pavements and sometimes on walls, but in all cases it consisted of cubes of coloured marble. In the fourth century tesserae of coloured glass were used. Because of their possibilities for colour and for the reflection of light, they have never been surpassed as an architectural adornment on a large scale. The broad simple treatment and the tendency towards abstraction and formalization, characteristic of the pictorial art of the day, were eminently suited to the technique of mosaic and to subjects that are meant to be seen from a distance.

Very much surface-accepting, these mosaics are completely at one, both physically and aesthetically, with the interior space they sheath. Even when scenes are depicted, as in S. Maria Maggiore, the figures are starkly frontal, offering no recession, and when backed with gold, which became very common from the fifth century onwards, all depth is ruled out. They have light-gathering properties too and animate the atmosphere of the interior volume which becomes alive with colour and with a twinkling effect due to the irregular setting of the tiny cubes. The glory of the heavenly Jerusalem seemed to have come down to earth, but greater glory was to come.

BYZANTINE ARCHITECTURE

It was in the sixth century that a decisive break with the basilican tradition was made in the East under the emperor Justinian. Then preference was given to churches with a centralized plan, like the martyria and baptisteries. The imperial architects made this the norm for congregational buildings, to such an extent that Balkan and Russian planners were still producing variants a millennium later. Moreover these architects began with the climax – Hagia Sophia was and is the supreme Byzantine achievement. All other buildings, fine though some of them are, are so many aspirations after it. But the subtlety of this masterpiece is such that consideration of it must wait until some insight has been conveyed into the various elements that were combined to produce it.

THE BALDACHIN PRINCIPLE

One of the fundamental facts to grasp about Byzantine churches is that each and every one has been constructed in accordance with the baldachin principle. This means that it is the dome that is the primary space-defining element; the church as a whole is conceived as a complete baldachin, i.e. as a hemisphere on four supports, and so the walls between these four are not needed for load-bearing and can be perforated, replaced by columnar screens, given a curved form or simply eliminated, reducing the enveloping system to a mere skin stretched on a skeleton.

The feel of such a building can perhaps be made more evident by contrasting it with previous Roman structures. The Roman domes were either like the one crowning the Pantheon, i.e. lids on cylinders, or they were continuing vaults rounded upwards-and-over to roof some of the large volumes in the imperial baths. But the Byzantine dome is not a lid and it does not read up-and-over but downwards; the lower parts exist for it and would be meaningless without it. It is for that reason that, despite the fact that construction has to begin at ground level, it is necessary to speak of a Byzantine church as planned from the top downwards.

In S. Vitale at Ravenna, for example, it is the dome or rather

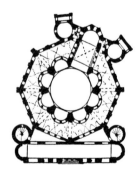

Fig. 40 Ravenna, S. Vitale

Ravenna, S. Vitale, interior

the domical vault that reigns supreme. Indeed the building cannot be explained from below upwards since it is the dome itself that determines the possibilities of the spaces below. The eight-sided vault sits upon an octagonal clerestory pierced with windows. The descending light makes the dome seem to brood over the building and directs ones gaze downwards. The roof and the clerestory are now seen to be supported by eight great pillars between which there is of course no need for any structure; instead tall arches span the openings. However the octagonal space beneath the dome expands through these arches into another eight-sided figure which forms an ambulatory, the expansion taking the form of billowing outwards into semicircular niches. These niches are divided into two zones with arcades in both lower and upper. At ground level they lead up to the gallery, while on the first floor they culminate in half-domes. This vertical division has been left out of the eastern arch which opens into a projecting choir and apse where the altar is located. The entire structure is therefore a baldachin with eight legs, which constitutes a space-frame, embraced by an ambulatory and gallery that create a space-trap, with a sanctuary and a great narthex or entrance porch attached. The narthex itself is off-axis, touching only a corner of the outer wall and leading into the church through subordinate triangular volumes. The vistas on entrance are very complex and the visitor at first is uncertain of his position and so finds himself under compulsion by the design itself to clarify it, and this he can only do if he penetrates to the core of the building and stands beneath the crowning dome.

HANGING ARCHITECTURE

In S. Vitale and similar Byzantine buildings the dome then does not appear to be a carried load but a self-supporting heavenly sphere hovering or descending from above. Despite this supremacy of the burden over the supports, the latter do not give the impression of being crushed nor in fact of being load-bearing. The general effect is that of a hanging architecture; the vaults have apparently no weight of their own; the columns are not conceived as supporting elements but as descending tentacles or pendulous roots. The space radiates downwards: heaven, represented by the dome, condescends to earth, which corresponds with the flat pavement: incarnation is given architectural expression.

Interest centres in the contrast between the form of the dome and the space defined beneath. The chief Byzantine method of accommodating the roundness of the one to a rectangular or octagonal volume below was the pendentive – the very word emphasizing the hanging character of the architecture since it derives from the Latin *pendere* meaning 'to hang down'. Indeed a pendentive is a spherical triangle with its curved baseline helping to support a dome, either directly or indirectly on a drum, and its inverted vertex reaching down between two adjacent arches that meet at right angles. The bases of four such pendentives between four arches join to create a circle on which the dome or drum may rest. So the downward transition from the dome to the lower structure is effected very smoothly indeed, despite the contrast in shapes and without that slight break that cannot be avoided if the angles are bridged by slabs of stone or by small arches (squinches).

At the summit then there is the dome which, in the words of a sixth-century writer, Paul the Silentiary, describing Hagia Sophia but applicable to all Byzantine churches, 'is a great

Fig. 41 Pendentives

helmet, bending over on every side, like the radiant heavens, and embracing the roof of the church'. He continues: 'It is like the firmament that rests upon air.' It appears to float and this effect derives from the windows around its base which create a band or ring of light and so diffuse a glow of luminous atmosphere through the upper part of the volume. This diminishes in intensity and precision the lower it reaches and consequently the illumination both makes the dome appear to be suspended and at the same time pours down like a cataract emphasizing the 'hanging' character of the whole.

CAPITALS AND COLUMNS

Continuing the downward sweep, by means of the curving pendentives and the arches, the next feature to be enjoyed is either the impost block or the capital, since the classical entablature was dispensed with. The impost block, also known as a dosseret and a pulvin, was at first plain; it was next carved with a simple cross and then decorated all over. It finally merged with both Ionic and Corinthian capitals to create an entirely new form, namely the impost capital that streamlines the passage from the square bottom of the arch to the circle of the column, effecting it smoothly within its own block-shaped body. It therefore assists the continuing movement of descent. Its shape is sometimes conical and sometimes cubical and when it has grooves or channels running down the sides it is known as a melon capital.

Other Byzantine capitals include the basket type, its designation pointing both to its shape and to its decoration. There is also the so-called Theodosian form which is essentially Composite with the replacement of the egg-and-dart ornament between the volutes by a band of acanthus leaves and of the rosette on the abacus by a monogram or a cross in a circle. When the acanthus leaves are flattened and given a sideways profile, the capital is known as windblown acanthus.

It is the ornament that provides the clue to the appreciation of these capitals which were designed to fit exactly with the character of the building as a whole. They are purely decorative, appealing not to the sense of touch but to the eye. Continuing the use of undercutting, there is a rich and elaborate patternization with no modelling so that the stress is on the two-dimensional resulting in a lacelike effect. This suggests that the capitals are not really supporting the dominant burden; they seem to be too delicate to perform such an onerous function and to be

Istanbul, Hagia Sophia, capital

capable only of transferring the weight from one leg of an arch to the next. So the capital does not act as the burden's resting point but as the arch's turning point.

The columns too are not intended to convey an impression of active support and hence there is a universal absence of fluting. Even where there are coupled columns, i.e. columns set in pairs through the thickness of a wall, their load-bearing nature is contradicted by the polish and variety of the marble graining that directs attention to the surface once more. Finally the tentacle-like character of the shafts is enhanced at the point where they are about to reach the ground by inserting a narrow slab or plinth beneath the Attic base and so preventing its coming into contact with the pavement.

The flooring has its own special importance within a centralized building because it is the one common element among all the volumes and so helps to unify the several forms. It is not of course visible in its entirety from any one position, but the way it recedes in every direction contributes to a sense of expansion and so of exhilarating liberation. Byzantine space is radial; the

visitor is not drawn to a centre as in an Early Christian baptistery, rather he experiences the space as in a process of moving
outwards until it meets the walls that define it. However this is
not excavated architecture because the interiors have not been
created by a subtraction of mass but by the design of enveloping
shells with particular attention paid to their surface quality.

SURFACE QUALITY AND MOSAICS

All surfaces in a Byzantine church are smooth, free from plastic
decoration and with little in the way of projecting elements.
Where there is sculpture, this is like embroidery, two-
dimensional in character and therefore surface-affirming. This
is also the effect of the mosaics which, spreading over the walls
like a skin, completely hide the structures beneath.

Byzantine mosaics are planar and their accommodation to the
walls is most striking. The Gospel scenes in the top register in S.
Apollinare Nuovo, for example, are all starkly frontal; they
suggest no recession and many of them have golden grounds
which rule out any depth. Indeed to enjoy them fully it is
essential to forget Renaissance perspective according to which a
picture is a window opening on to a space beyond: on the
contrary, Byzantine pictures open on to the space before them.
This means that the depth of, say, an apse mosaic is in front of it
not behind it. From a Renaissance standpoint this could be
called a reversed perspective, i.e. the viewpoint of the picture is
behind the scene. Christ as the Pantokrator or All-Sovereign
looks down from the centre of a dome animating the space
between himself and the visitor, who is not regarded as a spectator looking at a picture but as a servant being himself looked at
and confronted by his Lord. Christ seems to inhabit the actual
space of the church and the architectural lines follow the direction of his gaze. In the course of time a complete iconographical
scheme was devised which embodied this descending and hierarchical sequence. At the summit naturally is heaven, inhabited,
as it were, by Christ surrounded by angels, prophets and the
four evangelists – all present in the dome, its drum or on the
pendentives. Then comes an intermediate zone represented frequently by the Virgin and Child in the apse and by scenes from
the life of Christ. Finally the nave and aisles correspond to the
earth and are provided with figures of the saints. The entire
scheme in this way affirms both incarnation and resurrection
and reinforces the descending character of the architecture.

Delight in such a church as St Mark's, Venice, is really only possible if all these factors are borne in mind, for the mosaics do not simply cling to its interior walls like pearls around a lady's neck. Remove such a string and her fairness need not be impaired, but strip off the mosaics and the nature of St Mark's would be entirely altered. Its interior is in fact unified by the mosaics because they cover both vaults and substructure.

With their uneven and iridescent surfaces, Byzantine mosaics are said to convey an air of incorporeality and to dissolve matter. The recognition of this so-called dematerialization is frequently regarded as an important key to delight in Byzantine churches. Nevertheless it rests upon a misinterpretation by western commentators who fail to take account of the eastern understanding of the nature of matter when it is related to the divine. Not dematerialization but transfiguration is at the heart of a Byzantine church. The technical term for this mysterious 'change' is metabolism: while the natural substances do remain themselves, they become Spirit-bearing; the divine and creaturely existences are unified. There is no conversion of matter – no dematerialization – so that it ceases to exist or becomes something else; instead there is transfiguration whereby the material reality is integrated with the divine life that pours down from above. Glory is then made visible.

CHURCH PLANS

While the dome is the characteristic feature of all Byzantine churches, there is some variety in the substructures. There is a compromise between the standard Early Christian design and the baldachin principle in the domed basilica, the dome usually being supported on four columns in front of the apse in the second bay of a two-bay nave. Hagia Irene in Istanbul, which is a Turkish rehandling of the church that was rebuilt after a fire in 564, is a fine example of this type.

It was however the centralized plan that carried all before it. Whereas this meant that a church could assume an octagonal shape, or, by putting four apses together, become a quatrefoil or tetraconch, the cross-in-square became the favoured plan and it usually took the form of a quincunx. A quincunx is a structure divided into nine bays; it has a central large square dominated by the principal dome. This square is abutted by four rectangular bays which are usually barrel-vaulted and at each of the four corners there is a further small square either domed or groin-vaulted. In order to provide for the liturgy, an apse appears at the east end and this is generally flanked by side chambers, while

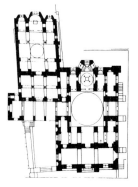

Fig. 42 Osios Loukas

at the west end there is a porch or narthex – galleries too are common. An attractive and typical example of this is the smaller church at Osios Loukas, probably built *c.* 1040 in honour of the Mother of God (Theotokos). By adding quincunx to quincunx even more complex plans could be created. So St Mark's in Venice, first consecrated in 1073, is basically five of these units interlocking, plus an apse to the east, to produce a Latin-cross plan, i.e. a cross with three short arms and one long one. The much earlier church of St John at Ephesus, completed in 565, is also a Latin-cross but this is formed of six baldachin units, four from west to east and one in each of the transepts.

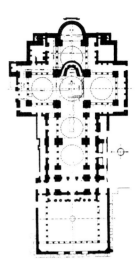

Fig. 43 *Ephesus, St John*

THE PRINCIPLE OF COMPOSITION: DIVISION

The various styles of architecture considered so far all have addition as the principle of design: part is added to part. Superficially it might seem that Byzantine follows the same procedure. Is not an apse something added to a nave? Is not a quincunx the sum of nine bays and a tripartite sanctuary? It would be over-hasty to reply in the affirmative and indeed further analysis will show that the principle of composition is division. Division does not begin with the parts but with the whole, the parts being subdivisions that have little or no independence. Now there is no doubt that in a Byzantine church it is the whole that both dominates and determines the parts, which are quite clearly subordinate and in themselves are no more than fragments. When, for example in Hagia Sophia, half-domes have been reared up to support the central hemisphere, they can of course be recognized by their form to be half-domes but they have no meaning apart from their relation to the design in its entirety. To consider them as separate entities would be a mistake; they are secondary fragments incomplete in themselves.

Within a Byzantine church then dome, half-dome, squinches, and so on coalesce instead of establishing separate forms. There is a relative lack of strong definition at corners so that the half-cylinder of the apse merges without seam or obstruction in a kind of sweeping flow with the cube of the centralized building. Even this however is not a sufficiently precise statement to avoid all suggestion of addition. Instead it is necessary to recall the extent to which a Byzantine church consists of expanding space that is centripetal and radiating. So one does not begin with the apse and regard it as juxtaposed against a cube, but with the central volume beneath the dome that swells outwards into the rounded apse which is then apprehended not as an

*Istanbul, SS. Sergius and
Bacchus, interior*

addition but as an extension of the nave.

The Byzantine apse, unlike the Early Christian one, is an extrusion of the flat end wall of the nave; it is not an appended structure abutting one extremity of the church. The sanctuary in Hagia Sophia illustrates this perfectly. There the curve of the apse is less than half a circle on plan: the effect of this shallowness is to make it belong to the nave and thus contribute to the spatial unity of the whole interior. Nevertheless since the crown of its semidome is lower than that of the main eastern arch beneath the dome, it has a certain distinctness that enables it to function as a focus of interest, but this distinction is not so great that it produces a semi-independent entity: the apse remains a subdivision.

A BYZANTINE CHURCH AS A PLACE

The modern visitor to a Byzantine church can be misled as to the original nature of the architecture by two factors: the presence of an iconostasis and the occupation of the nave by the laity. An iconostasis is a screen covered with large pictures or icons, separating the altar from the rest of the building. It was a late development, beginning in Russia towards the end of the fourteenth century. According to the previous arrangement the clergy were not completely fenced off in this way and indeed had a place in the nave, with the laity in the ambulatory and galleries. These galleries often enfold the central volume on three sides, i.e. over the aisles and over the inner vestibule (esonarthex) to the west. The domed central bay was used particularly for the Little Entrance, when the Bible was carried in, and for the Great Entrance when the eucharistic elements were conveyed to the altar. From the sixth century these processions no longer moved along a longitudinal axis through the church from the door but out from the chapels flanking the apse into the nave and back again. There was therefore no need to emphasize the horizontal axis and this was further rendered otiose by the growth of non-communicating attendance, which meant that the laity did not need to approach the altar and had simply to observe the drama of the divine liturgy. The pathlike quality of the basilica was now no longer required; the Byzantine church became a holy place. In keeping with this, processional mosaics were dispensed with and replaced by static and discontinuous scenes. Centralized architecture, as exemplified by SS. Sergius and Bacchus, *c.* 525, Istanbul, fits very well with this because it involves planning around a midpoint with stress on the vertical axis and this too accords with Orthodox worship.

EXTERIORS

Because a Byzantine church is a place without a strong directional quality, no great importance was initially attached to a façade, and indeed the sides of centralized buildings are frequently similar. Exterior decoration was at first limited. In time a concern for the outside appearance led to some decoration, and so in Greece many churches, such as those at Kastoria or in Athens, have their walls enriched with brick patterns. This means that Byzantine exteriors have a dual character. On the one hand they may be regarded as so many flat pictorial surfaces diversified by the use of stone, brick and slate; on the other hand they can be appreciated as a massing of forms with cylinders, prisms and blocks piling up dramatically to the climax of the dome, and witnessing to transcendence. But like the pyramids, they may be read both up and down since they express within the hanging interior the theme of the self-abasement of the divine love in Christ.

HAGIA SOPHIA – POINT OF DEPARTURE AND CLIMAX

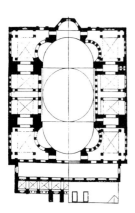

Fig. 44 Istanbul, Hagia Sophia

Hagia Sophia rises pyramidically on the exterior with verticality, width and depth all harmonized. Despite the added buttresses and Islamic minarets that somewhat obscure the original design, it is evident that the upper part, consisting of dome and half-domes, has a plastic effect with positive geometric forms handled to accentuate their mass and volume. The lower part on the other hand is a series of bounding surfaces, a mere curtaining, so that the whole corresponds to the inside with its downward accent. In other words, even from the outside the baldachin character of the great church is apparent, with the dome dominating and dropping its four tentacles earthwards and the voids between them provided with a skin to enclose the space.

In Justinian's day entrance was through a forecourt or atrium into an outer porch (exonarthex), an inner vestibule and so to the nave. The atrium no longer exists and the visitor enters directly into the exonarthex and from this point passes through a modelled sequence of space that leads to the main part of the cathedral. Both vestibules are narrow and oblong and both are shorter than the church front to which they are visibly subordinate. The exonarthex, to use musical terms, constitutes an overture introducing a simply rhythmical movement that is continued in a fuller tone in the inner porch and reaches a

Istanbul, Hagia Sophia, exterior

Istanbul, Hagia Sophia, interior

swelling crescendo in the nave. The esonarthex, while extensive in breadth, induces a feeling of being squeezed up against the entrance doors which are set in a wall that is flat and insubstantial. This wall suggests a veil waiting to be penetrated and when this is done there is a sensation of sudden expansion. One breathes freely again in the volume of the main church that appears not only long in depth, vast in size and toweringly high but also much brighter after the relatively dark vestibules.

Light and spatial amplification are indeed the first overriding impressions. Light always attracts attention to itself. If one moves from somewhere dark into an adjacent room that is more illuminated, then one's gaze immediately seeks the source of light. So standing inside the main door of Hagia Sophia, eyes are inevitably drawn to the windows ringing the base of the dome.

Above them the dome itself seems suspended, and from on high the light is then graduated downwards, becoming more subdued and uniform at the lower levels, with galleries and aisles in half darkness providing a firm contrast and all contributing to the hanging effect of the design.

Space expands. The dome slides smoothly down into the pendentives and bulges gracefully into longitudinally disposed semi-domes. To the east the half-dome swells into three niches, one where the altar formerly stood. To the right and left of the main entrance door two other exedrae spread outwards. The aisles and galleries are further interlocking volumes with ever-changing vistas. It is difficult to remain still; movement itself brings delight when harmonious space-enclosure is present to such a high degree.

Despite the vastness of Hagia Sophia, the magnitude is not diminished by lack of measure and indeed there are three elements that provide this. First, all the utilitarian features such as steps and parapets have been designed with an eye to human dimensions, (whereas if the size of a classical temple is doubled everything is doubled to maintain the proportions). Second, the architectural members have been related proportionally to one another – the radius of the dome to that of the arches, the columns on ground-floor level to those in the galleries. Third, there are the mosaics that originally sheathed the whole and consisted of a multitude of minute cubes together with the drill-carved capitals that introduce the infinitesimal – these diminutive elements combine to magnify the interior space and transfigure the material that moulds it.

In Hagia Sophia the central volume has a well-defined axis, parallel to the aisles that serve as edges and reinforce the eastward movement. This axis is created by the screens that close two of the four arches supporting the dome; they consist of tympana and columns, the latter being drawn back into the same visual plane as the walls. In this way movement is channelled to be received eventually in the embrace of the apse and then turned back on itself. At vault level this horizontal axis is also marked by the half-domes to east and west and the smaller semidomes of the niches, since these elongate the central square. In this way the architects achieved a successful combination of verticality and horizontality, i.e. there is a simultaneous operation of both vertical and horizontal axes. This is a place which, more so than any later Byzantine churches, is also a triumphal path.

All this is to consider Hagia Sophia from the nave, but one must turn to the aisles and galleries for a complete appreciation of the church. While on plan they may appear to be independent units, from the nave it is possible to obtain only glimpses of them. From this position they appear as fragments of subordinate space. Since these parts have neither completeness nor a life of their own this endorses the conclusion that Byzantine architecture is designed according to the principle of division. From the aisles and galleries the nave remains to some extent hidden behind screens of columns and it too presents itself only in fragments. Each feature indeed is to be comprehended as a subdivision of the whole.

Byzantine architecture began with its masterpiece and no one who has visited Istanbul is likely to question this verdict nor to query the legend that when Justinian first entered the completed cathedral, he cried: 'Solomon, I have triumphed over you.'

6

MOSQUES AND MADRASAS

Without question one of the most beautiful buildings in the world is the Dome of the Rock at Jerusalem (690–2). Yet despite the fact that its tile-encrusted exterior is a superb example of Islamic art, its interior, both in plan and elevation, is essentially Byzantine. Equally Byzantine in detail but very different in overall conception is the Great Mosque at Kairouan (rebuilt 836). The arched colonnades that surround the main court have been created out of a remarkable mixture of ancient shafts and capitals, some of the latter still bearing the sign of the cross. Columns of different height have been used, some standing on the pavement, others on bases and others again on pedestals. To the purist the result is disturbing – yet the general effect is most impressive as the arches march around the vast open space and lead towards the prayer hall. However unlike the disposition of the centralized Dome of the Rock, with its Christian fore-runners, that of the Great Mosque is not readily comprehensible and some knowledge is required of the worship that has determined its design.

ISLAMIC WORSHIP AND THE MOSQUE

The individual Muslim is required to observe the ritual of prayer (*salat*) five times a day. This ritual consists of recitations from the Koran accompanied by a series of movements – standing, bowing, sitting, kneeling, prostrating. While these devotions can be carried out anywhere, it is recommended for men that they perform them in a building where they can associate with others. Every Friday however the *salat* must be congregational. It will now be apparent why the special building was called a mosque, for the term derives from the Arabic *masjid* meaning 'prostration'. It will also be evident why the principal mosque in any town is designated the Friday mosque.

Since the worship is very simple, mosques require little in the way of liturgical furniture. Chairs are unnecessary because sitting is simply a squatting back on the haunches, but there are two items that are normal, namely a stand for the Koran and a pulpit or *minbar* for the Friday sermon. It is important not to be misled into assuming that the shape of the pulpit is anything like those in Christian churches. The *minbar* takes the form of a miniature flight of stairs rising away from the congregation

Cordoba, mihrab *of the Great Mosque*

whom the preacher faces down the steps. The decorative possibilities of this feature do not need stressing. Usually enclosed,
with a handrail down one side, it was provided with a canopy
from the mid eleventh century and with an elaborate entrance
portal. Although universal, the most remarkable examples are
perhaps to be seen in Turkey where the huge Ottoman interiors
require, both visually and acoustically, tall and elegant structures.

Equally important acoustically, since it enables the voice to
resonate, is the niche (*mihrab*) in the wall pointing in the direction (*qibla*) of Mecca, the birthplace of the prophet. This soon
became a focal point of mosque decoration and achieved great
magnificence, e.g. the *mihrab* of Oldjaitou Khodabendeh
(1310) in the Friday Mosque at Isfahan. In the Middle East it is
frequently circular, while in Spain and Morocco it is polygonal.
It is often accented by having a dome over or just in front of it,
which appears to have been adopted from Islamic tombs where
the hemispherical vault was regarded as a symbol of paradise.
Symbolism is also the reason for the lavish use of lights, hanging
from the ceiling and flanking the *mihrab*, for, according to the
Koran, Allah himself is the light of the heavens and of the earth.

Over every mosque floor there is spread either a multitude of
prayer rugs or a single large carpet. This most typical of nomadic
arts recalls the past when the Arabs were by no means a seden-
tary race. The covering fulfils three functions: it deadens the
noise of footsteps and so preserves an atmosphere of quiet; it
enhances the beauty of the building by its intricate patterns and
its colours; and it ensures the purity of the worshippers who not
only leave their shoes outside but also perform a ritual ablution
of face, hands and feet before entering. For this, there are
fountains, tanks, rows of taps, and so on, either in the centre of a
forecourt or otherwise close to the main door. Many a fountain
is finely decorated, and when a tank is used the expanse of water
sets off the architecture by the reflection it produces.

Observing that the Jews used horns and the Christians a
wooden clapper to summon to prayer, Mohammad ordered his
followers to mount the highest roof in the neighbourhood and
thence call the faithful to their devotions. It was to provide for
this that there eventually evolved the minaret, from which the
call-to-prayer (*adhan*) could be given by the muezzin.

The earliest minarets in Syria were square and consisted of
several storeys; this became the normal type in North Africa and
Spain. In Iraq a spiral form was popular, seen occasionally
outside the country of its origin as in the mosque of Ibn Tulun in
Cairo (876–9). Iran favoured a cylindrical form and this appears
as a tall column with an enormous capital, which is in fact the

balcony for the muezzin. In Turkey needle-like or pencil shapes with one or more balconies present graceful profiles. Soon minarets ceased to be regarded simply as objects with a function and, as with so many Islamic architectural elements, they became decorative features. Although only one is needed for the *adhan*, paired minarets flanking a façade appeared in Iran and sometimes as many as six can frame a building. Indeed to the adherents of Islam, minarets, together with domes, are signs of the worship of Allah and the presence of a mosque, just as a spire and pointed doors and windows suggest a church to many Christians.

MOSQUE TYPES

To devise a typology of mosques is by no means simple because there is a great number of variables that may be combined in many ways. Nevertheless all mosques belong to one or other of two major categories: they have either an open or a closed plan. In the first instance the mosque is a single space of which one part is covered and the other not. In the second instance the mosque comprises two distinct volumes set side by side: a prayer hall and a forecourt.

Open-plan mosques

This design was the most primitive and the original plan of the great ninth-century mosque at Cordoba is an admirable illustration (figure 45). This is a large rectangular structure of which part is roofed and part is open, thus providing a shelter from the cold and wet and an area for hot weather.

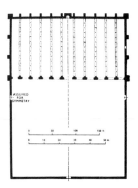

Fig. 45 Cordoba, Great Mosque

    The covered section is usually a hypostyle hall, i.e. its roof is borne on rows of columns. Any four adjacent columns create a bay, which is the module for the whole in that bay is added to bay to allow infinite growth in any direction. The spaces between the rows are so many 'aisles' and these can run either laterally or longitudinally. On the one hand then there is the mosque of Ibn Tulun where the hall is wider than it is deep with aisles extending from side to side, on the other is the one at Cordoba which is longer from end to end, with the aisles stretching from the entrance to the far wall.

    The longitudinal plan is occasionally modified by making the central aisle wider than the rest to produce a 'nave'. If this then meets a transverse aisle, also larger than the others, crossing the hall from side to side in front of the *mihrab*, there is produced an

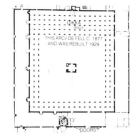

Fig. 46 Cairo, Mosque of Ibn Tulun

Cairo, mosque of Ibn Tulun

upright-T-shaped mosque which is widespread in Egypt and North Africa and for which Kairouan probably provided the model. Sometimes, as in the mosque of al-Hakim, Cairo (990–1013) the roof of this 'nave' is elevated to create a clerestory: by this means the central passageway is accentuated and the direction towards Mecca very clearly defined.

The uncovered section of the open-plan mosque, like its roofed counterpart, can be either longitudinal or lateral. Four combinations are possible and these have differing effects upon the rhythmical relationship of the two parts. Transverse court may be joined to transverse hall (Marrakesh, twelfth century); a transverse court may precede a longitudinal hall (Cordoba); a

longitudinal court may lead into a lateral hall (Ibn al-'As, Cairo, 827); finally both parts may be longitudinal (Kairouan).

The court area was elaborated by introducing colonnades along its sides. Here again differing effects are to be noted: with the longitudinal plan greater prominence is given to the open space in the middle than to the porticoes that frame it, whereas by the lateral disposition attention is directed to the colonnades and there is a tendency to multiply them, for example at Kairouan there are two aisles, at Marrakesh, four. In Iran, as well as northwards around Samarkand and in Afghanistan, the rhythm of these colonnades was refined and accents were provided by inserting open porches (*iwans*) with vaulted ceilings at points corresponding to the main axes. The result was the creation of two sub-types: the axial and the cross-axial *iwan* mosques. The former is constituted by one or two porches – one if there is a single *iwan* either for the entrance or for the prayer hall opposite it and two if each possesses one. The cross-axial *iwan* type has four porches, one in the centre of each side – both the Friday Mosque (eighth century onwards) and the Royal Mosque (seventeenth century) at Isfahan are superb examples, together with the Mosque Kalan (fifteenth century) at Bukhara (see

Isfahan, Friday Mosque, south-east iwan

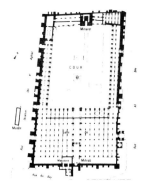

Fig. 47   Kairouan, Great Mosque

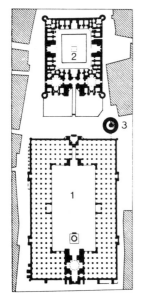

Fig. 48 Bukhara, Poy-Kalan complex

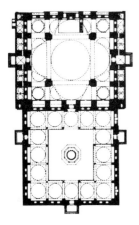

Fig. 49 Istanbul, Şehzade complex

figure 48(1)). The contribution of these *iwans* to the enjoyment of the buildings is an important one: although much larger, the profiles of their arches are the same as those of the colonnades and in this way a sense of proportion is introduced and the courts are unified.

Closed-plan mosques

The second principal mosque type emerged when the building ceased to be regarded as a single entity, part roofed, part unroofed, and instead was designed in two halves, each with a character of its own. The prayer hall was given a composed façade with its own monumental porch. The open-air section then became a kind of atrium, with colonnades on all four sides. There is a progression into the forecourt through a fine *iwan* and then, opposite this, through a second impressive portal, often echoing the outer one, into the prayer hall itself. There is consequently something of a contrast between a mosque of the open-plan type, such as Kairouan with its fairly austere containing wall, and one of the closed-plan such as the Blue Mosque at Istanbul (early seventeenth century) with its interlocked shapes.

The structural and spatial system of the closed-plan prayer hall can consist of one or more units, each of which is a square defined by walls or by piers at the four corners and it is usually covered by a dome. So a single-unit mosque is a domed square with porch and minaret. It has few, if any, internal supports, with the dome initially resting on the walls. The character of the latter was changed when the baldachin principle was adopted and the load concentrated on the four corners; walls ceased to be structural elements and became space-definers.

When several of these units are combined the plan necessarily is more involved and perhaps the most striking is the inverted-T which seems to have been devised at Bursa in Turkey. Sinan, the greatest of all Islamic architects, adopted this design in 1583 for the Atik Valide Camii at Üsküdar. This is a domed square plus three semi-domed units, one at each side of the square to form the cross-bar of the T and the third, jutting towards Mecca, constituting its upright.

Sinan's first major work in Istanbul had been the Şehzade complex (1548) which reveals the influence of Hagia Sophia. It is a baldachin with its central core extended by four semi-domes. There is consequently an identical symmetry along both main axes and this has a repetitive effect that fosters a sense of peace. In the Süleymaniye (1550–7) the plan is even closer to that of the cathedral, but with essential differences: the space is

Istanbul, Blue Mosque, interior

not divided up but is centralized and continuous and the general effect is one of simple grandeur.

THE SPACE-POSITIVE CHARACTER OF MOSQUE ARCHITECTURE

Islamic architecture, as will be apparent by now, is neither mass- nor surface-positive; rather it is to be regarded as space-positive. However this does not mean that space is handled in the open-plan and in the closed-plan in identical ways – there are differences.

First, space in the open-plan flows from the uncovered to the covered portion and back again, whereas in the closed-plan the forecourt and prayer hall are distinct. At Kairouan, for instance, emphasis is upon the central area and not on the colonnades which simply provide a rhythmical accompaniment along the length of the court to the covered area. In the forecourt of the Süleymaniye, in contrast, one is invited to linger. Its porticoes are constructed from columns of the richest porphyry, marble and granite, extending uniformly around all four sides to embrace the visitor. At each corner rises a great minaret, designating the area as a place.

Second, there is a difference to be noted in the handling of space within the prayer halls. In the open-plan, with its aisles and bays extending on all sides, it is the limitlessness of space that is emphasized; with the closed-plan the unity of space is to the fore. This infinity and oneness are in fact the architectural embodiments of an understanding of the divine nature. Islamic architecture is the projection into the visual order of these two essential aspects of Allah himself; the building expresses *tawhid*, which is the metaphysical doctrine of the Divine Unity as the source and culmination of all diversity.

To enter a hypostyle hall, such as el-Aksa (715) in Jerusalem or the mosque of 'Amr (827) in Cairo, is to enjoy an experience of spaciousness. The major impression given is one of breadth, of outwards and sideways spread, and of depth too, so that space extends in all directions. Indeed it is time to recognize that a mosque is multidirectional. On the one hand the members of the congregation face towards Mecca and this suggests a longitudinal movement, but on the other hand they arrange themselves side by side and this involves lateral extension. This multidirectionality is to be understood as another means of witnessing to the divine infinity which is also stressed when there is a profusion of pillars and arches, such as may be enjoyed at Cordoba. In the closed-plan, particularly as exemplified by the Ottoman mosques, there is the same concern for the infinite but this is revealed no longer by multiplicity but by the sheer size of each edifice. However what is even more striking than this immensity is the way these huge volumes have been unified, and this may be illustrated from the Süleymaniye.

Although the plan of the Süleymaniye (see figure 50), as previously noted, is indebted to that of Hagia Sophia, with central dome supported by semi-domes, there are significant differences. In the cathedral the aisles are divided from the nave by columns; in the mosque this separation has been suppressed. Not only have columns been reduced to a minimum throughout but the central volume has been integrated with those on either side by means of alternating large and small domed units – there is no rigid line between them and the interior is open and visible

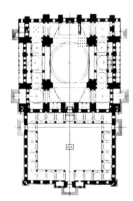

Fig. 50 Istanbul, Süleymaniye

from all parts. The galleries too, which in Hagia Sophia are as wide as the aisles, are here reduced to narrow balconies. This opening up is carried even further in the Şehzade (see figure 49) by adding two semi-domes to the north and south so that the central dome is borne by four of them. The relative proportions of these domes also have a bearing on the character of the spaces that they enclose. In Hagia Sophia each semi-dome is exactly half the central one, but in both the Şehzade and the Süleymaniye the base of each semi-dome is less than half a circle. The effect in Hagia Sophia is longitudinal as befits a building with a strong directional pull towards an altar set within an apse. In the mosque however the different proportions and the suppression of the eastern apse serve to centralize the space, to unify it and so to affirm the oneness of the Creator. The interior is then one unit to be perceived in its entirety at a single view. Its reality is not to be found in the domes and arcades but in the cavities they define. Plenitude of space . . . majestic space . . . continuous space . . . *tawhid* (the consciousness of divine unity) made visible.

Cairo, mosque of 'Amr, interior

THE MADRASA

Side by side with the mosque and indeed influencing its plan was
the Koranic school or *madrasa*. This category of sacred building
was introduced by the Seljuk Turks in the late eleventh century
to train theologians as defenders of orthodoxy. Modelled after
the houses of Khurasan which have four arched openings off a
central court, these colleges assumed a cruciform plan. This
design spread into Egypt and was found convenient because
each *iwan* could serve as a lecture hall for the students of one of
the four legal schools: Hanafite, Hanbalite, Malikite and
Shafeyite. It was this arrangement that affected the open-plan
mosque in Iran and elsewhere, resulting in the cross-axial *iwan*
mosque. So the two building types and their functions tended to
merge. Examples include the Madrasa Mir-i Arab at Bukhara,
1535 (see figure 48(2)) and the earlier mosque-madrasa of
Sultan Hasan in Cairo (1356–9). The latter has the four lecture
rooms, but the one that points towards Mecca (and is on the
same axis as the founder's domed tomb) is the largest with both
a *mihrab* and a *minbar* furnishing it for public worship.

To accommodate students, cells were required and these were
inserted between the *iwans* in one or two storeys. This means
that the typical madrasa is a court with four inward-looking
façades; each façade has its central porch flanked on either side
by the smaller arches of the cells, the latter providing rhythm
and the former constituting an accent.

Space is handled in the manner characteristic of the open-
plan, i.e. there is a gentle flow between the unroofed section and
the barrel-vaulted *iwans* which become integral parts of the
central space. In the cross-axial *iwan* mosque a prayer hall, in
the form of a domed square, was often introduced behind the
porch, as in the Royal Mosque at Isfahan. This unit, having a
completeness of its own, preserves some independence and
there is no strong movement between it and the *iwan*. Indeed the
eye is caught by the arches between them and a kind of optical
screen comes into operation and suggests a division, leaving the
porch as an extension of the open area while the dome pulls the
space beneath it towards its own centre.

ORNAMENT

However important for the enjoyment of Islamic architecture is
an understanding of the way space is handled, it is the decorative
quality of the buildings, especially those of the *iwan* design, that

is most immediately striking. This attraction is not misleading, in the sense that it diverts attention away from what is primary, such as space. On the contrary, the ornament is of the very essence of the architecture; it is not something applied to the buildings, it is integral to them. However the contribution it makes can only be fully assessed in the light of a knowledge of the materials employed and of the elements from which the designs are created.

Of the various ingredients at the architects' disposal there are seven that are especially favoured, namely terra-cotta, stucco, brick, stone, colour, water and light. The first two in this list are really techniques, while the second two are materials, with colour as a property of all four; the remaining pair are of course natural elements. Each of these has to be considered in turn to discover how it is used and to what effect.

Terra-cotta

Terra-cotta or baked earth denotes both the material and the technique whereby pottery is made. As an ingredient of Islamic architecture it refers to ceramic tiles, of which there are three principal types. First, there are those in single colours, with a cross or star or foliage pattern spreading over any two. Second, there is mosaic faience, i.e. tiles cut into small shapes and fitted into complex designs. Third, there are those known as 'seven colours', the seven being applied to a single tile with each colour outlined in manganese to prevent mingling. Ottoman tiles, which in many respects set the fashion throughout the Muslim world, were combinations of blues, purples and olive greens, and the famous Iznik factory produced its own special hue that was a red between tomato and flame.

Much of the appeal of these tiles lies in the fluctuating lines of their designs and in their brilliant colours. They are employed to articulate façades, breaking up flat walls; they frame doorways and windows and enhance the splendour of the *mihrab* area and of the domes inside and out. The effect of this decoration is to call attention to the surface of a building and then to dissolve it. The ceramics disguise the substance from which the building has been made – although they seldom obscure the forms. To call attention in this way to the surface is to de-emphasize the mass behind it: a façade ceases to be a wall and becomes a two-dimensional entity. By concealing or leaving unexpressed the real supports, any feeling of weight is counteracted and each building seems to float in the air like a summer cloud. Walls vanish into glowing colour; vaults and arches are overlaid;

domes are filled with radiant designs that banish the solidity of stone or masonry and give them an ephemeral quality as if the crystallization of the pattern is the only reality. This is not surface-positive architecture because the surface itself strains towards the immaterial.

Stucco

Stucco is plasterwork; it is applied wet to a wall and is carved while still moist, with small new portions added as necessary. The resulting patterns do not have rounded or carefully graded planes; they look more like stencilled designs with a sharp contrast between the black shadows created by the incisions and the light-reflecting uppermost surface. They are two-dimensional reliefs or patterns in two planes, invariably shallow, flat and spread out. They add to but never obscure the primary forms of cylinder, cuboid, cone and dome because they are integral parts of their surfaces, their shapes neither resting upon a background nor against one. As with terra-cotta, so stucco dematerializes structure, and then in turn itself dissolves. This latter effect is achieved because, being small in proportion to the object it decorates, it is delicate and intricate and transforms a wall into a lacelike filigree as insubstantial as gossamer.

Brick and stone

It might be supposed that such substances as brick and stone cannot but inhibit the quest for dematerialization. Not only are they undeniably solid but they can be regarded as structural by their very nature. However Islamic architects have been sufficiently masters of their art to turn structure into decoration.

Unlike stone, brick does not create a feeling of weight, permanence or hardness; it makes for softer contours and it can be moulded. It was soon appreciated that decorative designs can be created by the very manner in which bricks are laid. They can be upright, diagonal or flat, sideways or end-on. The spaces between them can be of different widths and different depths thus providing a varying density of shadow. Repeat patterns, different border motifs, crosses, chevrons, grilles – all these are possible. In this way designs of disciplined mobility were devised, two outstanding examples being both preserved at Bukhara: the mausoleum of Ismael Samanid (tenth century) where the medium of construction has become its decoration, as is the case also with the Minaret Kalan (1127–9) (see figure 48(3)).

In certain areas where marble could be quarried, it was used as a veneer. This again emphasizes surface quality and the quest

Bukhara, mausoleum of Ismael Samanid

for dematerialization. The beauty of such a material resides chiefly in its graining which is frequently exposed and arranged in patterns, as in the interior of the Dome of the Rock. Sometimes stones are perforated to form a grille – another surface element lacking mass. Often pierced screens are placed in façades next to blind arches that are identical in shape and decoration, so that the distinction between solid substances and light openings is constantly denied.

Colour

Even those who have not visited Istanbul will have heard of the Blue Mosque, although this is not the official designation of the Sultan Ahmet Camii (1609–16). Yet this popular name underlines the importance of colour in Islamic architecture and derives from the predominance of Iznik tiles in subtle blues and greens which clothe the lower parts of the walls and the galleries.

Colour is of course a property of each of the previous four ingredients. Stucco is usually white but can be tinted; bricks come in all hues; marble and other stones have their own tones; tiles are varied in their colour range. Colour is used to add vitality to a building. It can also define form, keeping it simple and at the same time enriching it. In this respect the Islamic use of colour differs from that in western Europe where it is applied to form; in Islamic architecture it is integral with it. Many a dome, such as that of the Gur Emir, Samarkand, has its profile made more precise and comprehensible, precisely because of the ceramics that are part of it. Indeed so important is colour that the suggestion has been made that it has become structural. By this is meant, for example, that the tiles on a façade are not applied decoration, they *are* the façade. Colour is then treated as an architectural material that dictates the arrangement and composition of the whole. However this is based upon a mis-understanding of the extent to which the architecture denies structure and does not seek to replace it – colour is not structure reappearing in a different form; it is above all one more means of achieving dematerialization. To walk either around the perimeter of the shrine of Gawhar Shad at Mashhad (1419) or through the Royal Square at Isfahan to the portal of the Royal Mosque (1612–37) is to become aware that glowing hues can be expres-sive of the being of God.

Water

The importance of water for ablutions has already been men-tioned and many a mosque courtyard, such as those of the Royal Mosques at both Tehran and Isfahan, contains a large tank that reflects and, in so doing, acts as a complement to and unifies the arcades and *iwans* that surround it. Water channels can and do mark axes and constitute frames – they are seen brilliantly employed in the funeral garden of the Taj Mahal. Every Islamic garden is a carefully designed interior space; it is a living carpet. At Agra however there is a fourfold plot or *chahar bagh*, i.e. one that is divided into quadrants by water channels to symbolize the four rivers of Paradise. When the water is still, the reflection fosters peace and calm; when a slight breeze ruffles the surface then the architecture seems to be set in motion and to be dissolving before one's eyes.

Light

Since Allah is light, special attention is paid to this final ingredient by Islamic architects. Shiny floors catch and throw it up to the ceilings where it is sometimes trapped, sometimes refracted. Structures become chequered designs of light and shade. Tiles are placed at the base of walls to vibrate with light and dispel their heaviness. Other surfaces become perforated reliefs to filter light. Lamps have surface patterns corresponding to those on surrounding walls so that one design is cast upon another. Candelabra make interiors brilliant. In the great Ottoman mosques huge windows convert the walls into airy screens that allow the sun to stream in and dissolve the massive columns that support the domes and contribute to total dematerialization.

PATTERN ELEMENTS

Three of the six ingredients just reviewed involve patterns, namely terra-cotta, stucco and brick, and stone should probably be added because of its texture. To create patterns on or with these, four main elements were drawn upon: animal, vegetable and geometrical forms, together with writing.

Although the Koran does not condemn the representation of living beings, it was generally frowned upon and few examples are to be found in religious buildings. Notable among those that exist are the tigers on the façade of the Shir Dor at Samarkand. Much more popular were designs derived from natural vegetation such as flowers and leaves – these give a certain nervous life to the ornament. Vines, acanthus, palms, sometimes pomegranates and pine cones, all unfold in a continuous rhythm like a wave, with a tendency to become stylized. The most typical device is the arabesque which is a continuous line or stem that splits repeatedly to produce secondary stems which either split again or return to be reintegrated into the main one.

Islamic artists engage in all the usual pattern-making operations. They define the field by means of framing. Filling within the borders is effected by linking and this takes the form of branching, radiating and interlacing. The resulting decoration is not flat because, like a river that goes below ground only to reappear again, the lines pass under and over each other, their shapes on the surface being explicable only in terms of a hidden activity at a lower level. Nor is the pattern immobile; rather it is a visual transcription of rhythm. The wavy lines are indeed infinitely adaptable to any area that they are expected to fill: they can contract and extend: they can stretch along borders or

Fig. 51   Panel from the forecourt of the Şehzade complex, Istanbul

bridge gaps. The continuity of the interlacement too invites the eye to follow so that vision is transformed into a rhythmic experience.

All the patterns are based on mathematical calculations and are built up from one or more figures contained in a circle, using especially pentagons, hexagons and octagons. But they are not to be read in terms of solids and voids, or of the design and its ground. In arabesque the filled space and the empty areas demand equal attention; they balance one another and cannot be separated. In this way the very design is yet another embodiment of *tawhid*, that behind everything is the divine unity. At the same time the endless variety, which excludes monotony, is a further testimony to the boundlessness of God. Nor does the use of framing contradict this understanding because the Islamic border is not intended to delimit but to act as a window into the limitless. This conclusion means that the overall pattern is not the result of a *horror vacui*, of a dislike of the void, so that everything has to be covered up; on the contrary it is evidence of an *amor infiniti* or love of infinity.

Calligraphy

The fourth pattern element has been reserved for special mention because, consisting as it does of lettering, it differs from the other three. Muslims understand writing as the means of giving visible form to the revealed Word of God contained in the Koran. To develop and use a fine script (*kalle*, beautiful; *graphe*, writing) is therefore a religious duty. It is indeed a most appropriate type of decoration for a mosque where the Koran is read and expounded and for a madrasa where it is studied. To cover a façade with lettering combined with geometric and floral motifs is to stress its two-dimensionality and to dissolve its surface into ideas that are regarded as more real than its substance of brick and even faience. Decoration and lettering are totally integrated and at times it is not immediately evident whether one is contemplating a pattern or words – in fact it is best described as patterned words. This is achieved partly by the way the inscriptions are related to a façade – being used as frames along and around different sections – and partly from the proportions and forms of the alphabet selected.

STRUCTURAL ELEMENTS

To consider structure after decoration is to reverse the normal order. Without arches or columns there would be no building at all and so ornament is usually regarded as secondary. Not so with Islamic buildings where structure in effect has become an additional pattern element. Supports and loads are transformed into decoration.

Arches

Since Islamic architecture is arcuated, it is to the arch that attention must first be paid and especially to the profusion of graceful shapes that have been created. Although at first, following Rome and Byzantium, arches were semicircular, interest in varied effects soon led to other profiles of which the most favoured was the pointed arch, often keel-shaped. In North Africa it was the horseshoe, also frequently pointed, that was widely adopted. Other variations produced multifoil or cusped inside edges, as in front of the *mihrab* at Cordoba: what is structural has been resolved into an ornamental element.

Many Islamic arches are enclosed in a rectangular border which, with its static quality and stress on stability, acts as a counterbalance to the radiating energy of the arch itself. In other words, Islamic arches might suggest a movement from the centre outwards, thus denying fixity, but movement is countered by this frame and the result is a vibrant equilibrium or a tension in repose.

The Islamic arch is not only decorative in itself, with stress upon the delicate beauty of its lines, it can also be multiplied on different scales to create an overall pattern. The Taj Mahal exemplifies this to perfection (figure 52). The primary unit is a keel arch within a rectangle and as such it is used for the main

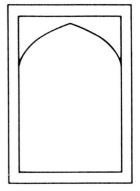

Fig. 52 Arch motif, Agra, Taj Mahal

entrance portal. However on either side of this it is repeated, somewhat smaller, as flanking niches, and, smaller still, inside the portals and niches as windows and doors. The platform on which the mausoleum stands, the walls and the drum of the principal dome all have the same motif as a flat design, while the dome's profile reproduces and brings to a climax the now familiar outline. The result is a unified whole with the arch not simply part of the construction but a pattern element as well.

Domes and their supports

When an arch is turned through 360 degrees and translated into three dimensions it becomes a dome which is a frequent structural element within arcuated systems. Because it symbolizes heaven, it was used for memorial buildings, such as the Dome of the Rock, and for tombs and thence passed into mosque design. It can be treated in a variety of ways: sometimes plain, sometimes fluted; coated with faience or pierced with geometrical shapes; often covered with a web of lacelike stucco. In India it assumes a lotus or bulbous shape and is placed on a drum; in Iran double domes are common, necessitated because the outer one tends to grow larger and loftier and out of scale with the chamber beneath it and so a second dome is inserted below. In Turkey great hemispheres dictate the size of the ground area and centralize the space. In Egypt the domes are low, while in Syria they are placed on top of octagonal drums.

From inside a mosque, the Islamic dome does not hover in the air like that of Hagia Sophia nor does it weigh down upon its supports like a Roman one; there is no suggestion of effort or tension; it is stable and secure as befits a haven of peace planned for contemplation. Abstract patterns cover the surface and some cupolas are ribbed. These ribs too are decorative not structural; they cross and recross, increasing the apparent height of the vault and giving it life and energy. They do not come together at the crown but leave the very centre free. The shape thus unfolds from the top downwards, its splendid unity being gradually differentiated by means of the panels framed by the ribs – in this way the Unity that exists everywhere and at all times is acknowledged.

As with Byzantine buildings, it is the contrast between the form of the dome and the enclosed, square space below that gives it its grandeur. Interest centres in the way the two halves of the structure are joined to create a satisfying synthesis of forms. Three methods are employed to achieve this, two being Byzantine techniques and the third an Anatolian innovation. This last device is known as Turkish triangles and it takes two forms;

either it consists of triangular panels whose apexes meet at a single point in each of the four corners, their bases supporting the bottom rim of the dome, or it is made up of a belt of triangles fitted together with their apexes alternatively upwards and downwards to form a continuous band. The squinch and the pendentive are the two Byzantine methods used, the one being a small arch thrown across a corner and the other a downward-curving spherical triangle that carries the weight at each corner to the ground – the baldachin principle.

These different ways of supporting the dome affect the overall shape and character of a building. Where the belt of triangles is employed, a mosque or madrasa retains its square character up to that level and so the lower part of the structure is a cube on to which the belt fits; in this way the walls are revealed as load-bearing elements, although this is often denied by covering them with patterns derived from textiles and suggestive of carpets. When squinches are employed the tendency is to turn the super-structure into an octagon so that the complete form consists of a cube supporting an eight-sided shape that in turn bears a hemis-phere – again the walls are structural. With pendentives the load is transmitted to the corners and so the walls lose their architectonic quality and become simply screens. Then, as clearly shown by Sinan's Mosque of Mihrimah (1555) at Istan-bul, the dome sits on four arches, not on the walls, with the pendentives between the arches. What is more the pendentives themselves have ceased to be solely structural elements and have become part of the visual appeal both within and without.

Stalactites

Following the more or less iron Islamic law that structure is to be transmuted into decoration, squinches too underwent a pro-found change. Initially single arches across each corner, they were next multiplied and organized in superimposed tiers. It is probable that it was their further combination in an interlacing geometric pattern that led to the creation of the stalactite or *mukarnas* vault. Such a vault is made up of rows of out-curving panels, on top of one another, generally shaped as miniature quarter-domes, with their apexes apparently hanging over empty space. They constitute a cluster of niches resembling the cells of a honeycomb, mounting up upon one another, being joined by prominent edges. *Mukarnas* can effect a transition from the angular to the circular, softening and enriching the broad masses and simple contours of a building. They have a static and a rhythmical character and so break and reflect light in fascinat-ing patterns. Decorative collars around minarets are formed from them, as are also the welcoming vaults of entrance portals. By this technique ceilings are dematerialized and the architecture acquires an ethereal character. Indeed, when the *mukarnas* are lined with mirrors, their structural function appears to vanish entirely.

*Isfahan, Shaykh
Lutfallah Mosque,
mukarnas*

Capitals

So ubiquitous was the *mukarnas* vault that it soon appeared in the form of stalactite capitals and indeed this was an original Islamic creation. Initially capitals were quarried from Roman and Byzantine remains with some preference, evident at Kairouan, for the Corinthian. When the artists came to produce their own, there was a tendency to stylize the Corinthian so that the double row of acanthus leaves was reduced to one V above another. In general the prohibition of graven images entirely discouraged sculpture in the round and the glory of Islamic architecture is but little reflected in its capitals. When they were part of a design – and often arches were supported on rectangular piers with little need for an elaborate terminal element – a simple bulbous form or a bell-shape with surface geometric patterning or even just a block was all that was regarded as necessary.

FAÇADES AND THE USE OF FORMS

Although there is undoubtedly such a thing as an Islamic style that enables immediate recognition of those buildings that embody it, yet there are sufficient contrasts between different types to make delight somewhat complex. It has already been noted how a hypostyle hall gives primary expression to the divine limitlessness while the domed square speaks of the divine unity. Space in the former is multidirectional while in the latter it is centralized. A volume composed of bays can be extended at will to express infinity, while in the Ottoman mosques witness to infinity takes the form of vastness and dematerialization. Enjoyment must then vary depending upon the category of building visited.

It is now necessary to draw attention to a further contrast, namely between buildings that belong to façade architecture and those that are to be appreciated in terms of forms. To the façade class obviously belong all those of the *iwan* type, whether mosque or madrasa. These buildings indeed consist of so many façades facing inwards around a central court. Islamic architects have no interest in the rear sides of their façades; only the fronts are encrusted with ceramics whose purpose, as we have seen, is to dematerialize them. The backs are left plain and might even be called shoddy. Stand on the terrace of the Ali Kapu palace at Isfahan and look towards the Royal Mosque and this contrast will be very evident. Indeed these mosques are two-dimensional and have really only one exterior view; any other angle would make visible the bare cement or masonry behind each *iwan*.

In the work of Sinan – to turn directly to the master of the centralized mosque – all the exterior façades have been developed and all perspectives taken into account. He permits the interior design to be revealed in exterior form and so three-dimensionality is evident and a play with form is revealed. Sinan indeed combined four simple and primary shapes: cube, hemisphere, cone and pyramid. He started from a circle within a square which when treated spatially became a dome upon a cube; the half-globe itself is really contained within an invisible cone, while the entire building fits within a pyramid. However it

*Istanbul, Blue Mosque,
exterior*

is perhaps the Blue Mosque that displays the most superb exterior of all. From the gilded crescent at the summit of the
central cupola, a pyramidal mass of semidomes and subsidiary
smaller domes cascades symmetrically down towards the four
lofty minarets at the corners of the prayer hall. If the gaze is
reversed to travel upwards, then the exterior mushrooms with a
total of 15 major and minor half-domes to produce a coordi-
nated hierarchy. Delight here derives from the perception of the
flow of the forms, their rhythm, their interrelationship, their
articulation and their unity. It rests too upon a recognition of
how the buttresses have been assimilated into the design, how
the arches are used to break up any monotony and how the
windows are no longer just a means of introducing light but
constitute a decorative adjunct that offsets any hint that the
mosque is ponderous.

Careful attention to proportion also enhances total effects.
To give one example: the Süleymaniye is placed in the centre of a
rectangle of which the sides are in the proportion of 2:3, while

the relationships of the distances between the main gate of the enclosure and that of the forecourt, forecourt to mosque and mosque to graveyard beyond are 4:5:5:7. In effect all the vital proportions of a building are derived from a harmonious division of a circle and this too expresses *tawhid*.

THE PRINCIPLE OF COMPOSITION AND THE MOSQUE AS A PLACE

To identify the principle of composition as addition is relatively simple. Just as an overall decorative pattern is built up by a systematic arrangement of repeat units, so a whole building involves the adding of bay to bay or aisle to aisle in a hypostyle hall and domes on top of cubes in a centralized building. When it does not matter whether there should be one, two, three or four *iwans*, or two, four or even six minarets – then the design has obviously been based upon readily identifiable units added together by both juxtaposition and superimposition. Each unit is clearly differentiated and possesses some independence. Nor does the impression of absolute unity conveyed by the designs of Sinan affect this conclusion; this simply testifies to his brilliance and to the way he has made the units cohere.

A Sinan interior also exemplifies the extent to which a mosque is a place. It is a point of reference and gathering; it is concentrated. Once within, there is no incentive to re-emerge and every enticement to stay. Embodying perfect equipoise, it promotes contemplation, as you study the intricate patterns and delight in the enfolding forms. It is indeed embracing architecture. Even a hypostyle hall, although not restricted in size and so seemingly without limit, invites one to linger and enjoy its

Lahore, Badshahi Mosque

spaciousness – though here, with the open plan, there is some flow out into the uncovered portion of the building. However with the Mogul adaptation of the open-plan to produce the Indian courtyard mosque there is a greater degree of centralization.

The Badshahi Mosque at Lahore may be taken as a typical example of this particular open-plan form. Built by the Master of Ordnance of Aurangzebe in 1678, it is essentially a two-*iwan* design, one leading into the prayer hall and the other transformed into a great monumental gateway at the top of an imposing flight of steps. The very extensive courtyard is surrounded by one-storey arcades, thus providing firm edges, and there is a tall minaret at each of the four corners visually framing the entire complex. The sanctuary pushes forward from the western perimeter and consists of a large *iwan* flanked by porticoes of five arches each. This leads into a domed square, the dome itself being of the lotus type with a most graceful exterior

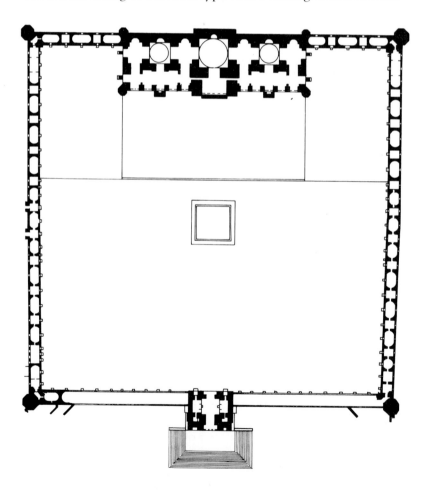

Fig. 53 Lahore, Badshahi Mosque

profile. It is set off in two ways: first, it is on a drum and, second, it is placed some distance back from the entrance so that it is not masked; smaller domes accompany it on either side. Although the eye is immediately drawn towards this *iwan*, with its foliate arches and its stripes of white marble and red sandstone, the great uninterrupted expanse in front of it tells against any forward impulsion. The whole is indeed one great place within which to walk gently at will.

This chapter began with the Dome of the Rock which can also supply a fitting climax if it too is analysed in terms of place. The Dome honours the rock whence the prophet ascended. The glittering mosaics and beautifully carved capitals, together with the grained marble, dance around it. The cupola serves it as a crown and also brings attention back downwards to the rock itself. Here the centralized plan completely fulfils itself as the ideal setting or place for an object in the midst.

7

ROMANESQUE ARCHITECTURE

Having followed the fortunes of the mosque up to the achieve-ments of the Ottomans in Turkey and the Moguls in India, it is now necessary to go backwards some hundreds of years to discover what had been happening to religious buildings in the West. There a new style had been developed which is usually called Romanesque, although in England it can be termed Norman. The period from which we can date its beginning is disputed, but the view is taken here that it is only after the year 1000 that something essentially new emerged. Admittedly fea-tures of Romanesque had been anticipated as early as the reign of Charlemagne, but it was not until the eleventh and twelfth centuries that fundamental changes in church buildings were achieved.

FACTORS PROMOTING CHANGE IN CHURCH DESIGN

Since a church is a devotional and liturgical centre, any changes in spiritual exercises or in the forms of worship are bound to have architectural effects. From the fifth century veneration of the saints had become intensely popular and this had two results: attention had to be given to the location and means of housing their relics and provision had to be made for the large crowds who came in pilgrimages to honour them. From the latter stemmed greatly increased circulation space and from the former the creation of crypts and the multiplication of altars to enshrine the sacred treasures. The proliferation of altars was also encouraged by the expanding ranks of the clergy, each one being required to celebrate mass daily, as well as by the practice of votive masses and the building of chantry chapels. It was the combination of these factors that led to the elaboration of the plan of the Early Christian basilica by the addition of ambulatories, galleries, transepts, crypts, side chapels, chevets and choirs. Pilgrimages required the first two and contributed to the development of the third; the remainder, except the last, were the architectural response to the veneration of relics and to the greater number of masses, while choirs constituted centres for monks and/or clergy and shielded them from the profane laity.

THE CIRCULATION SYSTEM

An ambulatory is an area in which to amble or walk (Latin *ambulare*) and in Romanesque churches it takes the form of a continuation of the aisles around the eastern apse. It is never a simple corridor but an important part of the processional way whose unimpeded movement helps to integrate the building as a whole. It is also an extension of the main sanctuary and shares in its majesty by means of the arches pierced into it through the apse wall. On its outside edge it gives access to radiating chapels that house additional altars. This arrangement of the east end is known by the French term *chevet*, which derives from the Latin for a head.

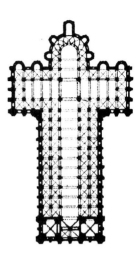

Fig. 54 Toulouse, St-Sernin

With a chevet the importance of the high altar, which had previously stood alone and thereby acquired positional enhancement, is not lost however because the subsidiary altars are so located that competition is avoided. But the radiating plan does result in inaccurate orientation because, while the principal apse points to the east, its adjuncts cannot do so. To overcome this disadvantage, staggered apses may be employed, i.e. arranged in steps (*en échelon*) and consequently parallel. Three is not infrequent, for example as in Cefalù cathedral, but as many as five can be added, graded outward from the main sanctuary.

Yet more chapels are projected eastward from transepts in large monastic churches and cathedrals. Like the ambulatory, these Romanesque transepts are elements in the circulation system, either as a swelling of the nave or, if separated from it like wings, as links between the north and south aisles and the chevet. This latter function is particularly noticeable in those churches, such as the cathedral of Santiago de Compostela, where the aisles actually continue around three sides of the transepts. Transepts then do not interrupt but contribute to the circulation system; in addition they can provide auxiliary entrances and exits.

At a higher level circulation is along the galleries which also

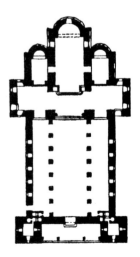

Fig. 55 Cefalù, cathedral

Conques, St-Foi,
ambulatory

permit the access of light and contribute to the equilibrium of
the building in the pilgrimage centres; they form an upper
church, often making a complete circuit of the building. From
there visitors appreciate the message conveyed by the otherwise
not very visible sculpted capitals; from there too there is a
magnificent view of any spectacle taking place on the floor of
the nave. Indeed a medieval guidebook to Compostela remarks
that whoever ascends to the gallery in a sad condition will
become joyful as he contemplates the beauty of the church.

Below ground the crypt housed the all-important relics that
drew the crowds. This is a vaulted, pillared chamber and is the
product of a long transformation of the tombs of the early
martyrs. Each one possesses the essential characteristics of a

place, designed with considerable care. Indeed the Romanesque period is the golden age of the crypt which was to disappear in the thirteenth century when the saint's remains were exposed to view in reliquaries either behind or above an altar in the body of the church. Often subterranean, they are sometimes not completely below ground level and then they are surmounted by a high choir, i.e. the sanctuary area is lifted up and steps ascend to it. Such stairways are either single and central or double with one on either side. Examples include S. Zeno in Verona and S. Miniato al Monte in Florence, but while the raised choir is often regarded as a Lombardic peculiarity, examples are found elsewhere, for example, Worcester Cathedral which has a Gothic choir on top of its Romanesque crypt.

The medieval choir is without question an elaboration of the sanctuary area of the Early Christian basilica. Originally this space consisted of the half-circle defined by the apse plus a further section demarcated by balustrades or *cancelli*. The latter component was much increased in size to accommodate the great numbers of clergy and/or monks so that to the half-circle was added a long rectangle that could stretch a third of the way down a church or cathedral.

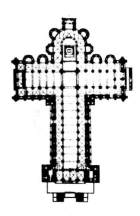

Fig. 56 Santiago de Compostela, cathedral

ELEVATION – ROMANESQUE VAULTING

So far the elaboration of the basilica has been presented in terms exclusively of plan, whether under the ground, at ground level or in the form of the gallery. However appreciation of the character of any style depends not only on two-dimensional plans but especially on the elevation, which brings in the third dimension. In relation to Romanesque churches, this requires a knowledge of the vaulting employed and of the treatment of the walls of the nave that supported it.

The basilica, it will be recalled, usually has a wooden roof which is a kind of lid. In Romanesque buildings vaulting began to be employed – a technique known to the Romans, although they used concrete whereas in the eleventh and twelfth centuries brick and stone were the materials employed. At first introduced into the crypt, which has to have a very strong top if it is to support the sanctuary above, vaults appear next in the aisles, in annular galleries and finally take over the nave.

The simplest form is the barrel vault which is an arch so thickened that it produces a continuous covering of semicircular section. Its alternative designation – tunnel vault – more vividly represents its effect. A nave with such a roof is therefore a rectangular cuboid with half a cylinder on top. This type provides an uninterrupted covering for a processional way towards the east, more fluid in its movement and more integrated with the substructure than the wooden ceiling of the basilica. Where there is a tunnel vault over the side aisles as well as the nave, there is a certain homogeneity of the interior volume. This arrangement appeals to the eye since it leads the gaze smoothly towards the visual climax ahead. Nevertheless it has some aesthetic drawbacks. It tends to be inert and inanimate, suggesting no differentiation between activity (upward thrust) and passivity (weight). It can appear heavy and also seem monotonous, although this may be relieved by frescoes, as in St-Savin-sur-Gartempe, near Poitiers, *c.* 1080. Further it lacks features to tie it directly to the structure below. It was factors such as these that led to the banded barrel vault, the groin vault and finally the rib vault.

The first of these is still a semicylindrical vault but now it is divided at intervals by transverse arches. What had previously been a continuous ceiling was now compartmentalized and given more scale, being brought into an appearance of closer size relationship with the subdivided lower parts of the interior –

Tournus, St-Philibert, nave vaulting

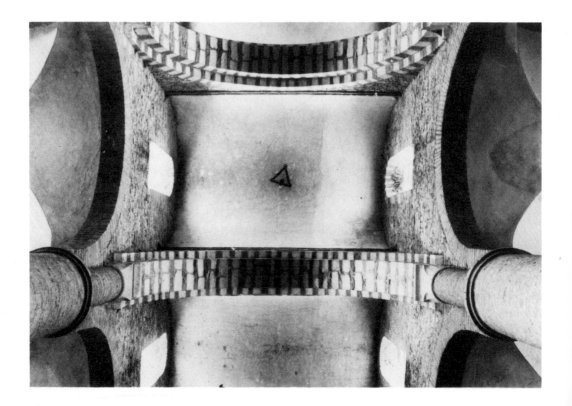

a fine example of this is St-Sernin at Toulouse, consecrated in 1096, one of the pilgrimage churches on the route to Compostela. Continuity is of course preserved, but now the forward movement is less precipitous and can be even slower when, as in St-Philibert, Tournus, of the eleventh and twelfth centuries, its vaults were themselves transverse so that instead of a single long tunnel, sectionalized by arches from one side of the nave to the other, there is a series of short tunnels sideways across the nave.

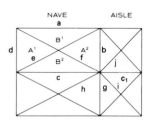

Fig. 57 *Romanesque vaulting*

St-Philibert also provides examples in its aisles of the groin vault. Much used by the Romans, this consists of the intersection at right angles of two identical tunnel vaults and so it can also be called a cross vault. Where these surfaces meet, there are folds, just as where the upper thigh joins the abdomen there is a groin. There is also spatial interpenetration since the two parts of each barrel vault lie opposite one another and are horizontal continuations without separation. In other words, in figure 57 A1 and A2 are parts of one tunnel and B1 and B2 of the other. The same diagram shows how a groin vault comprises six arches: four at right angles along the sides (a,b,c,d) and two diagonal ones (e,f). This gives rise to constructional problems. If a rectangular bay is being built, then clearly the diameter of the arches will be different, i.e. a diameter on a narrow side (d) has to be shorter than on a long side (a), and both will not be as great as that of a diagonal arch (f). The effect of this is that the arches cannot reach the same height nor will their apexes be at the same level unless the side ones are raised or stilted so that they spring at a higher point than do the diagonals. Hence to stand at the corner of such a vault and to look along a diagonal is to become aware that the curve of the groin is irregular – it has in fact a double curvature. This did not disturb the architects because, as will be seen below, they were interested in orthogonal design and frontality and not in diagonals.

The outcome of this was to provide a cross vault that is lighter and more open and flexible than the tunnel variety. Moreover, unlike the inertia of the barrel vault, the cross vault is active; its crown gives the impression of rising towards the centre and this is stressed by the groins with their interplay of lines. This line-play is further emphasized by the use of ribs that follow the folds. Such mouldings had been employed by the Romans for structural reinforcement, but in Romanesque buildings they have become decorative features giving delight by their linearity and by the variety of their profiles.

THE BAY SYSTEM AND THE NAVE WALLS

Once architects began to design with vaulting in mind, then it necessarily became a controlling feature; hence in Romanesque as in Byzantine churches, the supported members have precedence over the supporting ones. A vault indeed affects its substructure in two ways: first, it creates a spatial unit and, second, it determines the form and shape of its supports.

A groin vault is the uppermost limit of a spatial unit or bay, defined along its sides by four arches and at the base by a pavement. These units did not exist in the basilica and so the bay is something essentially new and indeed is one of the important characteristics of the Romanesque church. A nave, with banded barrel or cross vaults, is not one long undifferentiated volume but a series of smaller volumes added together. When bays are created in the aisles, each has an arch to east and west and on the side opening into the nave, while the fourth edge is an outside wall. When a nave is covered with groin vaults the arrangement is more complex. Again there will be an arch to east and west, but now the north and south sides will be made of sections of the nave walls. The extent to which these have been affected by the vaulting, as the superior element, has now to be investigated.

The nave wall of a Romanesque church resembles that of its basilican predecessor in that it is formed of three bands. At the top there is the clerestory, with windows to light the interior; next there is a section of masonry and at ground level there is an arcade. Because of the heavy weight of the vaulting bearing down on this wall, the legs of the arches have to be very strong and this has been achieved by increasing their girth. Pillars rather than slender columns, they often assume the shape of a pier, which is a solid masonry support, square or rectangular in cross-section. The pier reveals very clearly the extent to which these supports are essentially pieces or remnants of wall; the arches correspondingly are to be read as holes cut out of this wall. The first effect of the vault then was to require a thickened, somewhat massive wall beneath it. The second effect was more subtle.

A nave pier is a meeting point of four arches. First there is the transverse arch thrown across the nave (fig. 57c); second, there is the smaller transverse arch over the aisle (c_1); third and fourth are the arches of the actual nave arcade (b, g). If the ribbing of the transverse arches is carried down two of the four faces of the pier and the moulding of the internal arches is similarly marked, the result is a compound pier composed of a bundle of vertical

Fig. 58 Compound piers elements. It can take the form either of a simple cross or of a

Vézelay, La Madeleine, nave

square with four projections. If one of the arches is not so marked, then a T-shaped pier is the result. But these forms are the direct outcome of the vaulting system and are evidence of how the supported members influence the supports whose shape is derived from their superstructure. Nor are the ribs and mouldings structurally essential: they may appear to bear weight but it is in fact the wall or the core of the pier behind the shaft that carries it. They are there for their decorative properties and serve to articulate the space in a perpendicular dimension. They also knit together head (vault) and sides (walls) by carrying the lines of the vault down to the ground and by bringing the north and south arcades into relation; in this way they contribute to the definition of the bay as a clearly perceived spatial unit.

With its emphasis upon these spatial units there can be no question but that Romanesque architecture is space-positive; at the same time it does show a concern for surface quality – this is very apparent in the design of the nave walls. The articulation of these differs very much from that in the basilica. The masonry band between arcades and clerestory is now provided with a sequence of arches, which can be either blind or opening on to a gallery, so creating the triforium. It is not however a feature of every design: in Germany the space between the arcading and the windows is often plain; but in the great pilgrimage churches there is a two-storey partition with a gallery over the main arcades and no clerestory. Whenever the triforium is used, a planar effect is preserved; the arches never protrude; they always recede, observing the surface as their outer limit, and indeed Romanesque arches have a series of graded mouldings moving from the outside edge of the wall to its inmost core.

The procession of arches and windows, each layer crisply defined by a projecting string course (corbelling), preserves the horizontal thrust of previous churches. The flatness of the piers, which makes them less linear in a perpendicular direction, also contributes to this. However the vertical unity of the building has also to be safeguarded and this is achieved by means of enfolding shapes. A semicircular vault, for example, is in fact a form of embracement. The encompassing of small arches within larger ones is a usual feature of triforia. In the nave of Christchurch Priory, Dorset (1090–1120), the triforium, within each bay, is composed of two arches springing from one central shaft and these are contained within a third. The vertical and horizontal axes are then in balance; the upward movement is gentle and does not compete with the equally gentle advance towards the altar.

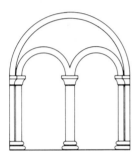

Fig. 59 Embracement: triforium of Christchurch Priory, Dorset

RHYTHM

While the basilica was spatially planned, its rhythm was primarily linear, made up of the regular colonnades or arcades edging the nave. The beat was a simple one: a–b–a–b–a–b, with 'a' representing a column and 'b' a space. The result is to march the visitor smoothly to the altar. In the Romanesque church this linear rhythm slows down because the succession of columns has been replaced by groupings that consist not only of columns but also of piers. The consequence is that equal strophes, following each other down the vista of the nave, have given way to alternating strong and weak stresses, i.e. of piers alternating with columns. The continuity of the Early Christian colonnade is in this way broken up, as in St Michael, Hildesheim (1001–33) where between each pier there are two columns, thus providing a new and more stately rhythm. The nave walls are now a linear sequence of individualized parts that retard any rapid flow towards the sanctuary and the beat is: A–b–a–b–a–b–A, where 'A' represents a pier.

However the Romanesque church has not only a linear rhythm, it has also a spatial one created by the system of bays. The aim is no longer to convey the visitor along the nave at maximum speed. The tempo is reduced; he is invited to linger within each bay which closes inwards towards its dominating centre in the middle of the semicircular vault. The nave has to be read as a recession of vertical volumes and the aisles equally echo the same rhythm with their corresponding bays.

An alternative spatial rhythm, favoured in smaller parish churches, such as at Kilpeck in Herefordshire *c.* 1134, treats nave, chancel and apse as three separate volumes, the second and third decreasing in size. So the width and height of the chancel are smaller than those of the nave, and the dimensions of the apse are less than those of the chancel. The visitor is thus led unhurriedly from west to east by the spatial progression. Whichever method of rhythm is used, the church interior is experienced in successive stages, each part having an aesthetic and structural existence of its own.

The rhythm is very even because of the proportions adopted. The ground plan is frequently composed of a series of squares. Since the aisles are often half the width of the naves, there is a clear relation between the components, two aisle bays being the equivalent of one nave bay. In Germany the dimensions of the square at the crossing were commonly used as the basis of the calculations, so St Michael, Hildesheim, has a nave divided into three such spaces. It is not surprising that there is a certain calmness and majesty about these interiors. There is a change of emphasis from the basilica in which everything depended upon the altar as the focal point. Now the church interior is a sum total of equal parts. The area around the altar, marked by the triumphal arch in the basilica, is no longer a centre of absolute attraction; it is the chancel arch, closed with a screen, that beckons. What has happened is that a choir has been inserted and this has pushed the sanctuary proper further away while the arch has ceased to be a frame for the altar and become an introduction to the chancel.

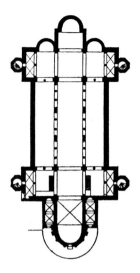

Fig. 60 Hildesheim, St Michael

PATHS AND PLACES

Rhythm requries movement for its enjoyment and this immediately suggests that a Romanesque church is to be assigned to the category of a path. Certainly there is no doubt of this as far as the pilgrimage churches were concerned; the disposition of naves, aisles and galleries enabled order to be imposed on the crowds by cutting, as it were, parallel furrows in the moving mass. An ambulatory too, by its very name, is for walking, but instead of the monodirectionality of the basilica, there is now a circular and embracing movement. The nave remains the main highway but the increased illumination of the aisles gives them more prominence after the comparative darkness of the basilica so that they are not so much edges as parts of a whole.

The whole is a circulatory system with all the characteristics of a well-defined path. There are edges, continuity and a directional quality. The choir screen acts as a prime goal, and when the sanctuary is raised above a crypt there is an even more striking terminal. Yet in the great cathedrals, abbeys and large parish churches where the full Romanesque plan is to be encountered, the path is a highly complex one after the simplicity of the basilica. This variety shows itself in several ways. The path embraces three levels, subterranean, on the floor of the church and in the galleries. It includes not just nave and aisles but transepts and ambulatories. There are numerous nodes with place characteristics, e.g. chapels and crypts, while the choir itself is screened off to constitute a centre. The transepts, especially when they are double, introduce differentiation, and the opening of their ends with porches (so that it is possible to enter or exit at points other than in the main façade) indicates that the west–east drive has been attenuated. The whole remains a path or series of paths but it now constitutes a place in itself: a focus for gathering, with a character of its own. It declares that instead of advancing to meet God – the message of the basilica – the faithful live in him and are embraced by him. The introduction of wheel windows, i.e. round with radiating spokes, into the west façade and the end walls of transepts, is a means of assuring visitors that the sun of Christ continues to shine on them as they go out into the everyday world.

ORNAMENT

Little has been said so far about ornament and yet it is so fused with the architecture that the one cannot be appreciated apart from the other. Sculpture dominates, but mosaic, fresco and stained glass are also to be noted.

Mosaic, in the main, is to be found in those areas open to continuing Byzantine influence such as Italy and Sicily. Indeed

the cathedrals at Cefalù, Monreale and Torcello are really basilicas with Byzantine mosaics. Frescoes were favoured further
north and in Spain too. In the nave there is often a sequence of
scenes that induce a harmonious pace as the visitor moves from
bay to bay and follows the story that is being unfolded. In the
apses, the frescoes, brilliantly coloured, have some of the
majesty of Byzantine mosaics, and evidence for this is conveni-
ently accessible in the Museo de Arte de Cataluña in Barcelona
where a very large number of magnificent paintings of the
eleventh and twelfth centuries has been preserved. Extra colour
is introduced by stained glass, which goes back to at least
Carolingian times, but few examples have survived and in any
case this technique had to await the Gothic era to achieve its
zenith.

However it was sculpture that provided the principal decorative element in Romanesque architecture. The chief focus for it
in the early eleventh century was the capital, but within 100
years emphasis shifted to the portal and to the façade as a whole.
To follow this historical movement will mean considering the
church interior first and then its exterior. But before undertak-
ing this the general characteristics of Romanesque sculpture
need to be specified in order to make evident its entire suitability
to the buildings of which it is so much an integral part: the
sculpture was in fact architecturally conceived.

SCULPTURE

General characteristics

Romanesque architecture is an architecture of walls, in the sense
that they are its main structural feature and that it is by them
that the vaulting is carried. Consequently if sculpture is to be
entirely at one with it, it too has to respect the wall surface and
this is precisely what has been achieved. The most striking
works are in the form of reliefs depicting scenes from the Bible
and the lives of saints. Whereas in Hellenistic reliefs movement
originates within the carved figures themselves, in Romanesque
they conform to conditions external to themselves; they are
fashioned with reference to the surface on which they are spread
out and flattened. Three results follow from this: first, there is
an increase in ornamental value in that the outlines are treated
freely in a decorative manner; second, there is a close relationship between the figures and the surface they decorate; third, the

planar character of the surface is preserved. So the figures are
contained within the front plane and the relief reads backwards
recessively from this as far as the innermost surface which is
parallel to the outer. Hence the decoration is itself wall and
never exceeds the strict limit imposed by the block of building
stone.

The carving also functions as an enrichment of the structural
forms. It is not just applied, like a mural painting, but integrated
with the lines of a church and used to give emphasis to certain
important features such as arches, capitals, windows and portals. In so doing, the designs are made completely dependent
upon the architectural shapes. The consequence is that figures
do not correspond with human or animal measurements but
with the dimensions of the space that is to be filled. In other
words, the designs illustrate the 'law of the framework', which
determines where they shall be located and within what limits
they are to fit. The same 'law' covers the attraction of the
carvings to the border so that postures are affected by its shape –
for example, within a round frame the figures will themselves be
circular. Figures are short, tall or twisted, not in accordance
with the norms of organic life but in order to match the architecture: they respect mouldings to the point that they can
become indistinguishable from them.

A Romanesque sculpture is also remarkable for its life and
movement, which accord admirably with the pathlike quality of
the typical church. The effect of mobility is achieved in three
ways: (i) by the triangulation of the space to be covered; (ii) by
making vertical figures resemble climbers, or by suggesting they
are performing a rhythmical dance or by having their legs
crossed to create an X; (iii) by making horizontal figures undulate so that they appear to swim or crawl.

With these features in mind, it is now possible to examine the
sculptured ornament in more detail, beginning with the interior
of the church.

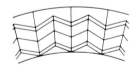

Interior use

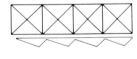

The sculptural enrichment of the vault had to await the introduction of the ribs which were adorned with a variety of geometric patterns: zigzag (chevron), a row of small pyramids
(nailhead), a band of cylinders or square pieces (billet), and a
twisted cord (cable). It is easy to appreciate how one or other of
these gives to the lines of arches and vaults an eye-catching
treatment, and nowhere is their effect better evident than in the
nave of Durham cathedral. Unlike all the others, which have
chevron mouldings, the two most eastward triforium arches

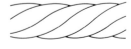

*Fig. 61 Chevron,
nailhead and cable*

Durham, cathedral, nave arcade

have been left plain. The contrast is quite striking. Those without the chevron attract less attention, look smaller and appear flatter than the others. The decorated ones draw the eye and in this way slow the ascent to the roof so that the vertical movement of the bay does not clash with the horizontality of Romanesque. They seem larger because the zigzag expresses the radiating effect of the round-headed arch, while the hood mould, bordering it above, keeps it in check. There is a concentrated liveliness without dissipation of forces so that the wall as a whole is animated and a certain plastic quality is achieved.

*Conques, St-Foi, capital
at base of south-west
tower*

Descending from the vault around the arch, the capital next
demands attention. A capital, it will be recalled, functions as the
terminal element of a column and as the means of transition
between the rectangular footing of an arch to the circle of a
shaft. To accomplish this latter task a square block was taken
and its lower parts rounded to produce a convex outline with
four flat faces – this is a cushion or block capital. The faces are
sometimes scalloped but more frequently carved with plant
forms and with figures. Here the principle of recession in parallel
planes is very evident. Palmettes and acanthus leaves are spread
out and look as if they have been compressed between the front
and back planes of the thickness of the relief. Even when figures
are represented, this principle is upheld: they are bound to the
block of stone, having no existence outside it and their shape
conforming to that of the capital.

Romanesque shafts, as previously stated, are not self-
contained sculptural units but pieces of wall (hence their eventual replacement by piers). However both shafts and piers were
treated sculpturally in a remarkable way. In many churches they
are composed of small figures on top of each other, so the
chancel arch at Kilpeck has three people superimposed per

column. Alternatively, they can consist of separate individuals as in the Portail Royal of Chartres or in the Fürsten portal of Bamberg cathedral. These figures either carry the capitals directly on their heads or are joined to them by short sections of column, their bodies being substitutes for most or all of the shafts. The wedding of sculpture and architectural forms could not be more complete.

The base, that is the bottom terminal element, obviating any suggestion that the shaft might be continuing downwards into the ground, is usually of the classical Attic type. This means that it is made of two large rings of convex mouldings, the lower of greater diameter, joined by a spreading concave moulding. Each base sits upon a plinth that consists of one or more chamfered or

Chartres, cathedral, centre doorway right of west portal

moulded projections and this acts as a visible footing from
which the wall or pillar can start. Plinths give a horizontal
emphasis and they also provide an opportunity for further
ornamentation. A round base upon a square plinth leaves small
triangles uncovered at each corner. These attract the eye and so
they are often decorated. There is delight in discovering and
admiring, for example, the stylized plant forms at the feet of the
columns in St-Germain-des-Prés, Paris.

By the mid twelfth century overall surface enrichment was
common. Linear patterns, for example, are incised on the great
pillars of the Durham nave. Blind arcading often runs along the
walls, edging the aisles, and the arches may intersect. String
courses mark the divisions of the nave walls and hood mouldings outline the windows. These latter were in fact initially
external features, being projections to throw off rain. In general
however the movement of decoration was in the opposite direction, i.e. the sculpture of the interior passed to the exterior.

The exterior

The exterior of a Romanesque church differs markedly from
that of the Early Christian basilica. The latter building had been
regarded as a home of the family of God and so stress had been
on the inside, which constitutes the essence of a house. However
there are houses that have a public character: that of the presi-
dent of the United States is one such example. By the early
Middle Ages churches too had become public buildings and
their exteriors were developed accordingly.

As you approach the front of a Romanesque church two
features immediately attract the eye: the doorway and the tympanum that surmounts it. The area between the lintel and the
arch is filled with sculptured figures which, as previously described, are subject to the 'law' of the framework. Within an
arcuated structure, where a rectangular border has no place,
shapes have to be adapted to a new field and so figures at the
extremities are bent inwards or shrunk, while the centre one,
frequently Christ in majesty, is elongated out of all proportion
to the rest. The result is a magnificent and impressive declaration of the Church's faith, characterized by harmony, rhythm,
vigour and balance. The arches that frame both tympana and
doorways recede inwards from the surface of the wall, in the
same way as the nave arcades, and their front edges are moulded
or carved to splendid effect. While this inward movement is a
welcoming one, the observer is kept at some distance by the
fixed plane of the wall surface itself and so is prompted to

Poitiers, Notre-Dame-la-Grande, façade

contemplate. There is no lack of opportunity for so doing – the inner porches at Santiago and Vézelay, the west portal of S. Domingo at Soria which combines episodes from the New Testament with scenes of the Last Judgement, the 'golden portal' of the Marienkirche at Freiburg, these and many more are an inexhaustible source of delight.

However this does not complete the tale of Romanesque façades. Seeking to stir the lifeless masonry into movement, Italian architects applied to the exterior the blind arcading of the interior and produced the so-called Lombard frieze which is a series of small round arches on pilasters. It can provide an accent to the fall of a roof, and when it is carried right round a church it embraces and unifies it. The Lombard frieze was also the source of the open arcaded gallery which preserves horizontality and so prevents a façade from soaring up into the sky, for example, as at S. Michele, Lucca, or the cathedral of Pisa. At the same time the galleries provide a contrast in planes, in openness and closure, which gives interest to the whole.

Lucca, S. Michele, façade

Another method of enriching the façade was to combine it with one or more towers. Campaniles began to appear in Italy, either round (Pisa) or rectangular (Pomposa), composed of superimposed layers and standing apart from the church. North of the Alps, integration of tower and church was undertaken. Functionally only a single tower is needed for the bells, but when it is treated as a decorative element, like the Islamic minaret, there is no need to limit its numbers. As far as the west end is concerned, single towers in the centre were an old tra-

*Hildesheim,
Godhardkirche,
westwerk*

dition in England and thousands of parish churches still stand to illustrate this integration. In France and especially in Germany twin towers, flanking and framing the main entrance and corresponding to the north and south aisles, give a monumental character to the façade. Dignified, handsome, majestic, they provide an ascending movement and an animated silhouette, as in the Abbey of Jumièges near Rouen. In Germany this relates to the 'west-work'.

The porch-church or Vollwestwerk, for example of the Godhardkirche at Hildesheim, had a west end composed of two elements; a crypt at ground level and, above it, an upper church complete with aisles and galleries. Externally this was given a central tower, while two others on each side gave access to the

upper church. This provided for the services of Holy Week and
was modelled in part on the Holy Sepulchre in Jerusalem: it
allowed for the many processions, for the celebrations of the
eucharist, the adoration of the cross, and so on. The first
examples pre-date full Romanesque, and include St-Riquier
near Abbeville (*c.* 775). A change in liturgical observance led to
the porch-church atrophying in Germany, first losing its crypt,
as in St Pantaleon, Cologne; then being transformed into a
western apse, for example, the cathedral of Paderborn, and
finally surviving only as a decorative feature of the façade, as in
the triple towers of Maria-Laach, near Koblenz, in the twelfth
century.

As an external feature towers were not confined to the west
end; they could occupy a variety of positions: at the end of
transepts or at the eastern extremities of aisles or over the
crossing. Always arranged symmetrically, they have a vital contribution to make to the external massing of Romanesque buildings. For example, a single central tower at a crossing provides
the roofs of nave, choir and transepts with something to stop up
against: it constitutes a focus and a terminus and also a link in
that, if there are no transepts for example, it allows the roofs
over the nave to the west and over the chancel to the east to be at
different levels without there being any ugly break between
them.

Romanesque architecture indeed, especially in France and
Germany, is characterized on the outside by a massing of simple
forms, just as impressive as Byzantine churches or Islamic
mosques. Each building is a collection of solids related to one
another, e.g. St-Etienne, Nevers. The exterior shapes – and this
applies equally to the triple apses in some Italian churches –
invariably correspond with the internal distribution of parts.
Roofs rise step by step from the small apses to the sanctuary and
they can be crowned by a central tower or sometimes a cupola,
like the remarkable one at Zamorra in northern Spain – the
compact silhouette appeals by the variety and firmness of its
outline.

THE PRINCIPLE OF COMPOSITION: ADDITION

The exterior demonstrates that a Romanesque church is a kind
of group building in the sense that it is an assembly of spatial
units, often with a rich contrast between different solid geometrical forms. Yet while the components retain some independence, it is their sum that creates the whole; the principle of

composition therefore is without question addition. Indeed one could say that the churches belong to a 'joined' type, i.e. they are a series of distinct spaces or volumes juxtaposed along an axis.

Whatever detail is analysed, it will be found to exemplify the principle of addition. Consideration of three external and three internal features will clarify this statement. The Romanesque tower, as previously mentioned, is a series of layers, one on top of another; it is the product of superimposition and therefore unquestionably of addition. The Romanesque tympanum is treated as a separate field for sculpture from the lintel upon which it rests – examples may be enjoyed at Moissac and at Autun – this differentiation too stems from addition (see figure 92). The Romanesque arch is also the sum of two elements: there is its semicircular head, which because of its inner regular cohesion is a subwhole, and there are its vertical supports with capitals to mark the point of juncture.

Moving inside the church and paying attention first to the vault: a groin vault exemplifies addition since, on the one hand, it is made by joining two barrel vaults together and, on the other, it forms its own space distinct from that which is below.

Nevers, St-Etienne,
chevet

The nave in its turn is sectionalized by bays which are juxtaposed – here are compact units of space added to one another – while the nave walls are three superimposed bands. The Romanesque design and use of capitals reveals the same principle. When each one can bear an entire scene from Scripture, they all stand out as entities in their own right. If it is also noted how the radiating chapels around the ambulatory are not usually adjacent but divided by short expanses of wall, then the statement that addition is the universal principle needs no further demonstration.

GENERAL CHARACTERISTICS AND REGIONAL DIFFERENCES

An account has now been given of most of the characteristics of Romanesque architecture: its vaulting, its embracing nature, its handling of space, its embodiment of rhythm, its delight in clear forms and massing, its respect of wall surfaces, its use of recession and its acceptance of addition. Reference has also been made to its axiality, and since there are mirror images on both sides of the horizontal and vertical axes – transept balancing transept and subsidiary apses likewise – bilateral symmetry is another characteristic and this adds to the atmosphere of calm.

The impression of dignity and sobriety is further enhanced by the way everything in a Romanesque church is in accordance with the dictates of frontality and is consequently orthogonal. Figures in fresco and stone have a frontal pose; block capitals have four distinct faces, touching at 90 degrees; each bay is a square or rectangle. Structural members have shallow profiles; arches are flat and stand four-square.

To descend to a crypt, with its more limited height and its horizontal spread, is to feel this frontal and orthogonal character even more strongly. Since the bays are so small and close together, there is a frontal robustness; plinths and capitals all look directly at one another. The short shafts convey a sense of pressure being exerted from above by the load of the vault, and because they are also thick, they are not so linear in a vertical direction as their classical predecessors; instead they repose in themselves. No wonder that Romanesque conveys a sense of solidity, strength and equilibrium. After the recumbent form of the basilican nave, the body of a church blends horizontality and verticality in a new way; aspiring and intersecting shapes have created the basis for a different kind of delight.

Despite much that is common, there are certain regional differences within Romanesque architecture. There are galleries above the aisles in Auvergne but none in Poitou; Rhenish churches often have double transepts; Aquitanian have domes and in Lombardy baldachin porches are frequent. However none of these items really affects the stylistic homogeneity. But there is one peculiarity – very much an English favourite – that needs closer attention and that is the flat east end.

After what has been said about the embracing quality of an apse and the way it resolves a longitudinal axis, what is to be made of the apparent abruptness of a straight east wall? The one receives, the other seems to halt the visitor in his tracks. To understand this flatness it is essential to realize that this form is not a substitute for an apse and should not be contrasted with it. In parish churches the square sanctuary is a separate room, i.e. the nave and the area around the altar are two distinct spaces, whereas previously nave and apse had been one unified volume. The result is that this flat wall becomes a backdrop for the altar, dimly perceived through the chancel arch; it is not primarily a means of defining the space within which the altar stands. Instead of being different forms of the same architectural element, apse and square-ended sanctuary are different volumes, the one terminating a nave – rounding it off, as it were – and the other a separate but not entirely inaccessible room. The nave with its arcading has become a stately processional way leading to an independent place created out of the choir and an orthogonal sanctuary.

In cathedrals the situation is not the same, in that the flat east end is invisible from the nave. Sanctuary and choir have been interposed and beyond them, e.g. in the cathedrals of Peterborough or St Albans, there is a Lady Chapel which is only reached by following the aisles into and around the ambulatory.

A warning about hybrids will be sufficient to bring this section to a close. Although vaulting is of the essence of Romanesque churches, there are some that have wooden roofs and there are others that have been given Gothic vaulting. In the former case the roof is still a lid and is not integrated with its substructure, although the nave walls may be marked out in bays. In the latter case roof and wall have been united but there is some clash of styles – the nature of that clash will be understandable only after we have discussed Gothic in the next chapter.

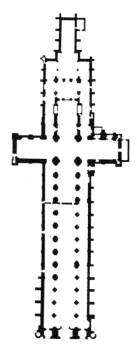

Fig. 62 St Albans, cathedral

8

THE AGE OF GOTHIC

Gothic architecture, which may be dated from the mid twelfth to the early fifteenth century, has often been the subject of controversy, with its critics dismissing it as barbarous (this was the intention behind the term 'Gothic') and its admirers declaring it to be the most perfect and only appropriate style for church buildings. Even those who have sympathetically analysed its character have held divergent views, as between, for example, two outstanding art historians, one from France and the other from England: Viollet-le-Duc (1814–79) and John Ruskin (1819–1900).

Viollet-le-Duc understood Gothic in terms of equilibrium: the whole structure is to be explained as the canalization of forces which are carried down to and neutralized at ground level. Ribs support vaults and are so many arches bearing the weight earthwards; the outward thrust of the arches is met by flying buttresses and is converted into a descending energy by means of pinnacles: the result is a tense stability. Ruskin's approach was more aesthetic and he distinguished between the form and the spirit of Gothic. The form lies in the use of the pointed arch surmounted by a steep gable, endlessly repeated in windows, porches, vaults, and so on. Its spirit he regarded as a compound of six elements: savageness, i.e. rude vigour; changefulness or continuous variety and novelty; naturalism, revealed by an interest in organic forms; grotesqueness, by which he understood a mixture of the fearsome and the ludicrous; rigidity, which he defined as the energy that gives tension to movement and stiffness to resistance; and redundance, i.e. richness of material, ornamentation, and so on. While the writings of these two scholars contain many insights into Gothic, neither of their central theses is acceptable at the present time.

Viollet-le-Duc's rationalistic theory does not correspond with what is now known to be the actuality. Ribs do not necessarily hold up vaults; vaults stay aloft through their own overall coherence even if ribs are destroyed. Flying buttresses are not so much structural members as fairy viaducts: remove them and scarcely a wall would collapse. Pinnacles do not counteract sideways thrust. Indeed the nature of Gothic architecture, as will become apparent as this chapter proceeds, is not based upon technical but upon aesthetic premises. But this does not mean that Ruskin is therefore to be preferred: his ingredients, which are basically ornamental and not strictly architectural qualities, can equally well be found in Romanesque, where rude vigour, variety, grotesqueness and so on can all be detected. However if two such outstanding students of the style can be faulted, then perhaps the way towards an appreciation should begin not by outlining further theories but by appealing to direct experience. When one enters a Gothic church, what is the first inescapable impression? Without question, it is one of soaring height with the gaze carried swiftly upwards to the ceiling where the vault reigns supreme. Since this is the most prominent feature, an analysis of the vault can be expected to provide a clue to the essential nature of Gothic.

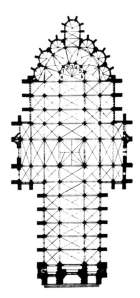

Fig. 63 Amiens, cathedral

THE GOTHIC VAULT

On plan the nave ceiling of any medieval Gothic cathedral, such as the one at Amiens (begun 1220), does not appear to differ from its Romanesque predecessors (figure 63). It looks like a series of rectangles which are the crowns of bays that are themselves baldachins with four legs. But when these ceilings are regarded *in situ*, the impression is no longer one of rectangular compartments but of triangles and diamonds outlined by ribs. What catches the eye in fact is the criss-cross of the ribs that diagonally span each bay. This diagonality has had a direct effect upon the four legs that support the vault. Each leg, standing at the junction of four vaults (two in the nave and two in the aisles – see figure 57), is formed of an inner core around which cluster eights shafts (figure 64). The shafts correspond with and are the bottom parts of the ribs and arches that rise to the vaults. So there is one for the transverse arch across the nave (c), a second for that which spans the aisle (c_1). There are two for the longitudinal arches (b,g) and there are four for the diagonals (f,h,i,j). The final result of this is to turn the pier into a diamond, half of which is like a V jutting out into the nave and has shafts that mount to the nave vault, while its other half – a second

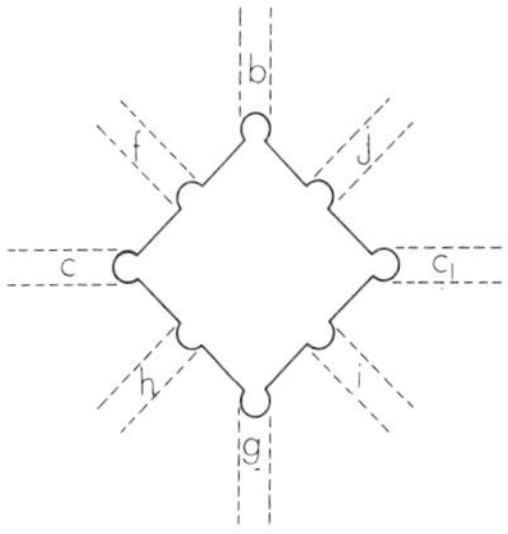

Fig. 64 Compound pier

Amiens, cathedral, nave and choir

V – projects into the aisle with a similar cluster of shafts ascending to its vault.

An elaboration of the quadripartite design is easily obtained by adding a transverse rib (AB), but this too is bound to have an effect below. The resulting sexpartite vault would have this transverse rib just hanging in the air without any termination, unless it were brought to the ground by means of a corresponding shaft. This was done and the shaft became a feature in what is known as the 'Alternate System'. In this the piers separating the nave from the aisles are alternately large (C,D) and small (B), the former supporting both nave and aisle vaults, the latter the descending shaft of the transverse rib. In this way the sexpartite vault was linked with the intermediate piers and a further relationship between top and bottom was established, continuity between them being expressed and head and body combined.

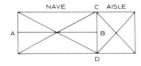

Fig. 65 Sexpartite vault and alternate system

Vaulting was rendered even more complex by means of longitudinal ridge ribs (1) and by other intermediate ones known as tiercerons (2), which stretch between the corners of the rectangle and the transverse rib (3). Insert yet more connecting links – liernes (4) that never start from the corners – and a variety of patterns is possible: a net vault, which resembles a combination of lozenges, and a stellar vault which is the one in figure 66. Ultimately, although in England alone, the Gothic masters produced the fan vault which may be regarded as the zenith of intricate linear decoration. A fan vault is like a concave-sided funnel and it probably originated in centrally planned buildings such as circular chapter houses. In these all the ribs emanate from the middle and so have the same curvature and profile. Transfer this to a square or oblong compartment and preserve the circular ridge rib, then all the ribs have identical curvature and the result is a pure rotational figure. This was first used in the cloisters at Gloucester (1351–77), but probably the most well-known example is the chapel of King's at Cambridge (1512–15), although Henry VII's Chapel at Westminster (1502–12) runs it a close second.

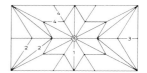

Fig. 66 Stellar vault

Enjoying these vaults involves recognizing the extent to which their design belongs to a graphic system that produces a surface pattern, linear in form. Indeed the ever-increasing intricacy tends to turn what appears to be structure into texture, held in place by ornamental knobs or projections known as bosses. These are located at the centre of each compartment (figure 66.5) and often where two ribs intersect. Here is symmetry and rhythm and a joy in interlocking geometrical shapes. The several operations involved in pattern making are all in evidence. Transverse ribs and longitudinal arches serve as framing. The ridge ribs and the diagonals are the means of filling, while the liernes and tiercerons perform the function of linking. They combine to articulate the surface and make it lively. Branching, radiating and interlacing are also visible. Tiercerons give a clustered effect that harmonizes with the equally clustered piers below, while the liernes both increase the decoration and provide some correspondence with the tracery in the windows where a similar linear interest has been at work.

THE RELATIONSHIP OF THE VAULT TO THE DESIGN AS A WHOLE

It will be apparent by now that it is the ribs that express the nature of the Gothic vault. Indeed they are responsible for its main aspects, which are equally discernible in every part of

Gloucester, cathedral, cloisters with fan vaulting

every building and are essential components of the style: diagonality, projection, division and unity.

Diagonality

Ribs that cross diagonally, demand, as we have seen, that their shafts be turned diagonally to correspond and their bases be changed to establish a smooth junction. Diagonality from above then descends to and affects what is below.

The ribs are of course arches and every arch, because it consists of a certain thickness between two upright planes, creates a vertical layer of space and, at the same time, it divides space. As soon as engaged shafts are placed beneath the Gothic ribs, then this division is continued downwards. Cross ribs and shafts become a diagonal archway between two piers that are opposite one another on a diagonal of the rectangular bay. No longer, as with Romanesque, is the transverse arch separating the bays important; in Gothic, it is the diagonals that are prominent and they do not separate but lead on from bay to bay.

Projection

Ribs stand on the surface of Gothic vaults, with the cells lying behind them, and so there is projection which contrasts with the recession of Romanesque groins. This principle of advancement is evident throughout Gothic churches. The members jut out; planes stand in front of one another rather than recede. The compound piers point across nave and aisles. The relative flatness of Romanesque has gone; the nave wall ceases to be a wall in any proper sense; its arches are not perforations in a surface but spaces between diagonal structural elements that open out to meet the visitor.

The projection on the interior finds its complement in a similar projection outside and this produces the typical Gothic exterior. So the portals are usually in front of the walls of the façades. At Rouen, or Reims, while the cathedral doors are in the same vertical plane as the wall, the porches splay out and contrast sharply with Romanesque entrances which step inwards.

Division and unity

Ribs divide vaults into four or more cells but these are incapable of having a separate existence; incomplete in themselves they are entirely interdependent and are fragments of a whole. This means that the principle of Gothic composition is division. The Gothic vault is not the outcome of adding single spaces together but of subdividing one space.

According to the principles of division, the subwholes cannot be rigidly separated from one another. In the vault this is frequently achieved by moulding the rib in the shape of a triangle (figure 67). Its protecting apex calls attention to the centre line (AB) and at the same time, because each of its two halves (c,d) belongs to an adjacent cell, it affirms the unity of the whole.

Throughout the rest of any Gothic building every part is united in a common design to which each is subordinate. This is very evident in the nave 'walls'. Apart from a group of French

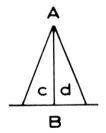

Fig. 67 Triangular rib

cathedrals of the second half of the twelfth century – such as Noyon and Laon which have both a gallery and a triforium between the arcade and the clerestory – most naves have a tripartite elevation. However, unlike Romanesque with its distinct

Rouen, St-Ouen, nave

superimposed layers, Gothic has little or no separation between them: they are subwholes within one totality. Sometimes, as in St Mary, Lübeck (completed 1330) the arch at ground level is embraced within a second that rises to include the clerestory. Sometimes triforium and clerestory are combined, although (since this wording suggests the adding of two parts) it would be more accurate to say that triforium and clerestory have been created by the division of a greater whole. Often the crowns of the arches, which in Romanesque are well below the next layer, leaving a wide expanse of wall, push up into the subwhole above, thus exemplifying one of the chief aspects of division, namely interpenetration. In the later Gothic centuries capitals tended to be reduced in size and even disappear as possible separating features. So in the nave of St-Ouen, Rouen (fifteenth century) the vaults are 110 feet high but there are no capitals to interrupt or divide the whole until the springing of the vault itself, i.e. some 10 feet only below the crown.

This interpenetration is very evident in Gothic porches and in the many niches that reproduce its outline – an outline that Ruskin saw as the quintessential form of Gothic: the tip of the arch pushes up into the triangle of the gable so that the latter is inflected and loses its baseline and its separate identity (see figure 95, page 243). Gothic towers reproduce the profile in further niches and windows; they have no separate storeys; bell openings embrace more than one floor; buttresses are vertically continuous and pinnacles override any possible division – for a superb example see the tower of Worcester Cathedral (1374).

When division reigns supreme, apse and choir cannot be two distinct entities; they must flow into one another so that each one is a subdivision of a whole. In the sanctuary of Amiens cathedral, begun 1220 (see figure 63, page 169) the two sides of the choir wall (a,b) continue and coalesce with the five sections (1–5) of the apse. Choir and apse interpenetrate and it is difficult to say where one ends and the other begins. At the east end the ambulatory and the radiating chapels are no longer distinct, as in the Romanesque chevet, but merge into a single flowing current. The chapels here and elsewhere, for example at Chartres (figure 68), have become gentle outward swellings of the ambulatory so that the minor volumes are integrated within the whole. The same principle led to the discarding of the crypt; the sanctuary is no longer higher than the nave; instead there is a pavement at a uniform level throughout the building. Transepts too have lost their independence. In France they often do not project beyond the line of the aisle walls and in all cases they have become subordinate to the design in its entirety.

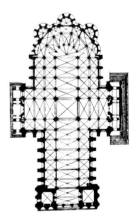

Fig. 68 Chartres, cathedral

Worcester, cathedral,
tower

The pointed arch and verticality

The Gothic vault owes much of its unity to the use of the pointed
arch, although this is not the most telling feature of the style nor
was it adopted for structural convenience but for aesthetic
reasons. Its great advantage is that it can bring uniformity to all
the arches throughout a building and it makes the design of the
vault independent of the shape of the bay beneath. The Romanesque vault was composed of semicircular arches which inevitably had different diameters and which could not all rise to the
same height unless they were stilted or segmented. Pointed
transverse, longitudinal and diagonal arches can all be carried
up to the same level, even when their spans differ, simply by
altering the angles at the crown. The result is a very harmonious

and therefore pleasing composition. Moreover the pointed arch helps to unite the vault and the lower structure vertically because, with such a shape, movement begins from both sides at the bottom at once and proceeds rapidly towards the apex; the two halves of the arch then unite when they are set in relation to the vertical axis. The pointed arch therefore promotes another characteristic of the Gothic style, namely verticality. Indeed its very designation as 'pointed' reveals this function since the arch points upwards, and it scarcely needs spelling out how it and other features combine to stress this heavenward movement.

Mention has already been made of four-storey elevation in certain naves; this probably emanated from a desire to achieve greater height and its demise may well have been due to a similar wish to foster the vertical development of the aisles. Nevertheless the height of Gothic naves contrasts with their comparative narrowness so that one seems to be in a chasm between towering cliffs. In the nave of Westminster Abbey, for example, there is no sensation of spaciousness but of spiritual through physical uplift.

It has also been pointed out how the nave walls within each bay are vertically united and in this connection it is to be noted that the hood moulds over the arches have received little decoration in order not to check the upward thrust. Verticality is evident in the soaring shafts and this effect is increased by making the capitals concave in their lower parts so that the re-entrant angle continues the vertical line. Indeed at Beauvais the capitals have been reduced to virtually nothing and the transverse band of the triforium has not been allowed to impede what, in Ruskinian vein, one might call the great water spouts of stone that rush to spend their force and spread themselves over the vault. All the elements of weight and downward pressure seemed dissolved so that the law of gravity no longer operates. There is a continuous flow of energy which creates an effect of growth as in plants. The entire building seems to rise freely and strain towards the skies. Yet another illustration of this is provided by the structure of the apse. Whereas in the Romanesque apse the masonry courses are horizontal and concentric to create a half-dome, in the Gothic the courses are upright and form a series of ribs rising to a common keystone. This changed direction of the courses corresponds to the difference between the horizontality of Romanesque and the verticality of Gothic.

On the exterior the same verticalism is apparent, multiplied by pinnacles and spires that seem to probe the clouds. Romanesque towers are either flat at their summit or provided with small pyramids – functionally they need no more to hang the bells. Gothic architects added the spire and so increased the general erectness of their buildings.

The dissolution of matter or the maximization of light

Structurally the vault is the superior element of a baldachin which is supported on four legs. Such a framework does not require anything between the legs and there can be an ascendancy of voids over solids. To many students of Gothic this is taken to mean that the architects aimed to dissolve the walls to produce a kind of dematerialization which is regarded as evidence of an aspiration towards the spiritual. This however is to misunderstand the nature of medieval spirituality – Christians of the Gothic age interpreted reality sacramentally: the material mediates the spiritual; one does not become more spiritual by denying physicality. In fact the dissolution of the walls is not the product of a quest for the immaterial; it is the only way to increase the illumination of the interior. The Gothic architects took their cue from I John 1:5 'God is light'. In the thought of such influential writers as Pseudo-Dionysius this means that light itself is a manifestation of the splendour of God. Consequently light became a basic constituent of medieval church architecture.

Whereas in a Romanesque church light is distinct from and in contrast with the tactile substance of the walls, in a Gothic building the walls have become porous; light filters through them, permeates them, merges with them and transfigures them. In other words, Gothic windows are not there to dematerialize the walls but to transform them into diaphanous screens that in themselves witness to the divine. They are architectural elements that are not evidence of dematerialization but of a desire to maximize illumination. The Gothic window indeed turns the light of day to Christian use, diffusing and transfiguring it into the light of the heavenly Jerusalem, this transfiguration being effected by means of stained glass.

GOTHIC ORNAMENT

Stained glass

Although known previously, it was only in the twelfth century that stained glass began to come into its own. To appreciate its contribution to architecture, it is important to note that colour prints of panes are entirely misleading about the character of the art. Such reproductions depend upon reflected light, i.e. light shining on to and up from the page. Mosaic similarly requires surface illumination to bring out the colour of the tesserae. Stained glass however lives from transmitted light. Daylight passes through it and in so doing is turned into blue or red or yellow light. There are indeed no colours in a stained-glass window, only coloured light emanating from it. Whereas all other art forms have to have some light from a source extraneous to themselves in order to be seen, stained glass, being translucent and non-reflecting, provides its own illumination.

Coloured prints mislead in yet another way in that they suggest that the spectator should seek to enjoy the individual episodes depicted, but in a cathedral such as Chartres the scenes are anything from 30 to 75 feet above the floor and the separate figures are no more than vehicles of vibrant colour.

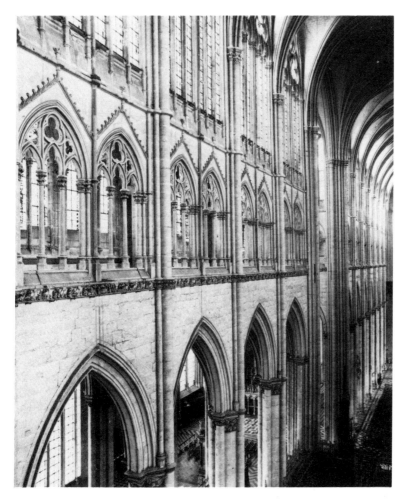

Amiens, cathedral, elevation of choir and nave from east

All this means that the windows are not composed of pictures that happen to be transparent; they are surfaces that are also planes of light, broken and enriched by the interposition of glass and lead. So the Sainte-Chapelle in Paris (*c.* 1243–8) is best perceived as a large lantern.

It scarcely needs pointing out that stained glass has to be enjoyed from inside a building; outside the panes look black and uniform because there is no illumination to pass through them from the interior to the exterior. Within however, because of what is known as halation, i.e. the tendency of light to spread around solid interruptions, the windows appear to be all light; outside they are interlocking patterns of bars and mullions with the glass itself scarcely registering.

Tracery

This mention of bars and mullions directs attention to another form of Gothic decoration – to stone carving and, in particular, to the tracery that frames and divides the window openings. The earliest Gothic windows were simple slender pointed arches. If a greater expanse of glass were to be held firmly enough in place to withstand the pressure of the wind, then there had to be some further supports and the result was the development of tracery. The various forms this took were sufficiently distinct at different times and in different areas to give their names to subdivisions of the Gothic style, such as Flamboyant and Perpendicular (these will be reviewed below). At this juncture what has to be considered is the way to look at tracery, without immediate concern for its variety of patterns.

Inside a church tracery appears black against the radiance of the glass. The grace of the window is in the light for which the tracery provides an outline, articulating it and giving it form. The tracery is entirely subordinate to the light and interest in it for itself is minimal. Outside however the tracery appears white against the virtual blackness of the glass; it then attracts attention to itself, as pattern in stone. The grace of the window on the exterior thus lies in the stonework and not in the glazing. Hence while inside enjoyment springs from appreciating the way the tracery shapes the light, outside it derives from the linear rhythm and symmetry of the stone design.

So attractive was tracery found to be that it spread from windows and was applied to vaults, to screens and panels and to blank arches. When a pattern is uniform in this way, it acts as an integrating device and increases the sense of harmony, the repetition ensuring overall unity. The effect is especially noticeable in the development of the rose window. This began as a wheel of fortune, complete with hub and spokes. On Romanesque façades it was isolated, corresponding with that style's principle of addition. The Gothic vision could not tolerate this and so the form was altered. The spokes were turned into pure tracery by transplanting the design of the more or less rectangular windows in the clerestory and narrowing them at the bottom so that they converge on the centre, e.g. at Reims. In this way the rose window has similar tracery to the others and ceases to be an independent entity.

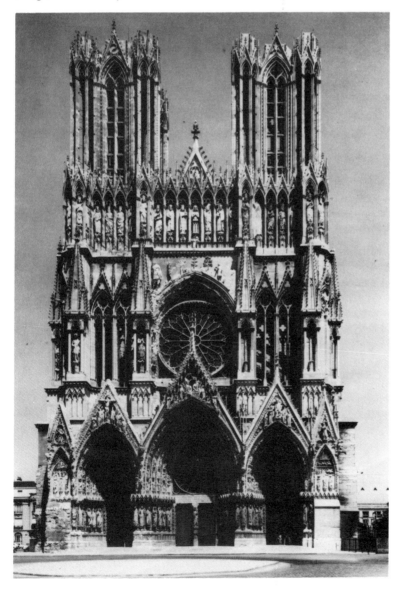

Reims, cathedral, west front

Sculpture

Stone carving was used by the Gothic masons not only for tracery but also for bases, capitals and figures. In each case there is to be noted a preference for natural forms, which possess some life of their own, although never to such an extent that they become detached from the architecture.

Foliate mouldings are to be observed and enjoyed in the triangular areas at the corners of the plinths supporting the round Attic bases, as in the aisles of Rouen cathedral. When, later, the single columns were broken down into a cluster of shafts, each shaft was given its own footing, which no longer serves to fix the pillar to the floor, as in classical and other styles; rather they seem to emerge from it, embodying a feeling of organic growth.

A similar naturalism is to be noted in many capitals, carved with leaf mouldings. Yet the shape of the capital is always preserved: the foliage is attached by stems to the base and widens out to follow its upward expansion, in accordance with its curvature and chalice-like shape. In other words the leaves do not stand out as separate entities nor interrupt the vertical movement; rather they contribute to it. Instead of being natural forms reproduced in stone, they are the media through which the stone itself comes alive, like the leaves of Southwell Minster by the chapter house door. The Gothic capital avoids frontality and surface quality and is often set diagonally, in correspondence with the vault rib aloft; crockets or foliage projections at the corners stress this diagonality.

The same close association with the architecture, naturalism and diagonality are to be enjoyed in the figure sculpture. There are three features that emphasize its link with the architecture; the small pedestals on which so many of the characters stand, the little canopies above them that define their allotted space and the niches within which they are framed. Photographs of figures that omit their setting obscure the upward movement (from pedestal through the slightly elongated forms via the pointed arches towards the vault) that enables them to be harmonized with the vertical rhythm of the building. The statues, in other words, while having something of classical naturalism, are not free in space (although they seem to invade it and project into it). Their innermost surface is not parallel with their outer one; the figures turn and diagonality, already apparent throughout the building, is to be found here likewise.

The separate identity of the figures is only relative, since they are formally dependent upon their architectural background in

*Southwell Minster,
chapter house, capital*

accordance with the principle of division. Even when they people the screen-like façades of English cathedrals in imposing rows, they never become detached from their settings since they represent those who dwell in the heavenly Jerusalem of which the earthly church is intended to be a copy and embodiment. Certainly delight in Gothic architecture derives not a little from the appreciation of these magnificent works of sculpture that are so wedded to the buildings that they inhabit.

THE EXTERIOR

With its profusion of figures, crockets, and so on, the exterior of a Gothic church is very much a sculptural object and therefore, like the classical temple, it is mass-positive, or rather structure-positive. Although there is enjoyment in dwelling upon the main details, the unity of each masterpiece involves their subordination to the edifice as a whole.

Everything strains upwards: pointed arches penetrate gables; buttresses rise in steps; pinnacles act as direction pointers towards the sky; flying buttresses seem to press inwards to support the clerestory walls and mount as they do so. Indeed the baldachin principle appears reversed; instead of there being a downwards flow, as in Byzantine churches, there is an ascent. The horizontal body of each building simply serves as a first step to the summit where all the energy is finally gathered into the towers which surge up into spires, the transition between them being masked and smoothed by further pinnacles. Delight arises partly from the recognition how everything combines to achieve this flamelike verticality, partly from following the lines and forces visually and partly from an imaginative journey that brings the body on to its toes reaching for the heavens.

The typical western façade is a kind of screen whose design often contradicts the interior disposition to consist of tiered but penetrating compartments, framed between towers, and only related to the nave and aisles by the treatment of the main and subsidiary portals. Each façade is a kind of frontispiece, often recalling the gates of a Roman city and designed to represent the threshold of heaven. The Gothic exterior is indeed sculpturesque like the classical temple but its message is different. It does not forbid entrance, except to all but evil spirits (hence the fearful gargoyles to scare them away) – instead its aggressively projecting porches summon all within.

PROPORTIONS

Within or without, every church or cathedral was designed with considerable attention to proportions. All ground plans and elevations were determined by strictly geometrical means using as modules certain regular polygons, such as the square (the façade of Notre Dame in Paris is composed of a sequence of four such figures), or the pentagon which in turn leads to the Golden Section – this was used at Chartres. Spanish architects preferred a sesquialter proportion (1½:1) and this accounts for the squatness of their designs. The proportions were not regarded as in any sense arbitrary; it was held that all ultimately derived from God, the great architect of the cosmos; hence to use these measurements to create order was to follow in the footsteps of their Creator and to reveal something of heaven. If the strong sense of symmetry be also noted, then the way the concern for unity and harmony was given expression can be readily understood.

MOVEMENT AND RHYTHM

The harmony, to which reference has just been made, derives not only from carefully calculated proportions but also from the use of rhythm, which, on the exterior of a church, is rapid and up-soaring, contributing to endless movement as the subdivisions interpenetrate and merge. This rhythm is mainly linear and it is visible again inside the buildings, especially in the vertical sections of the nave arcades. The eye is kept constantly in motion, being led up to the vault to admire the beauty of the patterning and then down again, via the shafts, to the base and clustered plinths. Because of the diagonality of the bases the bays flow into one another. The criss-cross ribs and arches contradict the previous inner concentration of the Romanesque vault and open it up on all sides to the adjacent volumes. Visually this is first apparent at roof level. The subsections of the vault melt together becoming elements in a continuous rhythm. So in figure 69 the severy marked a, which is a triangular subdivision of the cross vault (ABCD), joins severy b (a section of ABEF) to create an onward pointing diamond (the shaded figure (AGBH) that smooths the passage from one vault to another. Where a longitudinal ridge rib is also employed, this continuity is stressed and the interpenetration of bays is intensified. Movement along the nave is no longer a slow progression, lingering in each semi-independent bay, as in Romanesque churches, but a steady, uninterrupted march.

To appreciate this, the best point of vantage is not in the centre of the nave looking east – the appropriate place in a Romanesque structure – but at either side of the nave close to the north or south arcade. From there it is possible to contemplate the rhythm of the nave wall opposite and also, because of the diagonal turning of the piers, the zigzag movement in the eastward direction. Physical locomotion, not simply sight, is now a means of enjoyment. The bays are no longer experienced as separate entities, slowing advance, nor are the piers stopping points but slanting indicators of the way forward. Corresponding with this rhythmical movement is the quality of energy that Gothic undoubtedly possesses: it is strength in action not in repose. There is an exuberance that is perhaps most strikingly

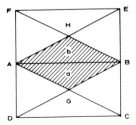

Fig. 69 Gothic vaulting

evident in the bursting of the vaulting shafts into the ribs of the groining.

PATHS AND PLACES

This embodiment of vigour and of rhythmical movement strongly suggests that a Gothic church belongs to the path category rather than to that of a place. Is this indeed so? As regards the vertical dimension, there can be no question: the different bays mount to the vaults, outlining paths that can be followed visually. In terms of horizontality, both parish churches and cathedrals still owe much to the original basilican plan with nave and aisles. Admittedly the edges required to define a path are less strong than in the early Christian and Romanesque buildings with their frontal arcades and their arches no more than holes in walls. Gothic arcades do not have this separating function, fencing off nave from aisles, because their piers are diagonal. Nevertheless the fact remains that the nave does constitute a main thoroughfare with the aisles as ancillary pathways. The continuity is ensured, first, by the sequence of bays, which form a spatial series drawing the visitor onwards; it is also maintained by the interpenetrating ribs of the vaults whose complex movement searches constantly for a place to rest. All this provides a directional quality that is reinforced by the longitudinal rib.

The goal towards which everything is leading cannot of course be foretold but it may be discovered by persevering in the direction indicated. The nave then is a way from expectancy to fulfilment; every Gothic church indeed corresponds in a sense with one of the greatest creations of the age, namely *The Divine Comedy* of Dante, who recounts how the poet is led ever onwards and upwards to the beatific vision.

Yet another characteristic of a path – very familiar by now – is end-from-end distinction and in this connection there is to be noted a difference between the parish church and many cathedrals. The former had gradually become a two-room edifice – the nave for the laity, and the sanctuary with altar a second room for the clergy, the separation of the two being marked by a chancel screen. The climax of such a disposition differs somewhat from that of a cathedral where a large choir has been inserted towards the east end to accommodate the clergy. This in effect is a space-frame within the overall space-trap of the building. In either case there is a noticeable contrast with the west end.

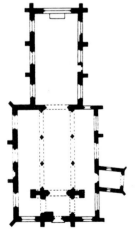

Fig. 70 Fenstanton, Huntingdonshire

This system of paths had already been elaborated within the Romanesque plan by the addition of ambulatories, transepts and side chapels. In Gothic buildings where division and not addition determines the design, these elements are no longer distinct and do not detract from the overall unity nor from the eastward drive – indeed transepts reinforce it, since they are frequently a cul-de-sac, united by interpenetration with the nave and being not so much a cross-street as a widening out of the main highway. In sum, these religious buildings were built for and were so well adapted to processions that they are best defined as processional ways, to such an extent that even when empty they produce the effect of one.

DIFFERENCES WITHIN GOTHIC

A path can be either horizontal or vertical and these two directions are often in antithesis and tension. The intensity of this contrast is in the relationship between the rectangle of the cross-section and the rectangle of the plan. This contrast becomes greater as one moves north within Europe. In Italy, for example, breadth is very noticeable compared with either height or length. In France height has the edge; in England length may be stressed. These variations within Gothic derive from national adaptations of the style, but they are also the outcome of some changes, particularly in decoration, which naturally occurred over the several centuries of the Gothic age. They are sufficiently noticeable to warrant attention, although it is to be stressed that they are all to be comprehended within Gothic.

Regional differences

Since the Gothic style may be said to have been launched by Abbot Suger at St-Denis in about 1140, it is fitting to begin with France itself. Luminosity, verticality and height are the most significant features, all three exemplified at Beauvais where the incredible altitude of 155 feet is attained. In the centre of the country and in the south churches were much wider up to the end of the thirteenth century. They were often of single span or of the hall type, i.e. with aisles of height equal to that of the nave, and they were sometimes buttressed by ranges of side chapels, as at Albi (1282).

Breadth, but now combined with lowness, is also to be found beyond the Alps in Italy and indeed quite a number of the features of northern Gothic that emphasize tallness have been avoided. On the exterior there are few spires, little in the way of pinnacles and only seven churches have flying buttresses. The interiors, such as that of the cathedral at Florence, have less stress on verticality with the lines of their roofs brought visually near to the ground by reducing the clerestory and thereby making the nave arcades relatively higher. Tie-rods, joining one side of an arch to the other to prevent their springing apart, also provide an interruption to any vertical accent. The brightness of the Italian sun favoured the use of small windows so that light is no longer a prime ingredient. Where narrow aisles and close-set shafts add to the appearance of loftiness and diminish any sense of breadth, in Italian Gothic there are spreading arches and the shafts are far apart so that it is the lateral spread of the building that impresses. Domes often appear, their circularity contrasting with the upward thrust of the pointed arch. Yet another

Florence, cathedral, nave

distinction between French and Italian Gothic is to be noted in the proportions of each bay. The French bay, as at Chartres, is rectangular with its shortest sides formed by the nave arcades; the Italian bay is generally square, as in SS. Giovanni e Paolo, Venice, *c.* 1250. The former creates a vertical accent; the latter a horizontal one.

All this does not mean that Gothic was simply a foreign importation into Italy, but it has to be acknowledged that it was never completely domiciled. There was still a hankering for the distant Roman past and for the more recent Romanesque era, so that the vigour of northern Gothic is tempered, Italian churches having a greater serenity, horizontality and spaciousness that makes delight in them less passionate and more contemplative. Spanish Gothic is somewhat similar, but it has a greater profusion of ornament which, however, as at Burgos, escapes vulgarity by the refinement of its detail. There is a gaiety about it that is constantly appealing. Many Spanish cathedrals are not as tall as their French models and they have a profusion of side chapels, for example Toledo, while others, such as León, are almost entirely French in character.

In Germany and those regions such as Czechoslovakia that were under its sway, Gothic enjoyed a prolonged vogue. Such structures as the nave of Cologne cathedral, begun in 1248, or the choir of the cathedral at Prague, begun in 1374, are among the finest examples of the style to be seen anywhere. It was however in the development of the hall church, of which there had been examples previously in the Romanesque period, that Germany excelled. This type was favoured throughout the era known as High Gothic, i.e. during the late fourteenth and early sixteenth centuries.

In the hall church there is less emphasis upon verticality and more upon the oneness of the space. Verticality is not so pronounced because the basilican profile, continued in Romanesque churches, with a sharp ascent from low aisles to the tall roof or vault of the nave, is replaced by one in which aisles and nave are approximately of equal height. Moreover the consequent suppression of the clerestory means that there is no band of bright light to draw the gaze upwards. Since each entire building now has a common source of illumination (through the windows in the exterior walls of the aisles), the unity of the design is the more readily grasped. Indeed there is no longer the slightest suggestion that the aisles are subordinate spaces, added to the nave in Romanesque fashion; being well lit, they are not edges but subdivisions of one volume. The primary boundary is then the outside wall within which the three subsections are on a par with one another. This means that the buildings correspond more nearly to the place category than to that of a path and this conclusion is further supported by the increased unity achieved through the suppression of ambulatories, transepts and side chapels. The interior has become one continuous fluid space with the piers as free-standing verticals – but verticals they remain, as in the Wiesenkirche at Soest, 1331, so that the upsoaring is not fully denied and this combines with that luminosity that is a feature of all northern Gothic.

In England, Gothic buildings are essentially pathlike and indeed differ most noticeably from their French prototypes in

Soest, Wiesenkirche, nave

that there is a greater concern for length, which necessarily decreases the impression of height. The plan is that of a long and continuous path not specifically aimed towards the chancel (if anything, the space beneath the central tower is a more important focus) and it proceeds through the building without coming to a halt. Transepts, especially when they are doubled, tend to be not stopping places but reinforcements of the longitudinal movement.

Stylistic differences

English Gothic is usually divided into three subperiods. In the thirteenth century it is designated Lancet, in the fourteenth Decorated, either Geometrical or Curvilinear, and in the fifteenth Perpendicular. These terms obviously derive from the forms of tracery and indeed the distinction between the three is principally one of ornament, which may modify but not profoundly alter the spirit of Gothic.

A lancet is a slender pointed arch – perhaps best exemplified in the Five Sisters window in York Minster. There is little carving and the shaping of the light is striking for its purity of line. When the window bars are combined in simple geometrical forms to create circles, quatrefoils, and so on, the linear pattern becomes more complex. Flowing tracery, making use of double curves, leads to the Curvilinear which favours ogee arches and pear-shaped mouldings. The effects correspond entirely with the nature of Gothic. The arches become pure texture and the shafts make the boundaries between bays so thin that the principle of division, together with diagonality, is further stressed.

The Perpendicular style, e.g. the nave of Winchester cathedral, has the vertical members of the tracery rising to cut without deflection the curve of the arch which is usually four-centred. It is often included within a square label or hood and this slightly modifies the previous verticality. When, as with the four-centred outline, the point of an arch is blunted and it is also contained within a frame, the upward thrust is less obvious. But this check on uplift is compensated for by the eye-catching quality of the vaulting, with the fan vault as the greatest achievement.

Equally eye-catching is the Flamboyant style favoured in France. Its name derives from the resemblance of its tracery to the leaping shape of flames. When these forms ceased to be a background element and became primary figures, as they did at Amiens in 1373–5, then the Flamboyant phase of French Gothic can be said to have begun. The figures consist of either one concave curve plus a double one (*mouchette* in French) or of

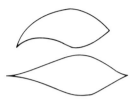

Fig. 71 Mouchette and soufflet

two double curves (*soufflet*). They spread from windows over the walls and balustrades to create a texture. At St-Riquier, near Abbeville, for example, these daggers have invaded doorways, arches and vaults. Since the glass is plain, daylight reveals them throughout the building and enables the visitor to appreciate how the very stone flickers with upsurging vitality. In this way the spirit of Gothic continued to find diversified expression.

Winchester, cathedral, nave arcade

9

THE RENAISSANCE
AND MANNERISM

For nearly 300 years the Gothic style dominated all countries in western Europe – from the foundation of the new St-Denis by Abbot Suger in 1140 to the designing of the Ospedale degli Innocenti, Florence, by Filippo Brunelleschi in 1419. Seeking to renew his architectural vision, Brunelleschi turned to the writings and ruins of ancient Rome and so promoted a renaissance of the former culture. This rebirth, which for its first 100 years was virtually confined to Italy, spreading from Florence through Tuscany and on to Rome, is usually divided into two periods: the Early and the High Renaissance. The first corresponds roughly with the fifteenth century (Quattrocento in Italian or 1400s), the second with the sixteenth century (Cinquecento).

THE EARLY RENAISSANCE

The contrasts between the buildings of the Quattrocento and those of the Middle Ages are immediately striking. Columns and pilasters have replaced clusters of shafts; round-headed arches are preferred to pointed ones; barrel vaults and coffered ceilings are introduced instead of rib vaults. The baldachin system has been largely discarded in favour of a wall architecture pierced with arches and having the antique orders applied to the surface. It is this last factor that emphasizes the extent to which imperial Rome, and not classical Greece, has provided the models.

THE TREATMENT OF THE ROMAN ARCHITECTURAL VOCABULARY

In terms of structure Roman architecture had depended upon walls, vaults and arches; in terms of ornament it employed the classical orders, their details serving as decorative adjuncts. Renaissance architecture is equally one of walls, with elements taken from the trabeated system applied to them, like a screen. But these elements – columns, capitals, and so on – are now made to tell a story about structure, i.e. features of the post-and-beam scheme have been adopted to articulate walls in a way that suggests they are structural, while in fact they are being used non-functionally. In Brunelleschi's Old Sacristy of S. Lorenzo (begun 1419) and his Pazzi Chapel (1430 onwards) the pilasters appear to have a supporting role although they are merely strips of stone that carry no weight. The result is an attractive pattern; it delights with a linear rhythm that animates the walls and gives them proportional values. The pilasters, entablature, and so on, are both compositionally ornamental and symbolically structural through their association with the classical post-and-beam system.

This attention to the functional meaning of the members, while not allowing their structural character to dominate, is particularly evident in the works of the second great Quattrocento master, namely Leone Battista Alberti (1404–72). Alberti created his buildings out of lines, planes and angles; walls

Florence, Pazzi Chapel, interior

provide the basic structure to such an extent that in his *De re aedificatoria* he can describe a row of columns as 'a wall opened and discontinued in several places'. His interest lies in what he calls design, i.e. visual effect, and not in structure. The appearance of a building is to be revealed by the former and not by the latter. The items of the Roman architectural vocabulary then become decorative expressions of structural concepts, ornament often suggesting a structural reality that does not in fact exist. This is most evident on a façade when it is divided by string courses that seem to indicate floor levels inside, and pilasters placed beneath them that suggest they are supporting these floors – in fact there are no such storeys and the pilasters are strips articulating the surface of a load-bearing wall, for example as at S. Maria Novella, Florence, by Alberti, begun in 1458.

The language of imperial Rome is uttered even more clearly by the façade of S. Andrea, Mantua, an Alberti design of 1470, two years before his death. It is in fact a great triumphal arch with a central opening flanked by two smaller ones. He thus revived an ancient symbolic form that speaks of heavenly authority. Inside too further triumphal arches, framing the side chapels, face the nave, and since both the west front and interior

Florence, S. Maria Novella, façade

Mantua, S. Andrea,
façade

arcades are designed to the same scale, the entire church is a
three-dimensional extension of the triumphal arch concept.

None of this should be taken to mean that Renaissance buildings were mere copies of Roman prototypes. The ancient orders
were treated with a certain casualness: Doric was exceptional;
Ionic rare, but more or less accurate when adopted; Corinthian
was developed in numerous ways. Brunelleschi, for instance,
produced an eight-voluted Corinthianesque capital; the Composite was highly favoured and the Tuscan was also employed.
The classical view that each of the orders is a complete system
and should entirely govern all the details employed had of
course not been followed by the Romans nor was it at the time
of the Renaissance. Brunelleschi used fluted pilasters to frame

corners; he placed roundels in spandrels, had shallow domes in the bays of loggia, and flat ceilings in his interiors. Alberti, on the other hand, was more concerned to design in strict accord with the practices of ancient Rome where, he believed, architecture, after reaching its first maturity in Greece, had attained its final perfection. However Vitruvius, upon whom he much relied and whose work he made widely familiar by incorporating many of his ideas into his own ten books on architecture, was sufficiently ambiguous to permit freedom of interpretation and to prevent slavish imitation.

PROPORTION AND PERSPECTIVE – PEACE AND SERENITY

From Vitruvius the importance of proportion was learned and this led Alberti to define beauty in his treatise as a 'harmony of all the parts, in whatever subject it appears, fitted together with such proportion and connection, that nothing could be added, diminished or altered, but for the worse'. Proportion was understood to be determined by numbers and therefore to be mathematically founded; hence the architect started from a module which he then mutliplied to produce the desired plan. Each part of a building was integrated into one and the same system of mathematical ratios and there were uniform proportions throughout. Every church designed in this way is a kind of mathematical mesh, a transparent cage of harmonious relationships. These proportions were used to develop both the plan and the elevation. S. Spirito is a foremost example of the first and the façade of S. Maria Novella of the second.

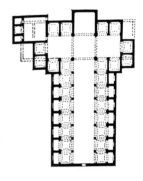

Fig. 72 Florence, S. Spirito

Brunelleschi's plan for S. Spirito, Florence, was approved in 1434. It was not completed until after his death, but, while modifications were introduced, it remains a masterpiece by any reckoning. The primary module is a square repeated again and again to create the aisles, which not only flank the nave but run round the transepts and the choir. Each transept is made up of four such squares as are the crossing and the chancel. The nave is two squares wide and adds up to four times four of the modules. The aisle bays are half the height of the nave bays and the arcade height is the same as the clerestory height.

Before commenting on the effect of these proportions, there is the Alberti façade to consider. The lower part of this, up to the base of the scrolls, suggests a rectangle but in fact it consists of two large squares, one on either side of a vertical line that runs up the centre of the door to the apex of the pediment. These two squares are each divisible into four smaller squares, making

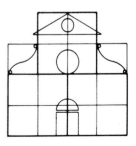

Fig. 73 Florence, S. Maria Novella, façade

eight in all. The upper storey fits into a third large square, which can also be divided into four smaller ones of the same dimensions as those in the lower section. Each scroll is contained in a similar small square. The height of the building is equal to its width and so a very large square embraces the entire façade.

Since the central concern of the designs is the embodiment of ideal proportions, both façade and interior can be regarded as attempts to present images of perfection at rest within themselves. Each whole is ordered further both by repetition of the primary module and by recourse to axial symmetry: the result is undeniably harmonious. The unexpected is ruled out; there is nothing uneasy or agitated and a feeling of peace predominates. There is a sense of equipoise that conveys authority, dignity and tranquillity; all is formal, coherent and lucid. To enter S. Spirito or S. Lorenzo is, within a few moments, to grasp the internal

Florence, S. Spirito, nave

disposition. The interrelationship of the parts is quickly perceived, since the parts themselves are well defined, being composed of such elementary forms as squares and circles. The
consequence is that the building does not take possession of the
observer, but the observer, by appreciating the fitting together
and connection (to use Alberti's terms), possesses the building.
There is no longer the propulsion of the Early Christian drive to
the altar, nor the dripping cascade of Byzantine space, the slow
succession of Romanesque bays, the dizzy heights of the Gothic
style. In a Renaissance church one feels at ease because man is
the measure of it all. There is the recognition of serene equilibrium: to enjoy this is to penetrate to the heart of Renaissance
ecclesiastical architecture where economy, precision and stillness are so effectively combined. While a Gothic church may stir
the soul, a Renaissance one confers quietness of mind. Believing
that the divine harmony is present throughout all creation, the
architects strove to make it visible.

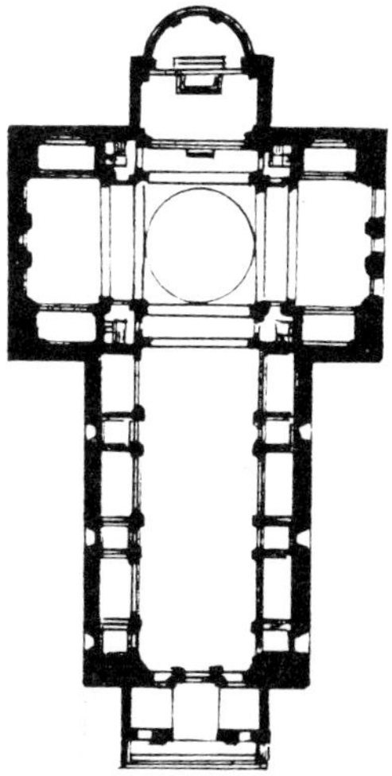

Fig. 74 Mantua, S. Andrea

This latter end was also served by linear perspective which
Brunelleschi virtually invented to replace the partial perspective
of preceding ages. He discovered a method of geometric construction by which it is possible to produce an accurate render-
ing of a system of objects as it appears to the eye and to present
all receding lines as converging to one vanishing point. A receding
barrel vault, as in Alberti's S. Andrea, Mantua, is one way of
embodying this perspective in architecture, and Brunelleschi too
used perspective planning to determine the total visual effect of
his buildings, which is usually to be grasped from a central
viewing point.

COLOUR AND LIGHT

The interest in sweeping, uninterrupted sight lines is complementary to the linear pattern drawn on the walls and consisting
of elements adopted from the trabeated system. This method of
decoration eliminates large expanses of plain surface suitable
for frescoes and so colour tends to be concentrated in the altar
paintings. Indeed the last 30 years of the Quattrocento are the
golden age of these works in Italy. Always subordinate to the
architecture, they nevertheless provide a focus. Elsewhere in the
churches colour is subdued; Brunelleschi, for example, favoured
a grey Florentine stone to pick out the supposed structural
features. Inlay was popular; some relief carving was introduced,
mainly localized in niches and medallions. Stained-glass windows were not suitable for such interiors since a neutral light is
needed to reveal all the elements impartially.

THE PRINCIPLE OF COMPOSITION: ADDITION

This uniform illumination is of course demanded by additive spatial structures. The identical compartments that have been juxtaposed to produce the aisles and nave of S. Spirito require similar lighting. Indeed every part of a Renaissance church appears as an easily recognizable and semi-independent form. Nothing is concealed – each section is clearly defined and stated in all its purity. Stone frameworks delineate crisply the geometrical shapes of the several elements. In the Pazzi Chapel, the circle of the dome, the borders of the pendentives, the edges of the arches and the framing of the panels are all precisely indicated – each entity seems separate and complete. Barrel vaults and coffered ceilings are self-contained and do not grow out of the walls – they are added to them.

The possibility of disunity inherent in such a system is prevented in numerous ways. Proportion of course has a part to play here. Unity is also undeniably achieved through cumulative addition: there is a lucid succession of equal compartments, each closed within itself, while the parts are tied together by repetition and continuity. Greater and lesser sectors are linked so that the smaller prepares for the larger by prefiguring the shape of the whole (see S. Spirito again, where the aisle-bays are multiplied to create naves, crossing, transepts and choir). A central axis also performs a unifying role and the use of bilateral symmetry establishes regularity and order – twin qualities favoured throughout the Renaissance, whether Early or High.

FAÇADES

Unity through addition is evident not only inside churches but also outside. A façade is of course simply the end of a building of which it can be treated as a filled-in cross-section. S. Maria dei Miracoli, Venice, designed by Pietro Lombardo (1481–9), is of this kind, its façade corresponding exactly with its interior. This church is an aisleless nave under a single barrel vault that terminates abruptly at the façade which is decorated with pilasters, architrave, arches, and so on to produce a pleasing pattern that relates it to the exterior space. The Roman vocabulary has in this way been attached to the front wall and the result is a regular succession of horizontal bays at two levels. This is known as a panel façade; Alberti's S. Maria Novella belongs to the same category, but here the continuity between within and without is more complex because its nave is flanked by aisles with lower roofs beneath the clerestory. This presents the problem of how to connect the termination of the nave with the more fragmentary ends of the aisles. Alberti's highly successful solution – much copied later – was to insert graceful scrolls to effect a smooth transition.

Alberti was also responsible for a second type of church front, namely the portico façade. For S. Andrea he not only used a triumphal arch but he combined it with a temple façade. This latter, consisting of four great pilasters apparently bearing a pediment, proclaims the view of the Renaissance architects that their churches are the modern equivalents of Roman temples. This was a very personal solution and it was not until the High Renaissance that a really viable alternative was to be devised.

Delight before these Early Renaissance façades lies in appreciating the way the axes of openings are vertically aligned, the clear-cut closure by emphatic cornices, the harmonious relations of the individual areas that, because of careful attention to proportions, never seem to have been placed haphazardly. The columnar series and the wall articulation combine into a fascinating pattern that demands quiet contemplation.

SURFACE-POSITIVE BUILDINGS

The panel façade is obviously less plastic than the portico type, and indeed its planar character more closely corresponds with the architectural vision of the Early Renaissance. Brunelleschi, in his initial works such as S. Lorenzo, designed in tiers of flat planes; his buildings are therefore two-dimensional in the sense that the stress is upon patterned walls rather than upon space-forming walls. While the basis of his works is geometry, it is not solid geometry. He is interested in the circle rather than the cylinder, in the square and not the cube. The Pazzi Chapel is then an examaple of pictorial space that has been created by surfaces alone; it is not a shaped volume. It is true that later, for example in S. Spirito, Brunelleschi began to conceive forms that are more sculptural, but in this he was anticipating the High Renaissance, whereas in the Early Renaissance surface-positive buildings were the norm.

Nevertheless walls do define volumes, but since these have been created in terms of stable proportions, they are fixed and have definite limits. There is no sensation of a beyond, of expanding energy bursting through confines – all is controlled, all is homogeneous, with churches static and self-sufficient in their tranquillity.

CENTRALIZATION

Inside these churches there is no great incentive to physical movement – delight is mainly visual and intellectual. This lack of propulsion is in part the outcome of Renaissance humanism and in part of a preference for centralized designs.

The Renaissance humanists, who were not atheists, believed that it was proper to make churches to human scale because man is in the image of God. They were concerned to create an architecture in which man can move with naturalness; hence the change from the dominating verticality of Gothic to horizontality, from arches pointing upwards to round-headed ones that lead the gaze gently onwards. The centralized plan is congruous with this outlook; within it man is the measure of all; he can stand at the centre of perfection and fully understand the environment that surrounds him.

The architects also favoured centralization because they believed – often incorrectly – that many circular buildings surviving from Roman times had been temples and also because they held the circle to be the ideal shape. According to Alberti, 'it is manifest that nature delights principally in round figures, since we find that most things which are generated, made or directed by nature are round'. In S. Sebastiano, Mantua, begun in 1460, Alberti produced a completely centralized design. It is a Greek cross formed of an entrance portico and a central domed square from which extend three apses.

Nevertheless despite the appeal of the 'perfect' shape, a completely centralized church was recognized as having some inconveniences. It is difficult to span a large area without intermediate supports; it is not easy for such a plan to be put into perspective; provision for processions is a problem as well as the siting of altar and congregation. However liturgical suitability was not at the centre of debate about such a plan; this turned on the question whether the altar should be placed in the middle or at the periphery. In favour of the latter it was argued that the altar should be as far away as possible from the entrance to demonstrate God's infinite distance; for the former it was contended that the centre is one and absolute, like God himself, and, being the point where all the building lines converge, best affirms the divine omnipresence. However the ecclesiastical authorities tended to favour modified central plans: the result can be envisaged as either an Early Christian basilica having nave and aisles but with a centralized portion at the east end replacing the simple apse, or as a centralized building enshrining the altar with one arm extended. It is the second of these that best

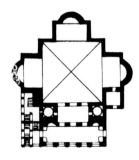

Fig. 75 Mantua, S. Sebastiano

characterizes Brunelleschi's S. Spirito and Alberti's S. Andrea, which are elongated central buildings rather than longitudinal naves with centralized spaces added.

MOVEMENT AND RHYTHM IN ELONGATED CENTRAL
BUILDINGS: PATHS AND PLACES

If one enters this new type of Renaissance church at the west end, the nave stretches forward into the distance but there is little encouragement to proceed along it. The roof, which is either a flat ceiling or a continuous barrel vault, is in no way sectionalized (there are no true bays) and so the nave becomes a single self-contained hall. Gothic diagonality has gone; the columns face one another across the nave and do not incite to movement; they are like a row of soldiers standing motionless and to attention. The observer may remain still and contemplate, helped thereto by the tranquil austerity of the building; or he may choose to advance but if so it will be at a gentle pace and a slow rhythm. It cannot be denied that the nave is a path, with well-defined edges, continuity, and so on, but at the end of it there is a centralized space that immediately brings physical progression to a halt. This is a point of rest and the visitor finds himself in a place: it is concentrated in form, readily comprehensible in shape, limited in size, and is a focus for gathering.

In this combined longitudinal and centralized plan, there is then minimal movement along its axis as far as the middle of the crossing. This is a hub from which radial arms – choir and transepts – branch off, but these are not extensive. At this centre, calmness and reassurance are experienced. What has taken place is that a spatial system composed of a series (nave colonnades and aisles) has been added to another spatial system composed of a group (crossing, transepts, choir). Obviously either one or the other can prevail. A series is supreme if the flow of movement is powerful enough to carry through the group; to extend the choir or to shorten the transepts would have given the longitudinal movement precedence over the group. However in the churches of the Early and High Renaissance the group is the determining factor – advance comes to a halt in a place where harmonious peace is the dominant sensation.

THE HIGH RENAISSANCE

The preceding introduction to the Early Renaissance has been illustrated by very few buildings simply because it did not see the erection of many outstanding churches. Moreover reference has been made to particular individuals and this is a change from previous chapters. Although some masons and builders are known from the Middle Ages, it was only with the dawn of the Renaissance that individual architects, responsible for more or less every detail of a design, came into their own. Yet while masters such as Brunelleschi and Alberti have their own characteristics, their works are not so idiosyncratic that they cannot serve as examples of the style of the period as a whole. The same is true of the High Renaissance which immediately introduces yet another outstanding individual – Donato Bramante (1444–1514).

BRAMANTE AND HARMONIOUS PLASTICITY

The first great monument of the High Renaissance is usually said to be the Tempietto of S. Pietro in Montorio, Rome, which Bramante began to build in 1502. Indeed this memorial chapel, on the spot where Peter had been martyred, shows the one fundamental difference between the Early and the High Renaissance in that it is plastic rather than planar. Prior to Bramante churches seem to be composed of planes. In the Tempietto however the third dimension is realized with circles and rectangles being now replaced by cylinders and cubes – articulation is no longer by lines but by forms. Bramante had begun to move in this direction as early as 1482 when he began the sacristy of S. Maria Presso Satiro, Milan. In plan this is a cross within a circle and in elevation a cylinder surmounted by four gables at right angles to form a cross above which is an octagonal drum crowned by a circular lantern. Plasticity is very evident and there is delight in admiring the lucidity of the forms and the way they have been added together to create a unity.

The building's simplicity together with the extremely clear solids, the formal unity and the regulated proportionality – characteristics of High Renaissance designs in general – are all present in the Tempietto. This is a combination of concentric circles in the plan with concentric cylinders in the elevation. The peristyle and cella are the two cylinders, and since the diameter of the former is equal to the height of the latter (up to but not including the dome), proportionality is very evident. However the intercolumniations are equal and give no hint of where the altar stands within the cella, while the inside is too small for a visitor to feel that the intention was to create an interior volume. Indeed this particular building is mass-positive, like a classical

Rome, Tempietto of S. Pietro in Montorio, exterior

Greek temple, but the exterior was also to be an element in spatial planning since it was to be set in a complex cloistered area. There is continuity also with certain Early Renaissance qualities: an interest in symmetry and in the use of purely architectural elements for articulation, with addition as the principle of composition and centralization dominant. The Tempietto is an expression of intellectual concerns and not of feeling or aspiration. It appeals to the trained eye, familiar with the Roman architectural language, and able to appreciate the formal logic and proportional qualities of the whole. This care for accurate detail, first noticeable in Alberti, led the men of the High Renaissance to lay great stress on the correspondence of their works with their prototypes. So Sebastiano Serlio (1475–1554), whose book on architecture was immensely influential, adapted to churches the Vitruvian characterization of the different orders in relation to the members of the Olympian pantheon. According to Serlio, Doric should be used for churches dedicated to Christ, Peter, Paul and the most virile saints, Ionic for gentler male saints and more matronly females and Corinthian for maidens.

Six years after the Tempietto was initiated, the foundations were laid of S. Maria della Consolazione at Todi. Designed probably by Cola da Caprarola, it further exemplifies some of the leading features of Bramante's architectural vision. It is a centralized building, and being quatrefoil, is the result of juxtaposing and so adding four separate and distinct apses to a square; it is harmoniously plastic on the exterior but inside there is a feeling for space which is treated as a kind of substance to be structured by the solid geometry. By their central planning both Tempietto and S. Maria suggest places rather than paths.

The dome of S. Maria was not in fact completed until 1606 and by this late date the High Renaissance was on the wane; indeed it had already been superceded in the eyes of some architects by Mannerism, which began as early as 1520. Yet the High Renaissance style continued side by side with the new movement and may be said to have reached its climax in the works of Palladio.

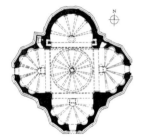

Fig. 76 Todi,
S. Maria della
Consolazione

PALLADIO AND THE CLIMAX OF THE HIGH RENAISSANCE

Andrea Palladio (1508–80) is probably best known for his villas, but two of his churches are quite outstanding, namely S. Giorgio Maggiore and Il Redentore, the first begun in 1566 and the second ten years later. Both are striking features on the skyline of Venice and their façades are particularly noticeable for the satisfying way they have solved the problems presented by each and every church front. A façade is both a terminal wall, with holes for doors and windows, and also part of a street or square. This latter public function demands a fine design and obviously this could be realized both structurally and functionally in complete separation from the interior of the building. The first problem then is how can a west end be made to look as if it belongs both to the church behind and to the space in front? The second is how to give it a spatial character and not just the appearance of a flat plane divided by horizontal and vertical strips. The third is how to unify in the design a tall nave and lower aisles when committed to the employment of classical orders with their relatively fixed proportions.

The Palladian solution, which was to be copied for 250 years, was to combine two classical temple fronts into one and by this expedient overcome all three difficulties. The façade of S. Giorgio consists of a central pediment on four tall columns, each borne on a pedestal; this section, which is a complete temple front in itself, corresponds with the nave in terms of width and height and of a similar large order. Behind this middle portion there is a second temple front, the apex of its triangular pediment not visible, but its baseline and angles carried on four small pilasters, two at each end; here the way is prepared for the aisles which have similar dimensions and the same type of pilasters resting on the ground. A like correspondence of outside and inside is manifested by Il Redentore, although here three pediments have been combined. At the same time both façades are intimately associated with the spaces in front of them, leading to their immediate small forecourts and to the vistas across the lagoon. S. Giorgio has to be approached by water,

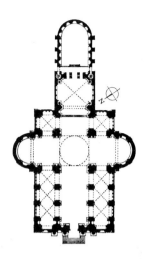

Fig. 77 Venice, S. Giorgio Maggiore

Venice, S. Giorgio Maggiore, façade

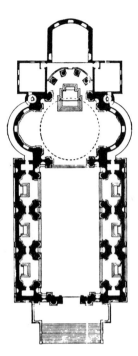

Fig. 78 Venice,
Il Redentore

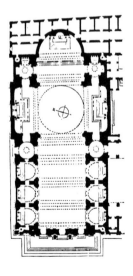

Fig. 79 Rome, Il Gesù

and the landing is directly by the entrance; Il Redentore was designed for an annual procession that crossed to it over a causeway of barges placed at right angles to the façade – in each case then the proper point from which to enjoy the façade is in the centre since here its axiality and symmetry are most evident and the unity of its design really striking.

Moving now inside and considering first S. Giorgio, it is evident from the plan (see figure 77) that it consists of four parts: a rectangular nave, a transept domed at its centre, a mainly square sanctuary and beyond that, terminating in an apse, the monastic choir. This is neither a centralized building nor one in which a longitudinal nave has been juxtaposed against a centralized crossing. It has a dominant axis in the longitudinal direction around which the design is completely symmetrical. The parts, though distinct, are fully united. The nave reaches an initial climax beneath the dome of the crossing; the semicircular ends of the transept embrace the visitor and draw him onwards to the altar which is backed by pillars revealing the choir beyond and this enables the whole to be integrated visually.

The plan of Il Redentore (see figure 78) is different and is more nearly akin to that of Il Gesù in Rome (figure 79) designed by Vignola in 1570. In both these buildings there are no longer distinct aisles; they have been fused with the side chapels that are then joined by open passages. The wings of the transepts scarcely project beyond the nave; the crossing piers are drawn into the mass of the walls and the crossing itself tends to merge with the altar area. The principle of composition is no longer addition but division, the parts becoming so many subsections. So the nave in Il Redentore cannot be experienced as an independent box because of the visual sequence provided by the vista towards the altar and through the columns behind it. However the interior of S. Giorgio is also so integrated that it too breathes almost the same atmosphere as Il Redentore. No sculpture or painted ornament invades the surfaces of the walls, vaults or domes. Light penetrates into every corner through the many windows and is employed subtly to differentiate the volumes a little so that in the Redentore the nave is lit diffusely, the tribune amply and the choir brilliantly.

Sophisticated purity of design reigns throughout. There is equilibrium to be enjoyed and the proportional relations have been extended into the third dimension so that plan and elevation are in absolute harmony. There is mathematical clarity and a sense of order. Nothing seems out of place; the beauty is so austere, so perfect, that it almost demands a tiptoe approach

Venice, Il Redentore, interior

as if a too hurried passage might disturb the tranquillity. The articulation of the walls, the details of the capitals, cannot be faulted – it is not surprising that Palladio earned and has preserved a reputation as an outstanding master always in complete control of all that he created.

MANNERISM

While majestic calm prevails in the Palladian churches, restlessness is characteristic of those built under the influence of Mannerism. This movement is usually regarded as beginning *c.* 1520 and continuing to the end of the century; consequently it is necessary to turn back in time from the later career of Palladio and to seek the origins of Mannerism in the genius of Michelangelo (1475–1564).

MICHELANGELO: THE INDIVIDUAL GENIUS

Palladio himself was no slave to the past and his aim was to surpass it. Michelangelo equally, while using the Roman vocabulary, was always its master, prepared to break the canons the better to express his artistic vision. Much of our delight in his works is therefore intellectual in the sense that it derives from the recognition of how the architectural elements have been used contrary to the norms of antiquity. Michelangelo affirmed the freedom of the artist as one who does not design simply according to rules. He retained classicism's outward appurtenances but replaced repose and balance with a tense and dissonant unity. This is nowhere more evident than at Florence in the Medici Chapel (1523–9) and in the vestibule to the Laurentian Library (begun 1524).

Unlike High Renaissance design, which is clear and simple, the details of the wall articulation of the Medici Chapel are extremely complex and indeed ambiguous. In each interior corner there is a door beneath a niche and these two are combined in a single unit. They share a horizontal member that serves as both the base of the niche and the lintel of the door. Beneath this member there are brackets which may be read as either supports for or pendents from it. At the top a segmental pediment appears too large for the space; it is double at the summit but its bottom is cut away. The supporting pilasters have no known capital and there are curious sunken panels in their faces. A block at its lower extremity seems to be a support for a missing piece of sculpture but the niche is too shallow for such an item and contains a carved patera and swag. This is relief architecture applied to plane surfaces, and it provides constant surprises.

To experience the chapel as a whole the visitor should stand behind the altar and face across it. On his right is a statue of Lorenzo above reclining figures of Dawn and Twilight; on his left Giuliano above Day and Night. There were to have been further figures at ground level to produce triangular compositions with the deceased at each apex. Their faces are turned away from the altar towards the far wall so directing attention to the Madonna and Child and unifying the space. Lorenzo and Giuliano each occupies a middle niche of three; the flanking ones have segmental pediments, but negative emphasis is given to the centre by framing it with pairs of pilasters while omitting the pediment.

Within this chapel movement is discouraged. The articulated walls combine with the sculpture as the dominant aesthetic

elements which are to be regarded steadily without the need for *Florence, Medici Chapel*
motion. Addition is the principle of design, as it is in the
Laurentian Library: every element is a separate entity. Nevertheless unity has been achieved through conflict and tension.
This is not the tranquillity of the Pazzi Chapel – astonishment,
even shock, accompany the recognition of what Michelangelo
has done and has achieved with the elements at his disposal.

To analyse the Laurentian Library is also to experience some
surprise, but here there is less of relief and more of kinetic
architecture, i.e. that which promotes motion. Indeed the very
walls seem to be on the move and the staircase draws one up and
onward (here Michelangelo was anticipating Baroque). Indeed
it is very difficult to allot him to a pigeonhole. While it has been
pointed out that some designs were achieved by addition, the
Cappella Sforza, in S. Maria Maggiore in Rome, is the result of
division; each space would be incomplete on its own and has
meaning only as a subdivision of a whole. Nevertheless sufficient of the leading characteristics of Mannerism are present in his
work for him to be included under this general heading.

GENERAL CHARACTERISTICS OF MANNERISM

The features of Mannerism mentioned so far, which involve a contrast with the style of the High Renaissance, are the substitution of tension and dissonance for repose and balance, of ambiguity for clarity and of complexity for simplicity. Negative rather than positive emphases are used and the initial effect is intended to be one of shock. However these contrasts are evidence not so much of a reaction to classic rigidity as of the individual artist's determination to treat the rules lightly in a creative urge to be master of his design. Because Mannerism applies to the works of gifted individuals, it was never really a universal style. Moreover it was an art for and by an elite that sought to go beyond tradition and was not afraid of a union of extremes. This combination of conflicting tendencies applies not only to structure but even to functions, for example Philip II's Escorial (1563–86) provides for monastic life, secular dignity, a royal household and mausoleum and the encouragement of learning. There is a virtuosity and strangeness about

Mantua, Palazzo del Te, courtyard

Mannerism and a defiance of the normal and the expected. All this is remarkably exemplified in a secular building: the Palazzo del Te in Mantua.

Built between 1526 and 1534 by Giulio Romano, the Palazzo at first sight appears to be a classical villa, but observation soon reveals that there is a constant rejection of antique norms and an adoption of a series of deliberate contrasts. In the inner court-yard no one side matches another. A giant order, first used by Michelangelo, embraces both the ground floor and the attic, unlike Hellenistic and Roman arrangements which had one order per storey. Pieces of the architrave which the columns support have slipped downwards and so have some triglyphs, thus creating an air of instability. The pediments have no base-lines. The several forms have no defined order and framing elements are missing. There are strong contrasts between rusti-cated stone and dressed surfaces, between the upward-thrusting inverted V of the pediments and the collapsing triglyphs above. Keystones have become exaggerated in size. The serenity of a Bramante has given way to a deliberate malaise which when recognized gives to the spectator who knows the classical orders a thrill of delighted horror at such capriciousness.

CHURCHES

Because of this penchant for the unusual, not many churches were commissioned in the Mannerist style. Really representa-tive buildings such as Il Gesù in Rome or Il Redentore in Venice have some Mannerist elements but are by no means Mannerist in overall conception. However Mantua has a Mannerist cath-edral and this also is by Romano (1545). In plan it has a nave and six aisles. An immediate contrast is to be noted in the ceilings: the nave and the outer aisles have flat coffered wooden ones, while the inner aisles have barrel vaults; the chapels are alternatively domed and barrel-vaulted. So there is a dynamic interplay of contrasting elements. Indeed side views from the aisles disclose the intention of the design more than the usual position on the axis of the nave. It can then be appreciated that there is no clear overall prospect but a juxtaposition of different spatial compartments. Space is disordered; it is enclosed in tunnel-like vistas with a preference for variety rather than unity. The clerestory is lighted by oblong windows alternating with pointed niches (aedicules) containing high reliefs; the windows are crowned with gabled pediments and the niches with arched ones – yet another inescapable contrast. Virtuosity is there to be admired.

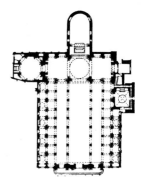

Fig. 80 Mantua, cathedral

Mantua, cathedral, nave   The passion for dynamic conflict also led to the oval plan being adopted for churches. First used by Vignola for S. Andrea in Via Flaminia, Rome (1550–5), the oval embodies a tension between the axes of length and breadth in contrast to the inherently restful shape of a circle. While a basilica is exclusively a monodirectional room and a centralized building is omnidirectional, the elliptical plan of the later sixteenth century is both central and directional and so suggests ambiguity.

THE SISTINE CHAPEL

Most Mannerist architects were primarily interested in other fields, such as sculpture and painting, and this explains the renewed interest in murals which had been little valued in the Early and High Renaissance. Certainly the Sistine Chapel exemplifies this concern for decoration, as well as other Mannerist features. Built in 1473–81, the chapel is famous mainly for the Michelangelo frescoes on the ceiling (1508–12) and on the end wall (1534–41). The series from Genesis has its own complex architectural framework at odds with the details of the building. The Last Judgement declares something much more dramatic and powerful than can be absorbed by the relatively small volume. It contradicts too the previous convention of murals that sought harmony between the solidity of the architecture and the space simulated by the paintings; here is a vast and violent scene within small dimensions. So while the chapel was not in origin Mannerist, Michelangelo has made it so by his titanic designs – previous rules are transcended and visual standards have been smashed by one whose genius not only falls within the scope of Mannerism but burst even the confines of that to anticipate a whole new epoch – that of the Baroque.

10

BAROQUE
AND ROCOCO

BAROQUE

By the end of the Cinquecento the Counter Reformation was in
full spate. The sessions of the Council of Trent were ended and
Loyola's shock troops – the Jesuits – had enabled the Roman
Catholic Church to move over from defence against the forces
of Protestantism to attack. A style appropriate to this situation
has to embody exultant vigour and overflowing strength; it
needs designs in the grand manner, imposing and massive in
size. Each building has to be a celebration of power, expressing
the self-assurance and authority of the Church as the vice-
gerent of God. Brilliance and exuberance, excitation and not
contemplation – these are what it has to display. It should aim
to stimulate religious experience, to incite to piety and devotion;
it should witness to the transcendent and so be concerned with
spiritual striving rather than with harmonious restfulness. It has
to instigate involvement by not simply demonstrating the truths
of religion but by actively persuading towards their acceptance.
Church façades should entice; church interiors should sweep
those who come inside off their feet by their splendour,
becoming no longer settings for a stately pageant but elements in
the action itself. Such a style was the Baroque, calculated to
delight the senses and kindle enthusiasm, to overthrow disbelief
and lead to rapture. A Baroque church is consequently like a
theatre but one in which every individual is assigned a role.
Deliberately created to impress the public in this way, Baroque
at its worst can be tawdry; it can be hysterical and even strident,
but it is always lively and never dull. To appreciate it an understanding is required of how these several aims were achieved.

CHURCH PLANS

The Counter Reformation emphasis upon teaching as a means to combat heresy meant that there was an ecclesiastical preference for longitudinal buildings with hall-like naves suitable for sermons. Indeed such a plan, suggesting a path, accords well with the aim of persuasion. There is a dominant direction, leading to a climax, and when the building is domed this impression is strengthened because the visitor is then drawn towards the light descending from above. This also explains why aisles are little favoured. Since they weaken the importance of the nave by repeating the same shape and direction, they now become merely sets of ancillary rooms and passages – Vignola's Gesù anticipated Baroque in this respect (see figure 79).

The centralized plan, on the other hand, suggests not so much a forward movement as a condition of contemplation; it creates a place and so is ideally suited to provide a setting for the adoration of the Sacrament. S. Ivo della Sapienza, Rome, 1643–8, is a superb example and also reveals the fertility of the Baroque creative imagination. The design by Francesco Borromini is a six-pointed star formed from two equilateral triangles. Its centre space is a regular hexagon that expands into three pairs of alternating bays: one type of bay is semicircular and the other follows the lines of the star but ends in a curved section that is convex inwards. The design is perfectly proportioned, symmetrical and balanced and at the same time is an ingenious representation of a bee (the Barberini family device), head, body and four wings corresponding to the six bays, and of the star of David, which is a symbol of wisdom.

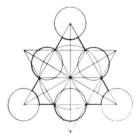

Fig. 81 Rome, S. Ivo della Sapienza

Also centralized, but using the typical Baroque oval, is Borromini's S. Carlo alle Quattro Fontane, Rome 1634–41. This is biaxial: there is an entrance bay and a main apse, each semicircular and facing one another on the longitudinal axis; at the ends of the shorter cross axis there are parts of flattened ovals enshrining two subsidiary altars. The walls undulate and are in fact four Ss, two connecting the high altar with the subsidiary ones and two running from the latter to the entrance. This is a reinterpretation of the centrally planned church in so far as, being a domed oval, it synthesizes centralization and extension. The oval fuses the embracing effect of the circle with the thrust of an axis directed towards the high altar; it binds and points; it unifies movement and concentration, linearity and radiation.

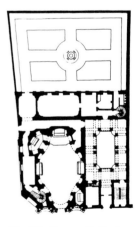

Fig. 82 Rome, S. Carlo alle Quattro Fontane

*Rome, S. Ivo della
Sapienza, interior*

MOVEMENT

Because an oval is a kind of dislocated though not misshapen
circle and is a form with both longitudinal and transverse axes,
it expresses dynamic tension. In a circle forces irradiate symmetrically in all directions and counterbalance one another, but
in an oval there is a directional tension along the greater axis
which provides a strong push forward so demanding movement –
this is one of the main characteristics of Baroque.

While the material nature of any building is opposed to
movement, architectural forms can suggest it: a column rises, a

Roman dome swells upwards and a Byzantine one cascades downwards. In a Baroque building everything is in motion. In contrast to Renaissance designs where each line looks like an edge and each volume a solid body, all boundaries are neutralized; there are no semi-independent parts with plastic value; instead there is a single totality around which the eyes constantly move. Spiral columns defy stability, appearing to twist and turn. Walls oscillate as convex and concave curves are contrasted. In S. Carlo, for example (see figure 82), the walls have become movement since they possess a wave-like surface. Even in such a centralized building as S. Ivo the effect is one of motion – the eye is carried around the entablature in a ceaseless manner, advancing from bay to bay, and yet the experience of this church is not simply visual; it can be felt with the whole body.

The passion for movement is discernible in even the smallest detail, such as the balusters or series of posts supporting rails. The Renaissance baluster, as designed by Bramante, was circular in cross-section and symmetrical around its midpoint. Michelangelo, in Mannerist vein, placed the bulge lower, thus combining symmetry with an appearance of greater stability. Borromini, in the cloister of S. Carlo, has balusters that are triangular in cross-section, with each side a concave arc, and he has furthermore alternated them so that the bulge comes now towards the top, now towards the bottom – the effect is a denial of stability and an affirmation of restless motion.

Baroque motion gives expression to the exultation and vigour demanded by the Church of the Counter Reformation. Overflowing strength, exuberance at play – for these no repose is required, except perhaps in the form of a final climax when all tension is resolved.

SPACE-POSITIVE BUILDINGS

Movement is also stimulated by the way space is handled. The Baroque architects did not conceive space as an abstract relationship between the plastic members but as the essential substance of a building that can be shaped and directed. This is achieved by means of the boundaries, which however remain always secondary. In other words the space has been so moulded that it has determined the form of the walls and piers, which are like seals that reflect the negative of a stamp. Consequently plans of Baroque churches are to be read in terms of the white areas and not of the lines.

It is of course impossible to recognize definite space without perceptible bounds, but simply to box in a volume is not to mould it in anything except a superficial manner. Consequently architects sought to enrich their spaces partly by an illusory negation of its bounds in order to direct attention to the infinity of God. The enclosing shell then is secondary: the end of the choir disappears in the golden gleam of the high altar; the dark chapels flanking the nave are hardly noticeable; the great painting on the ceiling seems to lead into the vastness of heaven itself.

This negation of limited space can be achieved in different ways as evidenced by three of the leading Baroque architects. Pietro da Cortona in his SS. Martina e Luca, Rome, 1650, concealed the walls behind columns, piers and pilasters, and broke up any remaining surfaces with doors and balconies. Borromini in S. Carlo fashioned the walls to suggest either that they are giving way to centrifugal pressure or that they are being compressed to bursting point. Bernini, in S. Andrea al Quirinale, Rome, 1658–70, achieved an effect of perplexity by the introduction of a screen of contrasting bright light between the comparatively dark volume of the nave and the luminous background provided by the apse. So Baroque church interiors, while defined, seem to have vanishing circumferences, giving the impression upon entry of spaciousness. There is a contrast between the limited volume and the apparent immensity. Space becomes perceptible because a desire is stimulated both to break its narrow confines and to traverse it in an imposed direction.

Indeed the visitor's progression through space has been carefully planned; the space flows through a dramatic sequence; there is movement in depth fostered by the recessional character of the design. Such movement requires a constant change of position, so that a static, frontal view is discouraged. Oblique sight lines are vital because the body of each building is never intended to settle down within a single frame. So while horizontality and verticality were the main directions in classical architecture, in Baroque, as in Gothic, the oblique is all important and leads on to a dramatic climax. Submerged in spatial experience, through physical advance, one is led to believe in the reality to which the church witnesses and to become involved in it. Bernini's S. Andrea is a remarkable example of this – its dramatically lighted interior is an episodic account of the martyrdom of the apostle which one is drawn to follow step by step. The main altarpiece, lit from a hidden source, depicts his crucifixion; above, on a cornice, St Andrew is being carried into heaven whence shafts of light descend. To delight in this is to appreciate how Bernini has used his art to turn the observer into

a participant who experiences the triumphant rapture of the resurrected saint. Such a church is a place for contemplation but it is also a path of pilgrimage. It is also an assemblage point for a community that is believed to embrace earth and heaven. The geometrical forms that have this embracing effect and so symbolize and express unity and community are, in plan, the circle and the oval, and, in elevation, the round arch and the dome. So, using these, Baroque churches were planned to lead worshippers to focus attention on the high altar and to experience a feeling of togetherness.

Rome, S. Andrea al Quirinale, interior

THE PRINCIPLE OF COMPOSITION: FUSION

Interior Baroque space is one single, overwhelming volume, within which there can be some differentiation, but not to such an extent that the unity of the whole is ever endangered. The space beneath the dome is an ampler version of the vaulted nave and the apse is meant to a be a narrower form of the same vault. The dome at the crossing in a longitudinal church is not the central dominant; it simply provides variation within the one composition. This means that, as previously noted, there is no resting place. Since everything interlocks, there are no semi-independent parts within or on which to dwell; everything is interdependent. It was natural therefore to favour barrel vaults that do not break up the unity of the nave – bays do not exist.

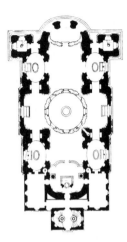

Fig. 83 Salzburg, Kollegienkirche

Each church interior is characterized by spatial integration. It is to be apprehended as a whole, since the parts have been welded together and merge with one another. Ceilings, for example, are neither lids, as in the basilica, nor the tops of ciboria, with walls no more than curtains, as in Gothic cathedrals – instead they have become fused with the walls into one complete space container. Elements are not independent but interdependent: columns, which are essentially round and free, are replaced by piers that can be regarded as aspects of a wall, and pilasters are preferred to half-columns. It is scarcely correct to speak any longer of transepts and aisles: the latter become a series of shallow chapels and the former often do not project beyond the side walls or, if they do, have their distinction reduced by being apsidal. In the Kollegienkirche at Salzburg, 1696–1707, by Fischer von Erlach, the transepts, dimly discernible in the light of a knowledge of the history of church plans, have become part of the progress from entrance to altar and so they belong to the nave; but, at the same time, the nave itself swells out momentarily into the transepts, embraces them, fuses with them, and continues its path to the east end. Interpenetration, whereby combining cells are clearly defined, gives way to fusion so that it is impossible to say where one unit ends and another begins.

One method of achieving this has been called pulsating juxtaposition. It is by no means easy to convey in words this impression of forms and spaces expanding and contracting. It operates when they are so mutually interdependent that they have a continual reciprocal effect, achieving their unity through their interacting relationship. Hence the vestibule of S. Maria dei Sette Dolori, Rome, designed by Borromini in 1642, can be described as a square that expands into the corners while its sides are contracting inwards. Delight in such a building is very much a matter of feeling rather than seeing, and is therefore not well represented by photographs.

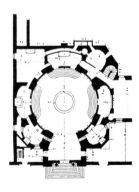

Fig. 84 Paris, Ste-Marie de la Visitation

The Church of the Visitation in Rue St Antoine, Paris, 1632–34, by the great French Baroque architect François Mansart, provides a further example of fusion and illustrates this method of composition. In plan it is round with five oval chapels, the three largest being one opposite the entrance and one on either side of it. These have quite evidently not been added to the main space; they are fused with it, integrated into a greater whole. The principle of composition is neither addition nor division but fusion.

DECORATION

The various features of Baroque already noted, such as movement, the negation of limited space and the quest for a unified vision through fusion, can all be promoted by means of the decorative arts. It is of course true that ornamentation is not absolutely essential to Baroque – Borromini, for example, used little colour and most of his interiors are painted white. Nevertheless nearly all Baroque churches are striking for their decorative effects, and indeed to some they are overdecorated. This however is a doubtful criticism: St Mark's, Venice, is as much decorated as any Baroque building, and it is impossible to distinguish between the churches of the Renaissance, of Mannerism, Baroque or Rococo on the basis of the amount of ornament. However decoration is more profuse than in classical buildings, but it is employed with a different intent, namely to create contrast and dynamic tensions. It also contributes to the sense of motion so dear to the Baroque spirit.

The visitor's gaze is not held captive by any isolated feature but flickers ever onward over the surface. There is no invitation to linger but a stimulation to the swift flight of the eye, possibly towards some distant climax. Each piece of sculpture is not to be regarded from one location; every aspect is an inseparable feature of a constantly changing form. From any point of observation planes lead beyond the given view and demand an endless change of position. The underlying structural pattern is often a screw or spiral, embodiments of movement.

Architecture, sculpture and painting are interdependent and mutually reinforce one another. Often it is impossible to be certain where one ends and another begins: paint simulates architectural members, while figures made of plaster (stucco) intrude into the space of the paintings. Columns can be fashioned as representations of Atlas, symbolizing a striving to endue architecture with the vitality of sculptural forms and to impart to the latter the significance of architectural members.

On the ceilings, panels with individual plaster frames are replaced by scenes that cover the entire area. These deny the church's enclosure from above and extend the earthly dimensions of the building into limitless realms of air and light. Immensity is thus created, while the message of the Church

Triumphant is proclaimed. In accordance with this programme Giovanni Battista Gaulli and his collaborators began work on the Gesù in 1668 and the result is that the roof appears to have been opened and the faithful look straight into the glories of heaven. The moulded frame is disregarded and this suggests that both stucco and painted beings are not confined to some ideal space beyond the surface but that they move in a sphere of their own, part of which is identical with the area below in which the spectators themselves are moving. There is an intermingling of the heavenly above, in which these lofty characters are in a lively relationship, and the earthly interior in which the worshippers find themselves. This is a means of promoting spiritual uplift through an appeal to sensual delight. All the vigour and self-assurance of the Church are there to the fore.

Rome, Il Gesù, ceiling of nave

Rome, S. Maria della Vittoria, sculpture of S. Teresa in the Cornaro Chapel

The propaganda function of each church is also served by the sculptures. However the effect of the figures now ceases to be restricted to the space they occupy; they impinge upon the surrounding volume in order to acquire their true being. In other words, the distinction between the space inside and the space outside the work of art is broken down. Figures obtrude into the spatial world of the observer and draw him into their activity. This is a rhetorical onslaught to involve the onlooker. In this provision of emotional stimulus to piety, Bernini was a key figure and his 'Ecstasy of S. Teresa', 1644–7, in the Cornaro Chapel of S. Maria della Vittoria, Rome, is an outstanding example. Here sculpture unites the physical space within which the worshipper stands with the metaphysical space of heaven – we become involved and learn to share in the saint's ecstasy. In the same church the high altar has a circular hole above it surrounded by clouds from which emanate shafts of glory: by this visual climax the declaration is made that heaven condescends to earth so that the Church may enjoy a foretaste of the age to come. Aesthetics is put at the service of spiritual experience.

LIGHT

Without question the decoration of a Baroque interior produces a theatrical effect. This is quite deliberate, since the aim is to make those who enter participators in the drama of salvation. This effect is heightened by the use of light. How this may be achieved has previously been noted in speaking of S. Andrea, but an even more conspicuous illustration is the east window of St Peter's. The 'Gloria', above the apostle's chair, is a gold oval which in bright sunlight overflows its bounds and spills out on to the surrounding sculptures. Here light has become almost a physical force with great visual impact, acting as a dramatic and unifying element.

Light then is handled by the architects not to give a uniform illumination, as during the Renaissance, but to provide accents. Nor are light and shade subservient to form, as in classical buildings; they are equal elements and appear to have a life of their own, by their contrasts serving as a further means to emphasize movement; light glides over the surface and plays with it.

FAÇADES

All the characteristics of the Baroque style noted previously are exemplified in the church façades, which have to be considered in two ways: first, in relation to outside space and, second, in themselves since they were often designed independently of the interior.

Baroque churches were seldom isolated like classical temples. In a rural setting, they were placed at focal points in the landscape, while in towns they were planned in relation to the urban space, which in its turn was designed in relation to them. There was then a continual interaction at the planning level, and this interaction persists once the building programme has been completed. Hence to enjoy a Baroque façade is to perceive its interplay with the space around it, as long as that has not been too much changed with the passage of time.

The space external to the church becomes space internal to a Baroque square, with the façade as one of its elements. S. Maria della Pace in Rome exemplifies this to perfection. Its front, designed by Pietro da Cortona, 1656–7, is to be enjoyed in combination with the piazza of which it is both a focus and an integral part. Indeed immediately upon entering the piazza, there is a feeling of being within the church because its façade projects into the square while at the same time remaining an organic part of the church behind it. The treatment of the house walls further unifies church and piazza: first, the cornice and the parapet of the attic storeys are continued behind the wings of the church; second, the houses are articulated by pilasters that reproduce the members of the church's upper storey. The church, through its façade, is both a projecting volume and a section of an uninterrupted wall around the piazza – church, square and elements belonging to both are fused. In this way the

Rome, S. Maria della Pace, façade

urban space conducts to the church which itself gives meaning to the whole. Many an impressive Baroque street is simply a sequence of façades – Sicily provides two superb examples. At Catania, in the Via Crociferi, palazzi and churches follow one another in an almost unbroken succession of Baroque exuberance, and the same description is applicable to the town of Noto whose situation on a steep hillside has also given rise to the skilful use of monumental flights of steps.

The façade seeks to embrace its environment and to entice people within; the straight line therefore gives way to the curve, and the circle with its equal radii to the more dynamic ellipse. A Baroque front bows in and out. This undulation – to consider the façade in itself – is evidence of the Baroque delight in movement. The double-S curve in the façade of S. Carlo, which probably derives from Borromini, is the most complete example of the desire for motion to be embodied in a church front. It seems to be the product of the interaction of internal and external forces, with the space within pushing outwards at the same time as the exterior space presses inwards, resulting in a wave-like wall that expresses tension and gives a dramatic accent to the centre.

It is indeed upon the centre that the architects laid their main emphasis. The two-storey scheme, inherited from Alberti's S. Maria Novella, is preserved but the parts have lost their independence in favour of emphasis on the middle axis, i.e. upon the entrance. Among many instances there are Christopher Wren's St Paul's, London, (1675–1710), and the abbey church of St Nicholas in the Aldstadt, Prague, designed by Kilian Dientzenhofer and begun in 1727; these both show the characteristic Baroque increase of plasticity towards the main doorway. This central domination is further stressed by denying any division between parts, for example corners are bevelled as in another Prague church, St Nicholas, Mala Strana, 1703–11, by Kilian's father Christopher. This is further evidence that fusion is the principle of composition and the impression is one of unity, with little separation between storeys, which are often integrated by the use of a giant order.

Every Baroque façade is a showpiece proclaiming the confidence and authority of the Church, and normally there is little interest in the sides and rear. An exception to this is S. Maria della Salute, Venice, but this is a centralized building; it is also a superb example of an architecture of power-celebration. Designed by Baldassare Longhena and begun in 1631, it is a focal point on the Venetian skyline at the entrance to the Grand Canal. Despite its imposing mass, it is in no sense inert but is

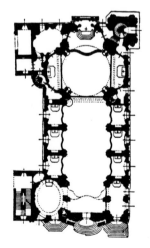

Fig. 85 Prague,
St Nicholas, Mala Strana

Venice, S. Maria della Salute, exterior

both unified and dynamic. The transition from the circle of the dome to the octagon below is perfectly made by means of a series of volutes. The outside walls of the chapels projecting from the ambulatory to either side of the entrance are treated like little church façades and their small order is taken up in the gigantic triumphal arch motif that frames the main doorway. The descending flow from the lantern through the dome and the scrolls is countered by the inverted V's of the pediments and the upright stance of the sculptured figures so that a degree of tension is introduced. The whole is like a pyramid with two-way vectors, towards the summit and down to the ground.

ST PETER'S

Equally striking are the approach to and the façade of St Peter's. An account of this impressive building does not fit easily into the form of this present study because its construction spanned several periods and almost every major architect of the High Renaissance was employed upon it – Bramante, Raphael, Antonio da Sangalo – as well as Michelangelo and Vignola representing Mannerism and Carlo Maderno and Bernini Baroque.

As it stands today however it does provide a total experience that is predominantly Baroque and begins as soon as you enter the Bernini piazza. This is a transverse oval defined by colonnades ranged on segments of concentric ellipses. Two fountains, to right and left, provide columns of mobile water that contrast with the severity of the central obelisk and with the motionless stone of the multitude of columns. This area is simultaneously closed and open; it interacts with the urban space; it embraces and leads onwards, the pattern of its paving pointing to the centre and then beyond into the trapezoidal forecourt. The obelisk serves as a node where all directions meet and also as an indicator of the longitudinal axis leading to the church.

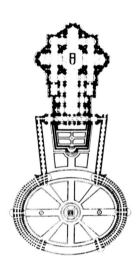

Fig. 86 Rome, St Peter's

The side of the trapezium next to the façade is longer than that which engages the piazza and this makes the front appear shorter and correspondingly taller than it really is. It has the typical Baroque concentration towards the centre and summons into the long nave which, with the façade, was designed by Maderno. The cathedral is essentially a martyrium extended with a Baroque longitudinal perspective and recession by an axial design. It is a continuum of space which, in plan, combines two squares and a rectangle and produces a pattern of cross axes (+ and x) which meet beneath the dome (see figure 86). There stands the Bernini baldachin over the tomb of the apostle – the climax and goal of this immense monumental highway.

As the mother church of Roman Catholicism, St Peter's is appropriately Baroque since that style spread universally, undergoing some local modifications in the process. In Austria, for example, a neo-classical spirit restricted its decorative aspect and the same is true of France. In Spain, on the other hand, profusion of ornament was favoured and this is to be enjoyed not only in the Iberian peninsula but also in the former Spanish dominions in Latin America. This decorative element was to become a major feature in the next stylistic movement – Rococo.

ROCOCO

Debate continues whether or not Rococo is to be regarded as the last phase of Baroque (*c.* 1720–60) or is sufficiently distinct to be an independent style. Certainly there are elements of continuity, but there are also contrasts. Like Baroque, Rococo employs all the visual arts in collaboration, seeks unity, delights in movement, favours the curvilinear and has fusion as its principle of composition. Unlike Baroque, however, Rococo rejects rhetoric, turns structure into ornament or disguises it, is atectonic (i.e. non-constructional), bright and cheerful, and is less concerned with a spatial climax than with making each church in its entirety the focus of experience.

Indeed in the buildings of this period by Johann Michael Fischer (1692–1766) it is possible to discern a division at the level of the cornice: below there is an articulated Baroque structure of considerable tectonic vigour but above there is a Rococo fluid unification of space by means of illusionistic painting and a profuse but delicate surface ornamentation. Hence it is possible to differentiate Rococo from its predecessor and not simply on the grounds of the presence of the decorative motif from which it derived its name, namely 'rocaille'.

ROCAILLE

Rocaille, which denotes rock-work or shell and coral-like forms, was devised in the office of Louis XIV's leading architect, J. Hardouin-Mansart, by the designer Pierre Le Pautre and was employed in the palace of Versailles *c*. 1700. In the country of its origin it was used for rooms of moderate size and is perhaps best seen in the Petit Trianon (1762–4). However it was in Germany and in Bavaria in particular that it was adapted for large-scale interiors and became the norm for a whole series of exquisite churches from the 1720s onwards.

Rocaille is established particularly at boundary positions, at the junctions of articulations, where two elements converge. It smoothes transitions between capitals and entablatures; it appears at the apex of an arch and in the spandrels of vaults. Sometimes frayed out like clouds, sometimes broken up into strips, it is spread over altars, confessionals, pulpits, fonts, organs, gallery railings and indeed over all forms of church furniture. Rocaille is used to create panels, constituting frames around more or less plain fields. Such ornament is essentially linear, long sweeping curves of slightly foliated mouldings forming elongated C and S patterns that often interlace and, like Islamic arabesques, delight with their movement and intricacy. Designs of scroll and counter-scrolls provide wave-like and asymmetrical outlines.

*Zwiefalten, abbey
church, side of nave*

MOVEMENT

Rocaille also embodies the mobility that Rococo inherited from
Baroque, but now the movement is neither restless nor tense but
gently flowing. The pattern of the ornament is continuous from
motif to motif, their asymmetry allowing no pause, and the
plain areas (which are just as important as the decorated ones)
inviting the glance to glide over their smooth surface. Even the
architectural articulation begins to sway because of its rocaille
form. The permanent and the solid are denied since the decor
suggests instability and fragility. There is no solid geometry;
nothing fixed, for all is fluid. C and S curves abound, enclosed in
one another or producing flame-like figures.

After 1720 there are few straight lines in the churches of southern Germany; altar steps are rounded, choir stalls semi-circular. The walls undulate to match the decor. The faces of pillars are made concave and gallery fronts convex, their S-shaped balconies projecting into the central space. By these means church interiors are vitalized through the swinging and dancing interplay of the curves. Ovalized planning is preferred, which is achieved in rectangular buildings either by turning the corners into quadrants, as in the Feldkirche, Füssen, rebuilt by J. G. Fischer 1724–5, or by placing altars across them, as at Birnau by Peter Thumb (1746–50). A natural climax was the complete oval, beloved of Baroque, as at Steinhausen (1728–33) (figure 89) and Die Wies (1745–54), both designed by Dominikus Zimmermann. This form is perfectly suited to the pilgrimage church, such as these two, which has to provide for circulating processions to admire the glory of the building. Appreciation is the result both of the eyes' pursuit and of the body's locomotion.

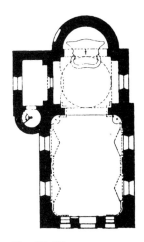

Fig. 87 Füssen, Feldkirche

Rococo movement does not depend upon dramatic spatial sequences, which are so apparent in the design of the Vierzehn-heiligen Church by J. B. Neumann. This church is really a hybrid: Baroque as regards its handling of space but Rococo in terms of its decoration. Neumann however had nothing to do with this latter aspect; the church was not actually completed until nearly 20 years after his death.

HOMOGENEITY

A Rococo church consists of a single homogenous space, unified in both horizontal and vertical directions. Horizontally there is an unbroken volume from entrance to choir and from side wall to side wall. This is particularly noticeable in the wall-pillar church, which is called the Vorarlberg type after the Austrian province. A typical example, such as J. M. Fischer's priory at Diessen (1732–9), has deep buttresses projecting inwards from the sides with chapels framed between them (figure 90). While these are connected by small transverse tunnel vaults, it would be inaccurate to suppose that there are any aisles properly so-called. Indeed the wall-pillar church is a single space, with imperfect transepts, a recessed apsidally ended choir and a gallery running through the pillars above the chapels. Vertically there is continuity from floor to ceiling, with the vaults of the chapels often of the same height as the nave to produce a kind of hall-church.

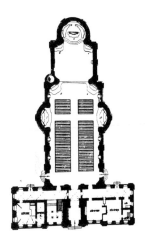

Fig. 88 Birnau, pilgrimage church

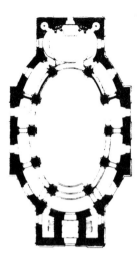

*Fig. 89   Steinhausen,
pilgrimage church*

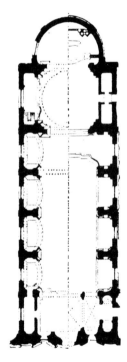

*Fig. 90   Diessen,
pilgrimage church*

Entablatures that may suggest a break are replaced by coves, that is, relatively narrow concave surfaces that provide a smooth transition from the vertical walls to the more or less horizontal ceilings. The divisions evident in the Renaissance church simply do not exist because fusion, not addition, is the principle of composition.

Rocaille both individualizes the forms and integrates them within a continuous whole. The eye is drawn to altar, pulpit, and so on, one after the other, but each is all-of-a-piece with, and so an element within, the architecture. This homogeneity means that there is no one overwhelming climax, which is the norm in Baroque churches. It is true that there is some emphasis upon the main altar which thus functions as a focus. Side altars are so arranged that they lead to it, either by being placed in pairs flanking the choir arch but obliquely so the gaze glances off them on to the high altar (for example as in the Church of St Katherine, Wolfegg, mid-1730s, by J. G. Fischer) or by setting them transversely in series on each side of the nave so that they stand to the high altar as successive flats do to a backcloth in a theatre, as at Diessen (figure 90), for example. Indeed in the latter church the high altar painting can be changed according to the festival precisely like a scene on a stage. Nevertheless while this accentuation is not to be missed, Rococo is in a sense indeterminate in that its centre is at the same time everywhere and nowhere. The visitor is drawn to contemplate a pulpit or an organ in a west gallery or a ceiling fresco just as much as the high altar. He feels he must look on all sides; he is surrounded as if in a jewel box. At Ottobeuren (1748–67), for example, there is really no spatial climax since the entire church provides the experience.

THE COLLABORATION OF THE ARTS

The sense of overall harmony is intensified by the collaboration of all the arts, in which previously Bernini had excelled. Whereas in a Renaissance church each art had its appointed place (a niche for sculpture, a pendentive for a fresco), while in a Baroque one they break out of their well-defined frames (statues emerging into the surrounding space and paintings exceeding their limits), according to the Rococo vision all the arts are to be fused – there is no longer classical hierarchy nor Baroque conflict but integration to the highest degree. All the tensions that in classical architecture were brought into equilibrium and in Baroque were increased and made deliberately antagonistic are

annihilated in Rococo. Paintings and sculpture, rocaille orna- ment, float all over the church, converting the entire building into a kind of intimate salon. Delicate colours are favoured – pinks, white and gold. Light floods through plain glass and ripples over the surface to produce an effect of airiness; clarity is everywhere and indeed every church is brought alive by the light.

There is variety and a wealth of decorative detail but it is all subordinate to an impression of unity. Frescoes of heaven, of saints glorified or the Virgin crowned, declare belief in a divinely ordained order pervading all and uniting earth with that which is above, where the source of harmony is to be found. The universe is set forth theocentrically and the world of sense is represented as part of a single whole and as a means of approach-

Wolfegg, St Katherine, interior to east

*Die Wies, Pilgrimage
church, interior to east*

ing the invisible realm. This is however no longer Baroque
rhetoric – there is little of persuasion and more of sensation,
visual and physical. Yet as in Baroque churches, the ceilings do
open to the sky as at Ottobeuren, and the separation of the
Church Militant and the Church Triumphant is overcome.
Identification with the mysteries of the Church is facilitated by
the use of natural details, and this personal involvement reaches
its pinnacle at Birnau where G. B. Götz has inserted a mirror
into one of his frescoes so that the pilgrim on the floor of the
church can see himself in heaven receiving the Virgin's blessing.
Yet another link between the visions in the frescoes and those
below is provided by altar paintings and statuary, for example
at Diessen the picture behind the high altar represents the

Assumption of the Virgin while above that the Trinity is waiting to greet her. Stucco elements are blended with the frescoes to facilitate the transition from the three-dimensional to the two-dimensional and so many of the figures around a scene in the vault are part-stucco and part-painted.

Birnau, pilgrimage church, fresco over choir

STRUCTURE AND ORNAMENT

Stucco becomes either an overgrowth, submerging all tectonic details, or constructed decoration. When it is the latter there is a

total substitution of rocaille elements for the traditional architectural forms. Indeed the Rococo architects were not interested
in structure; they did not seek to express it but instead denied,
attentuated and dissolved it. There is consequently a tension
between the architecture and the decoration, with the former
suggesting no more than a picturelike theatrical plane.

Structural function is denied, for example, at Zwiefalten,
another of J. M. Fischer's churches, 1740–65, where the nave
columns are engaged in pillars and seem to have nothing to
support. Structure is hidden when the building material is
covered with a skin of stucco and paint so that the walls are no
longer regarded as made up of individual stones but as single
uniform masses. Lastly structure is attenuated by becoming
more slender and graceful and by being set at the greatest
possible distance from the spectator so that he seems to behold a
marvellous vision rather than solid masonry. Clarity of classical
form is lost as the members become dematerialized or trans-
figured, an effect produced by the spilling of dazzling light over
them. Indeed they are dissolved into decoration with capitals
becoming concave, festooned with dangling garlands and all but
merging with the scroll work.

The consequence is that the achitectural elements become
insubstantial; they appear built up of ornament, which however
does not mean that Rococo is simply a scheme of interior
decoration. Rather its architectural features are fused into
a decorative scheme. They then become atectonic, i.e. non-
constructional, and have no sculpturesque character. Throughout, the tectonic elements are weakened or omitted. The shafts
of pilasters are panelled; heavy entablatures in the naves are left
out; thick mouldings at the arrises where the surfaces of different curvatures meet are avoided; the swelling of the vault is
reduced. There is an emphasis upon the continuity of an even-
tensioned surface. Rocaille itself is flat, unlike the full relief of
Baroque ornament; it is as thin as lace and so has a planar
character to such an extent that Rococo churches must be
regarded as surface-positive, possessing therefore a certain pictorial or painterly quality.

OVERALL CHARACTER

In the country of its origin Rococo found its main sphere in the
salon, the domain where the female was supreme and where
people assembled for diversion. To the salon the French hostess

gave a light tone, easy movement, gracefulness and harmony –
all these are characteristics of the Rococo churches of Germany.
Elegant, colourful, refined, delicate, opposed to heavy grandeur
and pompous gravity, Rococo is an *art de luxe* that encourages
enjoyment. It is not however ostentatious since it simply aims to
please. It is light, bright and cheerful, an expression of holy
gaiety. Die Wies has been appropriately called the dance-floor
of God. These churches are the product and the embodiment of
playful fantasy – they have a festive air, an appropriate setting
for the celebration of the marriage feast of the Lamb of God.

Rococo is an interior architecture, little concerned with the
outside. Although its examples are restricted in number and in
geographical location, it adds a new note to the multitude of
forms adopted by temples, churches and mosques throughout
the ages.

APPENDIX

INTRODUCING THE FUNDAMENTALS OF
ARCHITECTURAL APPRECIATION

The enjoyment of architecture involves the ability to identify buildings according to their main category and primary type and then to recognise which principle of composition has been used for the design.

THE TWO MAIN CATEGORIES

Most buildings belong either to the category of a path or to that of place, the one suggesting a journey and movement, the other a centre and stillness. Once the category has been established, the next step is to observe how well a building fits it and this requires familiarity with the characteristics of a clear path and a precisely defined place.

For a path to be identifiable, it must have (a) strong edges; (b) continuity; (c) directionality; (d) recognizable landmarks; (e) a sharp terminal; (f) end-from-end distinction.

For a place to be identifiable, it must be (a) concentrated in form with pronounced borders; (b) a readily comprehensible shape; (c) limited in size; (d) a focus for gathering; (e) capable of being experienced as an inside in contrast to a surrounding exterior; (f) largely non-directional.

While the appreciation of any building depends very much on sight, one that belongs to the path category can also be experienced by movement. Enjoyment then derives from the dynamic fit between the body and the architecture as one responds to the questions: how and where do I move? When visiting a place, this physical response has to be more limited. Static fit replaces dynamic fit, and the questions then are: where do I sit, lean, relax? Even so, some places do prompt movement, although it is not pronounced nor directed towards a goal – in fact it can be circular around a midpoint.

   Between these two main categories there are structures that combine features of both: such are paths that lead to and include places, the latter acting as foci or nodes.

THE THREE PRIMARY TYPES

The character of a building is further determined by the extent to which the design has been developed in terms of mass, or of surface or of space.

Mass-positive

When the essence is to be sought in the structure, such a building is of the mass-positive type. It is the stones, bricks, and so on that constitute its reality. Hence in examining a plan, it is the black lines and dots (representing walls, columns, etc.) that reveal its nature. Such structures can have a sculptural quality, since they are modelled or plastically shaped three-dimensional solids. They then appeal not only to the sense of vision but to that of touch.

Surface-positive

When the essence is to be sought in the bounding planes, such a building belongs to the planar or surface-positive type. The overall surface is constantly respected; depth is limited to a shallow stratification with one plane behind another. These structures have a two-dimensional aspect, but since blank areas can seem inert, they are often subject to articulation, that is they are divided into parts by the use of such devices as panels, ceramic tiles, and so on.

Space-positive

When the essential reality consists of the volume defined by the walls, roofs, and so on, such a building is space-positive. Its nature is revealed on plan by the white areas between the lines. The cavities within the mass are the substance from which it has been formed. Such space has a positive quality; it is not simply a hole that negates solidity. Movement is the primary means of experiencing it. We become aware of volumes that are long and narrow or curved or with stress on the vertical or horizontal, and so on. Lines of sight and movement are channelled by these forms; directions are indicated. Space awareness makes us realize that a building is not only three-dimensional, it actually occupies three dimensions, i.e. length, breadth and height are not only characteristics of the building's volume, they are the very substance out of which it has been created; it is not just something that exists in space, it makes space live in it.

Space-positive buildings can themselves be subdivided into: *Space-traps*, which encapsulate interior space and isolate it from the exterior. They are bubbles of space caught in solid shells; *Space-frames*, which reduce the separation of inside and outside to such an extent that they seem to flow into one another.

Awareness of these categories and types is important because without knowing the particular one to which a church or temple belongs, the essential character can escape detection and appreciation will be impaired.

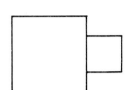

Fig. 91 Addition

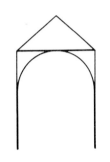

Fig. 92 Gable added to arch

OTHER CLASSES OF BUILDINGS

Knowledge of other variations is not so vital but there are two pairs of subsidiary classes with which it is helpful to be familiar:
(1a) *Excavated architecture*, which applies to an interior that appears to have been hacked out of a mass;
(1b) *Constructed architecture*, which refers to that which has been put together by means of supports, buttresses, and so on.

The first of these seems to have been approached from within and the second from outside, but the terms do not refer to methods of building; they are figurative ways of calling attention to an effect.
(2a) *The cave* designates a building whose emphasis is upon the interior; it is one planned exclusively with regard to its containing function.
(2b) *The crystal* stresses the exterior; such a building has virtually no inside and tends to suggest impenetrability.

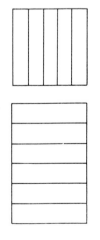

Fig. 93 Juxtaposition and superimposition

PRINCIPLES OF COMPOSITION

Whatever its category, type or class, every building is designed in accordance with one of three principles of composition: addition, division or fusion.

Addition

When a building is the product of addition, one starts with the parts which, even after they have been combined, retain a certain independence. Put one square against a larger one and the shape of each is still recognizable (figure 91). Unit is added to unit, without modification or inflection (figure 92). This addition is accomplished in two principal ways: by *juxtaposition*, when elements are placed side by side, or by *superimposition*, when they are on top of one another (figure 93). The principle of addition requires the architect to act as a coordinator, assembling everything to create a single totality, which is nevertheless characterized by multiplicity with its parts semi-independent.

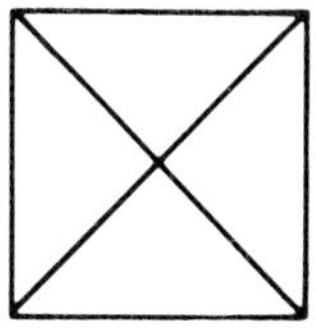

Fig. 94 Division

Division

When division is the determining factor, one begins with the whole and the parts are subdivisions, having little independence of their own. This principle is less easy to grasp because it is not just the opposite of addition – that would be subtraction, which involves a real taking away, whereas with architectural division the parts remain. If diagonals are inserted into a square (figure 94), four small triangles result but they remain sections of the original figure; the whole has been divided but nothing has been subtracted. Hence the units involved in addition and in subdivision are not of the same kind. Addition involves parts as subwholes, while division connotes parts that are really fragments. The principle of division requires the subordination of the elements to the whole; it is therefore characterized by unity with the parts dependent. Division can be accomplished in two main ways: by *inflection* (figure 95), when parts are modified to establish a relation to others or by *penetration* (figure 96), whereby one part overlaps with or in some other way permeates another.

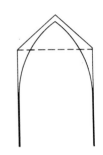

Fig. 95   Inflection

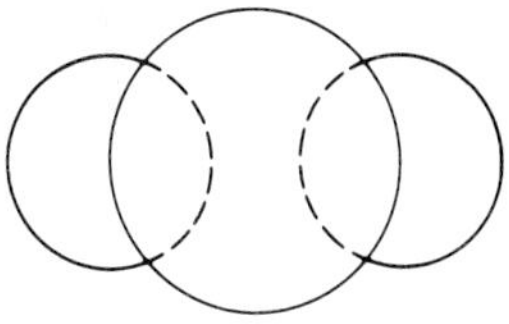

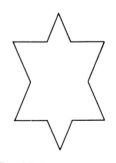

Fig. 96   Penetration

Fusion

The principle of fusion stands in sharp contrast to the previous two. When it is embodied in a building, that building has, in a sense, neither independent nor inflected but interdependent parts; it is one great single unit in itself (figure 97). In other words it is not possible to decompose such an edifice back into several elements. Unlike inflected parts which are still recognizable, the components of a design that aims at fusion cannot be so distinguished, except occasionally in analytic thought. One method of achieving fusion is *pulsating juxtaposition* (figure 98), the adjective serving to distinguish the phenomenon from the placing side by side that is characteristic of addition. Take a square that expands into its corners while its sides are contracting inwards; and then place circles on either side: the effect is that the circles seem to spread into the central figure

Fig. 97 Fusion

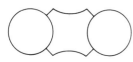

*Fig. 98 Pulsating
juxtaposition*

while it contracts under the impact of the juxtaposition – the
whole pulsates.

INGREDIENTS OF DESIGN

To be able to identify the general character of a building and its
principle of composition is not to exhaust the possibilities of
appreciation. Architects have at their disposal various components with which to create their designs and attention must now
be paid to them.

Structural elements

The simplest building is made of walls supporting a roof. This
supporting function can be performed either by columns, which
belong to the *post-and-beam* or *trabeated* system, or by arches,
in which case the system is named *arcuated*.

   The roof itself may be related to its supports in one of two
ways. It can be a kind of lid so that, while the walls bear it, they
and it are not markedly integrated. Alternatively it can be a kind
of head, dominating what is beneath it and leading to what is
known as the baldachin (ciborium) form. A baldachin is a
canopy, usually a dome on four columns. When the structure is
of this kind, the roof gives the impression of being reared on
high first, with the walls, if any are inserted, subsequently drawn
between its hanging tentacles like a curtain. The supporting and
protecting functions are then differentiated, since the walls
become mere fillings or flat screens between the major load-
bearing elements.

Sculpture

Both walls and roofs can be treated sculpturally. Pieces of
sculpture, either in relief or free-standing, may be enjoyed in and
for themselves. The use of carving for capitals, on façades and to
enliven walls must be taken into account, but it is the way they
enhance the architecture that has to be the main concern.

Ornament

Buildings can be given further visual interest by means of ornament, whereby one art contributes to another, as carvings and
mosaics may serve architecture. It is always part of something
else, but its use is by no means confined to making things look
more attractive. It can bring out the essential nature of an
architectural member, for example, fluting on a column draws

attention to its verticality. It can accentuate a plastic shape; it can change a plain surface into something lively; it can articulate the parts of a façade. It can contribute to unity on both the exterior and the interior by stylistic consistency.

When ornament is integrated with the object that bears it, it is not really possible to separate one from the other. Yet it may take on a life of its own and become self-contained; this is frequently the case with ceramic designs. Such patterns involve the artist in three operations: framing, filling, linking. *Framing* delimits a field; *filling* organizes the resulting area; *linking* joins the elements of the design and may itself take one of three forms: *branching*, when it proceeds from the frame inwards and sub-divides; *radiating*, when it spreads out from the centre, and *interlacing* when the lines cross above and behind one another.

Colour

Colour is not used merely to create attractive patterns, nor is it solely a medium for wall paintings, it can also accent form. It can elucidate the divisions of a building or different parts of architectural members, picking out significant details. It may express the character of an interior, now austere, now light and gay. It may assist balance and stability. It can enrich light flooding in from outside.

Light

The part played by light in architectural effect is far more than just illumination. The enjoyment of any style indeed requires an appreciation of the way light is handled. It can create shadows and then light and shade are components of the overall design. The direction of the light also affects the character of what is seen, for example, if it falls almost at right angles on a relief there is a minimum of shade and the plasticity of the effect is correspondingly decreased. In one style – Gothic – light is a primary material in the structure of churches and cathedrals with their vast expanses of stained glass.

Texture and materials

Texture refers in the first instance to everything that covers structure. It applies to whatever hangs upon and is held up by structure and to whatever is stuck on to it, such as plaster or mosaic. At the same time texture can be provided by the actual structure of the materials used, since their texture is the structure of their own surfaces. Marble, with its fine graining, appeals both to the eye and to the touch. Texture can accentuate form: it may stress massivity when large blocks of stone are used with deep joints between them (rustication).

ASPECTS OF GOOD DESIGN

By now it will be evident that an architect has at his disposal a host of ingredients with which to create a building. However buildings that are enjoyable have certain qualities and something has to be known about these in order to recognize them. What then are the aspects of good design that a visitor should seek to detect?

Proportion and scale

For a building to be pleasing it must not give the impression of a haphazard collection of elements. To ensure their coherence they have to be designed with harmonious proportions. Proportion concerns the relationship of the parts to one another and to a building as a whole. Throughout the ages attempts have been made to define ideal proportions, particular attention being paid to the Golden Section. This refers to a line divided into two unequal parts of which the ratio of the first to the second is equal to the ratio of the second to the whole. Measurements of ancient buildings indicate that this was known and used. Yet it has to be admitted that few people are spontaneously aware of simple proportions. Yet, for an acceptable order, disparities must be ruled out so that parts of a building correspond. This means that the scale too is important since this denotes relative size.

Rhythm and movement

When applied to buildings rhythm relates to a sequence of similar elements, either on a horizontal or a vertical plane. It involves spacing, repetition and grouping. Rhythm is apprehended either visually or by physical movement. The architecture functions as a stimulus for movement, either imagined or real – imagined, when the observer stands still and lets his eye travel; real, when the building incites to action and becomes a stage for movement. In the first instance the rhythm is linear, in the second, spatial. When it is spatial the building becomes a partner in a dialogue with the body and the individual recognizes that there are animate (himself) and inanimate (e.g. a row of columns) participants in the interaction. Rhythm is apparent, for example, in the way windows are arranged, vaults designed, storeys related.

Contrasts and accentuation

Attention can be paid to proportion and rhythm and yet the result may be monotonous. To avoid this architects use contrasts and accents. Contrasts can be created in many ways – there are possible contrasts between elementary forms, in size, in vertical and horizontal axes, in colour, and in the use of different materials and textures. Conversely, too great a contrast can destroy the unity of a design and it can also be impaired if accentuation is excessive; for example, if there is a large break in a rhythm, a hiatus will be created. Emphases here and there do preclude dullness, and among the methods of achieving this are the use of converging lines and of progressive and diminishing volumes. A visual accent can be provided if a sequence is slightly broken because human beings look for continuities and see a line as going on unless it is quite evidently stopped.

The different methods of accentuation call attention to what is the dominant factor in a design. The dominant is that to which the gaze is first drawn and naturally returns after an examination of the subordinate details of the composition. Enjoyment involves detecting the dominant and appreciating how it unifies the whole so that contrasts and accents are enriching and not disturbing factors.

Axiality and symmetry

The unity of a building can also be assisted by axiality and symmetry. An axis is the centre line of a figure and can be on either a horizontal or a vertical plane. To stress axiality is to make this centre line the pivot of a design. When the parts of a building are related to this line, they are also related to one another. This relationship takes the form of a symmetrical disposition.

The most common type of symmetry is bilateral: if a figure is folded along the axis, the two halves will coincide, each being a mirror image of the other. Symmetry may in this way provide a solution to what otherwise could look incomplete, and it is to be distinguished from balance and equilibrium. Take scales and uniform weights as illustrations: symmetry is achieved if an equal number of weights is arranged in the same pattern in each pan. For balance, the weights, equal in number, may be heaped on one side and laid in a row on the other, while equilibrium requires no more than the same number of weights on either side no matter how disposed. Symmetry tends to give greater enjoyment than asymmetry because of the apparent human need for regularity and order.

In addition to the bilateral there is also rotational and broken symmetry. The latter designates a certain correspondence between two halves but not an exact mirror image, for example, Mary and John at the foot of the cross establish a certain balance, although the two forms are not identical. Rotational symmetry is the product of movement around a central point or axis. In a plane this produces a circle, while in space it generates a sphere.

To sum up, appreciation of a building involves:
(a) recognizing whether it is primarily a path or a place and observing how well it corresponds to the appropriate characteristics; (b) perceiving its essential character by determining whether it is mass-, surface- or space-positive; (c) discovering the principle of composition and noting how that principle has determined the design: (d) paying attention to the contribution made by structural elements, sculpture, ornament, colour, light, texture and materials; (e) enjoying, visually and physically, the qualities of proportion and scale, rhythm and movement, contrasts and accentuation, axiality and symmetry.

FURTHER READING

GENERAL

Christian Norberg-Schulz, *Meaning in Western Architecture*, Studio Vista, London, 1975.

R. L. Scranton, *Aesthetic Aspects of Ancient Art*, University of Chicago, Chicago and London, 1964.

J. Summerson, *The Classical Language of Architecture*, Methuen, London, 1964.

1   THE TEMPLES OF THE NILE

H. Schäfer, *The Principles of Egyptian Art*, Oxford University Press, Oxford, 1974.

E. Baldwin Smith, *Egyptian Architecture as Cultural Expression*, Appleton-Century, New York, 1938.

2   AEGEAN ARCHITECTURE

James Walter Graham, *The Palaces of Crete*, Princeton University, Princeton, 1962.

3   THE SANCTUARIES OF CLASSICAL GREECE

Rhys Carpenter, *Greek Art. A Study of the Formal Evolution of Style*, University of Pennsylvania, Philadelphia, 1963.

Vincent Scully, *The Earth, the Temple and the Gods*, Yale University, Yale 1962.

4   THE HELLENISTIC AND ROMAN PERIODS

W. L. Macdonald, *The Architecture of the Roman Empire*, Yale

University, Yale, 1965.

T. B. L. Webster, *Hellenistic Art*, Methuen, London, 1967.

5   EARLY CHRISTIAN ARCHITECTURE AND THE BYZANTINE
ACHIEVEMENT

W. L. Macdonald, *Early Christian and Byzantine Architecture*,
Braziller, New York, 1963.

P. A. Michelis, *An Aesthetic Approach to Byzantine Art*, Bats-
ford, London, 1955.

6   MOSQUES AND MADRASAS

George Michell (ed.), *Architecture of the Islamic World*, Thames
and Hudson, London, 1978.

7   ROMANESQUE ARCHITECTURE

Kenneth J. Conant, *Carolingian and Romanesque Architecture
800 to 1200*, Penguin, Harmondsworth, 1959.

8   THE AGE OF GOTHIC

Paul Frankl, *Gothic Architecture*, Penguin, Harmondsworth,
1962.

9   THE RENAISSANCE AND MANNERISM

Peter Murray, *The Architecture of the Italian Renaissance*,
Thames and Hudson, London, 1969.

F. Würtemberger, *Mannerism*, Weidenfeld and Nicolson,
London, 1963.

10   BAROQUE AND ROCOCO

A. Blunt *et al.*, *Baroque and Rococo. Architecture and Decoration*, Elek, London, 1978.

John Bourke, *Baroque Churches of Central Europe*, Faber and
Faber, London, 1958 (despite the title, this excellent work is
concerned chiefly with Rococo).

APPENDIX

Rudolf Arnheim, *The Dynamics of Architectural Form*, University of California, Berkeley, 1977.

S. Gauldie, *Architecture*, Oxford University Press, Oxford, 1969.

Kevin Lynch, *The Image of the City*, Michigan Institute of Technology, Cambridge, Mass., 1960.

S. E. Rasmussen, *Experiencing Architecture*, Chapman and Hall, London, 1959.

INDEX OF PLACES
AND BUILDINGS

Italic page numbers refer to figures; **bold** to photographs

GENERAL INDEX

Italic page numbers refer to figures; **bold** to photographs

MAP OF PLACES